# TEST CRICKET

A *Golden Hands* book

Marshall Cavendish, London

# Contents

Edited by Martin Tyler

Statistics by Irving Rosenwater

Published by Marshall Cavendish Publications Ltd,
58 Old Compton Street, London W1V 5PA

Some of this material was first published
by Marshall Cavendish Limited in
the partwork The Game.

This book first published 1974

Updated to time of going to press, September 1973

Printed and bound by Morrison & Gibb, Edinburgh

ISBN 0 85685 052 7

## Introduction by Richie Benaud

There is no greater event in world sport than the battle for the Ashes, whether the series be played in England or Australia. This pictorial history of Test cricket contains much of the excitement of these clashes, originating way back in 1882 when Australia managed to defeat the full strength of England for the first time on English soil. Over the years, when playing for Australia, it was always a wonderful thing to gain a Test place but, with due respect to all, my pulse did beat a little quicker when I was lucky enough to play against the old enemy, England.

This pictorial history of Test cricket fills a gap in the many types of cricket book on the market. All play their part in enhancing the enjoyment of cricket—both to the young fan and to the older follower steeped in the traditions of the game. But nowhere else will you find such an all-embracing variety of photographs, picturing the whole history of the game in a vividly exciting and instructive way.

In fact, having seen this book, I can say that it will be a must for all who follow cricket, covering as it does the various test series between all the cricketing countries, with special biographies of the greatest players and splendid statistical analyses by Irving Rosenwater. Above all, however, it is the sheer number and breadth of the illustrations which make this book an indispensable addition to the literature of cricket.

As I write this, cricket has never been more appreciated. And cricket followers browsing through this excellent pictorial history will have extra information to add to their own enjoyment of the glorious contests to come. This is one of the beauties of a game that has captivated millions in the time since Australia won that famous first victory.

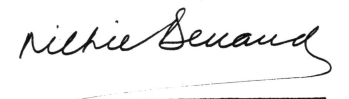

# Test cricket—
# series by series

Peter Parfitt falls another victim to Dennis Lillee in the 5th Test of the 1972 England v Australia series, at the Oval.

The five-match Test series is now universally accepted as the most important event of all in cricket. Like many of cricket's older fixtures and customs, Test cricket developed gradually, even haphazardly. There was never a moment when any one person stood up and announced Test matches would start. Indeed, it was not until 1894-95 that the term 'Test' was used, and it was not until later in the decade that the Board of Control was formed in England for Test matches held there.

In modern times, elevation to Test status has been a big step in the cricketing history of West Indies, New Zealand, India, and Pakistan, but originally there was just Australia and England, joined later in the 19th century by South Africa. The first Test is now acknowledged to have been played at Melbourne on March 15, 16,

and 17, 1877—and these early encounters were known merely as matches between an Australian XI and an England XI.

Not that these matches always evoked the partisanship they do now. Tours then were organized privately—official MCC tours did not start until 1903-04—and many players had little incentive to make themselves available. W. G. Grace, for example, made only one tour of Australia, though he played in Tests at home for over 20 years after they started. Some idea of the Australian outlook in those days can be gleaned from the fact that their original tour programme of 1880 did not include the representative match at the Oval in September that is now on record as the first Test played in England. And their methods of selection are cast in some doubt by the frequently told story of the second wicket-keeper who, when on the

high seas bound for England, was found never to have kept wicket.

South Africa entered Test cricket in 1888-89, and became with England and Australia one of the founder members of the Imperial (now International) Cricket Conference (ICC) when it was formed, on a South African suggestion, in 1909. South Africa left the ICC in 1961, because, under the constitution, membership was restricted to countries within the Commonwealth, but they continued to play Test matches, which were known as 'unofficial'. Nevertheless, they were still included in the record books and aroused no less public interest. Strictly speaking, however, only those matches between the full members of the ICC— England, Australia, West Indies, New Zealand, India, and Pakistan —warrant the designation 'Test'.

Test cricket is only loosely con-

**Particularly in England, Test cricket is extensively covered by television. The television companies pay well for the privilege, but do they keep the spectators away?**

trolled by the ICC, the arranging of matches and series being purely a matter for the individual governing bodies of the countries concerned. Thus South Africa never played West Indies, India, or Pakistan, and since 1960-61 India and Pakistan have not played each other.

It was not until 1928 that the fourth Test-playing country joined the other three, West Indies playing three Test matches that year in England. Eighteen months later, they were host to the Hon. F. S. G. Calthorpe's team in the Caribbean, and that same season, 1929-30, England sent another team to New Zealand under A. H.

H. Gilligan, so bringing the number of Test playing countries to five. India's first Test was played against England at Lord's in 1932, and after partition Pakistan began with a series in India in 1952-53.

From this, it can be seen that the conception of Test matches being the meeting of the strongest teams that could be put in the field is, outside the England-Australia series, relatively new. In the days when several amateurs were good enough for most England teams, many were prevented by business from touring, and only since World War II have full-strength England teams gone to West Indies, India, and Pakistan. Many of the early Test matches against South Africa, too, were played by what would have passed as 'second XIs'.

Though the series between England and Australia have overall been evenly fought, South Africa have been only fitfully successful in Test cricket. They did not win a Test until 1905-06, when they won four matches against P. F. Warner's side, and though they won again four years later it was another 21 years after that before their next rubber was won. And it was not until 1935 that, by beating England at Lord's, they won their first series overseas. Thirty years later, they were again in England, heralding in a golden era of South African cricket that included two annihilations of Australia.

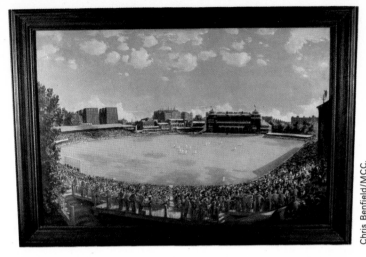

'England v Australia at Lord's, 1938' by Charles Cundall. The matches between the two countries date from 1877 and a series for the Ashes rarely fails to arouse most ardent partisanship.

Chris Benfield/MCC.

West Indies cricket soon established its huge potential by drawing the first home series with Calthorpe's team, and it was not until 1960 that England, under Peter May, won a series in the West Indies. Prior to that, only Ian Johnson's Australians of 1954-55 had been successful, their 3-0 victory halting the triumphs of the Worrell-Walcott-Weekes era. The Sobers-Hall-Griffith period followed in the 1960s, when they defeated all-comers, and if the late 1960s witnessed a recession, West Indies had long established themselves on the same level as their three senior Test-playing countries.

New Zealand, on the other hand, have known repeated frustrations. With the perennial handicap of playing cricket on rugby grounds that produce poor cricket pitches, they have not fulfilled the promise of the early and immediate post-war years when players of the calibre of Stewart Dempster, Bert Sutcliffe, and Martin Donnelly were among the best in the world. In 1961-62 New Zealand drew in South Africa, and later in the 1960s showed marked improvement with victories over West Indies and India and a series win in Pakistan. But after 42 years and 42 Test matches New Zealand had still not beaten England. Even more amazing perhaps was the fact that by 1971 they had played only one full Test match against neighbours Australia—in 1946. As a result of increasingly frequent visits by Australian 'second XIs' in the 1960s, and New Zealand matches in Australia against state sides, it was decided to remedy this unsatisfactory situation by reciprocal tours in 1973-74.

India and Pakistan, hard to beat at home, have generally failed to live up to the potential of much of their cricket when they tour. One of the principal reasons for this is that, for reasons of climate, diet, and physique, they find it difficult to produce the fast bowlers needed in England and Australia.

As a result of the general tendency, encouraged by television, to concentrate on the main events of each sport and on the best players, the Test match has tended to become increasingly important in modern times at the expense of ordinary first-class cricket. In England, especially, where the county matches are the game's bread and butter, there is a danger that there could be too many Test matches. Fortunately, it has been recognized that they could lose their novelty, and that the goose that lays the golden egg could well be killing itself off. Should this happen in England, the sufferers would be the first-class counties, who share in the Test match profits. Test cricket is not, however, subsidizing county cricket, as is sometimes thought. Rather it is compensating it. The counties find the players, develop them, and employ them, only, when they reach Test standard, to lose them for a number of matches every year—usually at a time when they might hope their stars would be attracting the public to their home grounds.

There is not the same problem in the other countries, though. In

1 England and Yorkshire fast bowler Fred Trueman retired with a record 307 wickets in Test cricket and the knowledge that whoever beat this figure would 'be bloody tired'.
2 Colin Cowdrey, with 7,459 runs from a record 109 Tests, is England's most prolific Test batsman, surpassing Wally Hammond by 210 runs.
3 Not always peaceful, the political demonstration has become a Test cricket sideshow in several countries.

Patrick Eagar

Australia, there are fewer Test series, and the country is big enough to absorb an extension of a rubber from five matches to six, as in 1970-71. This was to allow Perth to become the latest addition to the list of Test centres, and it resulted in an aggregate gate there of nearly 90,000.

England first had six Test matches in the season of 1965, and has had them at two-yearly intervals since. This recent innovation of half-season visits to England, which does not involve Australia, was instituted for a number of reasons, the original inspiration being the general desire of many to see the attractive West Indians of 1963 again as soon as possible. It has numerous advantages, even though the first half of an English summer is apt to be a much less congenial and profitable time to tour. It is appreciated in South Africa, where players often have trouble in obtaining more than three months leave from their jobs. And it is especially appreciated in New Zealand, because they can now visit England every four years instead of every eight, with the result that they can tour with a good number of players with previous experience. The system is also appreciated in England because a one-sided series of three matches is much less painful to watch than one of five.

From being a three-day fixture in the beginning, the Test match grew until, in the period between the wars, there was no time limit in Australia, but elsewhere matches of three or four days were played, with provision in certain circumstances for the final match of a series to be 'timeless'. It has since contracted again to the general norm of five days. This, like other playing conditions, however, is purely a matter for the two countries concerned, and in many circumstances — when England visit New Zealand for example — the matches are of four days duration.

Test match grounds vary from the colossus of Melbourne, with its increased capacity of 121,000, to the relatively small but exotic grounds of the West Indies or the scenic splendours of Newlands in the Cape, which requires extra stands to be erected in order to accommodate 18,000. In Australia, the second biggest ground is the Sydney Cricket Ground, which holds nearly 50,000. The capacity of England's six Test grounds is now less than it once was because seating accommodation has been improved at the cost of larger crowds. Most of them, when full, rarely take as much as 30,000. In South Africa, the splendid new Wanderers Ground in Johannesburg holds over 30,000, and crowds of 40,000, although packed in acute discomfort, are frequent in India irrespective of the state of the game.

There is only one exception to the concept of a Test series being a simple clash between two countries. In 1912, a triangular tournament was played in England between Australia, England, and South Africa, but for several reasons it was a failure. The weather was bad; South Africa, passing through a transitional period, were extremely weak; and Australia, because of domestic squabbles, were without six of their leading players. There has often been talk since of assembling the world's Test sides in a big international festival, but the difficulties are enormous, the precedent is discouraging, and so, by the early 1970s, nothing had come of it.

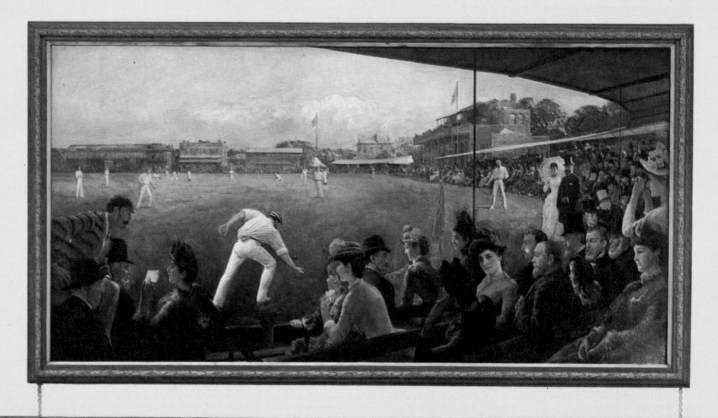

## England v Australia

When those players representing England and Australia took the field at Melbourne in 1877, little could they have realized they were not just playing the first match between the two countries but that they were initiating one of the great sporting institutions. Other series may be more adventurous and entertaining, but none receive the attention and generate the same feeling as that between England and Australia, which from 1883 has been a battle for the Ashes.

The very existence of the Ashes themselves is proof of the importance of the series. It was considered a national disaster when England were beaten by Australia at the Oval in 1882; defeat by either side in a series is still a great blow to national prestige. Players have been unceremoniously dropped from Test sides, their previous record disregarded, if a series is going badly.

After the 1970-71 series, the 50th in the history of encounters between the two countries, honours were even in regard to rubbers won. Each side had won 22 series with 6 drawn. Australia, however, were well ahead in matches won—80 to 68, with 61 drawn. England dominated most series played in the 19th century, but Australia remained unbeaten in a series from 1934 until 1953— a period coinciding largely with the presence of Don Bradman.

### ENGLAND v AUSTRALIA

Tests won by England:     70
Tests won by Australia:    82
Tests drawn:              62†

**Highest team innings**
England:   903-7 dec, Oval, 1938
Australia: 729-6 dec, Lord's, 1930

**Highest individual innings**
England:   364 by L. Hutton, Oval, 1938
Australia: 334 by D. G. Bradman, Leeds, 1930

**Most runs in the matches**
England:   3,636 (*average* 54.26) by J. B. Hobbs
Australia: 5,028 (*average* 89.78) by D. G. Bradman

**Most runs in a series**
England:   905 (*average* 113.12) by W. R. Hammond, 1928-29
Australia: 974 (*average* 139.14) by D. G. Bradman, 1930

**Most wickets in the matches**
England:   109 (*average* 24.00) by W. Rhodes
Australia: 141 (*average* 20.88) by H. Trumble

**Most wickets in a series**
England:   46 (*average* 9.60) by J. C. Laker, 1956
Australia: 36 (*average* 26.27) by A. A. Mailey, 1920-21

**Best bowling in an innings**
England:   10-53 by J. C. Laker, Old Trafford, 1956
Australia: 9-121 by A. A. Mailey, Melbourne, 1920-21

†Following the precedent accepted regarding the abandoned Old Trafford Tests of 1890 and 1938, the abandoned Melbourne Test of 1970-71 is not included in these statistics. Figures up to and including the 1972 series

**Series of the 19th century**
**1876-77 in Australia**
Australia 1   England 1
**1878-79 in Australia**
Australia 1   England 0
**1880 in England**
England 1   Australia 0
**1881-82 in Australia**
Australia 2   England 0   Drawn 2
**1882 in England**
England 0   Australia 1
**1882-83 in Australia**
Australia 2   England 2
**1884 in England**
England 1   Australia 0   Drawn 2
**1884-85 in Australia**
Australia 2   England 3
**1886 in England**
England 3   Australia 0
**1886-87 in Australia**
Australia 0   England 2
**1887-88 in Australia**
Australia 0   England 1

**1888 in England**
England 2   Australia 1
**1890 in England**
England 2   Australia 0
**1891-92 in Australia**
Australia 2   England 1
**1893 in England**
England 1   Australia 0   Drawn 2
**1894-95 in Australia**
Australia 2   England 3
**1896 in England**
England 2   Australia 1
**1897-98 in Australia**
Australia 4   England 1
**1899 in England**
England 0   Australia 1   Drawn 4

England's captain Lord Harris races to cut off a four in the first Test on English soil—at the Oval in 1880. England, with W. G. Grace to the fore, won by five wickets.

**1** A composite picture of a Lord's 'Test' between England and Australia. The Prince of Wales, later Edward VII, and his wife stroll on the outfield as the Australians field to W. G. Grace and W. W. Read. The portraits are of Test players of the early 1880s: R. G. Barlow, W. H. Scotton, W. Barnes, A. N. Hornby, Hon A. Lyttelton, W. G. Grace, A. G. Steel, Lord Harris, G. Ulyett, W. W. Read, and A. Shrewsbury; T. W. Garrett, P. S. McDonnell, S. P. Jones, A. C. Bannerman, H. J. H. Scott, F. R. Spofforth, G. Giffen, G. E. Palmer, J. McC. Blackham, W. L. Murdock, and G. J. Bonnor.

THE AUSTRALIAN ELEVEN, 1880.

G. E. PALMER.   W. H. MOULE.   G. J. BONNOR.   G. ALEXANDER.   T. U. GROUBE.
R. SPOFFORTH.   H. F. BOYLE.   W. L. MURDOCH.   P. S. M'DONNELL.   A. C. BANNERMAN.
A. H. JARVIS.   J. SLIGHT.   J. M. BLACKHAM.

**2** The Australian side that toured England in 1880 and played a single Test, at the Oval. Their performance in this match should have given England warning that the Australians, formidable on their home wickets, would be a strength to be reckoned with in England in the near future. **3** This they proved in 1882 when they won by 7 runs—England's defeat being the cause of the now-famous obituary for English cricket and the start of the Ashes. The Australian victory was in no small part due to the devastating bowling of 'The Demon', F. R. Spofforth (**4**).

Australia could not hope to beat England at full strength on level terms: that was the view of English cricket followers up to the time of the first of all 'Test' matches, played at Melbourne in March 1877. Yet Australia won a notable victory by 45 runs. The English touring party was all-professional, so it was not quite fully representative, but it was a strong team, and few had doubted beforehand that it would be good enough to win.

Right from this first encounter no quarter was asked and none given. Charles Bannerman, whose hard-hitting 165 set Australia on the road to victory, had his knuckles so badly bruised by the fast rising deliveries of George Ulyett of Yorkshire that he was eventually forced to retire. The English tourists won the return, but the Australians confirmed their new status as international cricketers at Melbourne in 1879 by beating another touring English side by 10 wickets.

These three matches introduced some of the greatest of all names to Test cricket, especially on the Australian side. The Bannermans, Charlie and Alec; W. L. Murdoch, batsman and later captain; the bearded wicket-keeper Blackham; and the legendary Spofforth, first of the great modern bowlers. All bear comparison with the illustrious names of later years. The batting on the whole was less accomplished than England's, and the fielding at first was inferior, as was the understanding of tactics. But in this early period the strength and penetration of Australian bowling was a revelation.

Those who maintained, despite these reverses, that England at full strength on her own ground would prove invincible found confirmation of their view at the Oval in 1880, in the first Test match in England and the only one of that Australian tour. Grace's 152 in his first Test was bettered by Murdoch's 153 not out, but not before Australia had followed on. England were left with only 57 to win, yet they lost five wickets in the process, and received such a fright that complacency should have been dispelled for ever.

Another all-professional party visited Australia in 1881-82, a strong combination that included Ulyett, R. G. Barlow, W. Bates, Arthur Shrewsbury, W. H. Scotton, Thomas Emmett, Alfred Shaw, and E. Peate, but it lost two of the four Tests played and failed to win any. These men must have been well aware what England would be up against in 1882, but belief in invincibility at home remained.

As in 1880, only one Test was played, at the Oval, and it set the seal on Australian maturity. Needing only 85 to win in a low-scoring match, England were bowled out for 77, a feat immortalized by the famous lament in the *Sporting Times* on the death of English cricket: 'the body will be cremated and the ashes taken to Australia.' Spofforth in this match took 14 for 90—figures that, until 1972, had never been beaten by an Australian.

England regained the 'Ashes' somewhat luckily in 1882-83 by winning two of a rubber of three matches. Australia squared the series by winning a fourth match, but the fate of the Ashes was held to have been decided already. Following this somewhat hollow revenge, England went on to retain the Ashes for the next nine years, but they were often fortunate to do so. Up to 1885 the Australians probably had the stronger side. Their great quartet

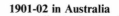

Australia 4 England 1
This English tour, led by A. C. MacLaren, was the 15th and last of Australia under private management. A number of leading players were not available, but the inclusion of S. F. Barnes, plucked out of league cricket with very little first-class experience and plunged straight into the turmoil of an Australian tour, was a surprise. In the first two Tests, of which the two countries won one each, Barnes took 19 wickets, but he was over-bowled, and early in the third Test he broke down. Australia won the last three Tests and proved their superiority beyond doubt.

Without Barnes, the England bowling lacked a spearhead, and the batting, apart from MacLaren and Tom Hayward, was disappointing, though Braund proved a valuable all-rounder. For Australia, the left-handed Clem Hill was outstanding as a batsman, making 521 runs and becoming the second man to exceed 500 in a series (another left-hander, Joe Darling, was the first, in 1897-98). Medium-pacers Noble and Trumble took 60 wickets between them. The Australians had picked up the rudiments of swerve bowling in Philadelphia on their way home from previous tours, and this was the first series in which it was exploited to any degree.

**1902 in England**

England 1 Australia 2 Drawn 2
Victory in this unsatisfactory series probably went to the better of two great sides. But the traumatic events of Old Trafford, linked for all time with the name of Fred Tate, and the exhilarating victory at the Oval, inspired by Gilbert Jessop, have long tortured English cricket followers with what might have been. England began the series with a substantial score at Edgbaston, then shot the Australians out for 36 after heavy rain—their lowest-ever score. But the rain that had treated the tourists so unkindly returned to save them, and the second Test, too, was spoilt by rain.

Bearing the results of the fourth and fifth Tests in mind, the decisive game was the third Test at Sheffield, played against a drab background in appalling light. Here, after Australia had gained a first-innings lead of 49, Trumper and Hill decided the issue by aggressive batting, sweeping aside the combined efforts of Barnes, Hirst, Braund, Jackson, and Rhodes, and 339 to win was too much for England.

At Old Trafford, Australia, 37 ahead on the first innings, had soon lost 3 wickets for 10 runs. Then Darling was missed on the square leg boundary by Tate, and the score was advanced to 64 before another wicket fell. The runs were crucial—and Tate could still have redeemed himself, but with four runs wanted and one

---

of bowlers—Spofforth and T. W. Garrett, fast or fast-medium, and G. E. Palmer and H. F. Boyle, medium pace—were more dangerous than any English combination, the fielding had improved dramatically, and only a tendency to rashness in the batting, and disputes that affected selection, allowed English teams to prevail.

After a disappointing tour of England in 1886, when several leading Australians were absent, and with the great quartet of bowlers ageing or anyway less effective, Australian cricket went into decline. From 1886 to 1890, 11 Tests were played and England won 10 of them, losing only once. This period coincided with the peak of the Surrey fast-medium bowler George Lohmann, and it also saw the emergence of the slow left-arm bowlers Johnny Briggs and Bobbie Peel. Yet no pair of bowlers has ever been quite so destructive on English wickets as

**England's nine-wicket victory in the first Test at Sydney was their only win in the five-match series of 1897-98.**

With several of their leading players absent and with their great bowlers less effective, the Australians of 1886 lost all three Tests that year.

were the Australians C. T. B. Turner and J. J. Ferris—right arm fast-medium and left arm above-medium respectively—in 1888. Poorly supported, they often had to bowl at impossible targets because of batting that lacked the necessary skill and concentration, and for all their effectiveness they could not triumph on their own over the great all round strength of the English teams of the period.

The recovery of Australian cricket came at last in the winter of 1891-92, when England sent a strong side, led by W. G. Grace, but lost the first two Tests of a three-match rubber. Australian batsmen had learnt to play steadily, with stonewaller Alec Bannerman the great stumbling-block, and Turner found a new bowling partner in George Giffen. Giffen's record places him, with Noble, Armstrong, and Miller, among the greatest of Australian

all-rounders. Abel, A. E. Stoddart, Briggs, and Lohmann did best for England in a series that brought a timely revival of interest in Australia.

England came back to win the next three series, in 1893, 1894-95, and 1896, and they owed much to their batting strength, Shrewsbury, F. S. Jackson, William Gunn, Grace, Stoddart, and Ranjitsinhji being outstanding. But the power that tipped the scales in this period was fast bowling, especially that of Tom Richardson. In his first nine Tests he took 66 wickets, and in the early 1970s he still held the career record of more wickets per match than any other bowler. It was not until his power began to wane that Australia won another rubber. But then, with the emergence of players of the calibre of Victor Trumper, Clem Hill, M. A. Noble, Joe Darling, Hugh Trumble, and fast bowler Ernest Jones, they finished the 1890s strongly by winning the last two series. The Australian side of 1899, led by Darling, was by general consent the strongest seen in England since 1882.

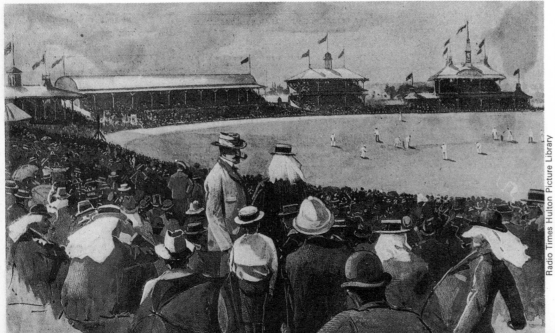

wicket to fall, he was clean bowled. At the Oval, England looked hopelessly placed in the fourth innings at 48-5 with 263 wanted, but Jessop arrived to complete an astonishing hundred in 75 minutes, and George Hirst and Wilfred Rhodes, coming together for the last wicket, made the 15 runs needed to win the characteristic aplomb.

## 1903-04 in Australia
Australia 2   England 3

After winning four consecutive series, Australia were overthrown by the extraordinary variety of the English attack, in which B. J. T. Bosanquet with his googlies, although sometimes expensive, was the decisive factor. The first Test was remarkable for two of the greatest innings ever played, one of 287 by R. E. Foster that gave England a long first-innings lead, and another by Trumper of 185 not out that helped set Eng-

Radio Times Hulton Picture Library

**The 1905 series was a personal triumph for England's captain, the Hon. S. F. Jackson. Playing in his last series, he scored centuries in the third and fourth Tests, headed the batting and bowling averages, and led England to victory by two Tests.**

land a sizeable fourth-innings task. This they proved equal to, and they won the next Test through getting in their first knock before the rain came. An unaccountable batting collapse then cost them the third.

Winning the toss in the vital fourth Test, England again faltered; but a fine defensive innings by A. E. Knight dominated their recovery, and the Australians, handicapped by rain that quickened the wicket, and mesmerized by Bosanquet, never got in the game. In the fifth Test England had the same wretched luck with the weather as the Australians had had in the second, and were easily beaten.

A section of the crowd demonstrated against the umpire in the first Test at Sydney when Hill was run out, and only a personal appeal from Noble, the Australian captain, dissuaded 'Plum' Warner from withdrawing his team. The hooting and bottle-throwing were even worse in the fourth Test, when the crowd were incensed by the repeated stoppages for rain.

## 1905 in England
England 2   Australia 0   Drawn 3

The Australian side again looked a strong one, but it was soon apparent that the bowling, weakened by the decline of Noble, was below Test match standard, and the powerful England batting, led by Jackson, C. B. Fry, J. T. Tyldesley, and MacLaren, was rarely in difficulty. England for their part always managed to find bowlers to suit the conditions, while the Australian batting could not surmount the wretched form of Trumper and Hill. Some fast bumpers from A. Cotter gave Australia an encouraging start at Trent Bridge, but Jessop replied in kind, and the bumpers were withheld from then on. England amassed 426-5 in their second innings, and then Bosanquet (8-107) ran through the Austra-

Joe Darling's Australians of 1902 contained many great names of Australian cricket, and in a series in which both individual brilliance and the weather were prominent they won by two Tests to one.

lians, England winning by 213 runs.

The second and third Tests, although drawn, went very much in England's favour, and England won the fourth by an innings. Jackson, the England captain, got his second hundred in successive Tests, and the Australians batted recklessly when caution might have saved the day. The most even game was the last, when both sides scored heavily and when Australia came within sight of victory on the last morning. Stubborn defence and the benefit of some hotly disputed umpiring decisions, however, enabled England to draw.

Jackson crowned a highly successful career in home Tests by topping both the batting and the bowling averages (492 runs for an average of 70.28 and 13 wickets at 15.46 each). He also won the toss in all five Tests.

## 1907-08 in Australia
Australia 4   England 1

The extraordinary depth and resilience of the Australian batting finally mastered an England attack that relied chiefly on pace. The England batting, weakened by withdrawals through financial disagreements, was unexpectedly stiffened by George Gunn, who happened to be wintering in Australia. His innings of 119 and 74 should have won the first Test, but England could not polish off the Australian tail. In the second match, in which Hobbs made 83 in his first Test, it was the English tail that wagged, the last pair putting on 39 for victory. But in the third Test England, after outplaying their opponents for more than three days, were demoralized

Mary Evans

in the Australian second innings by an eighth wicket stand of 243 between Hill and R. J. Hartigan.

In the fourth Test England had the worst of the wicket and they were led on the first innings by 109, but they hit back so well that the Australians slumped to 77-5. Then came another demoralizing recovery, the Australian total reached 385, and the Ashes were won. In the final Test England actually gained a lead of 144 on the first innings, but again the Australian batting, led by Trumper (166), came back to ensure victory.

J. N. Crawford, A. Fielder, and Barnes took 79 of the 93 Australian wickets that fell, heavily underlining the spin-bowling weakness that nourished Australia's powers of recovery. Four times in succession the side scored more runs at the second attempt.

### 1909 in England
England 1  Australia 2  Drawn 2
Australia began their tour badly and were beaten in the first Test. They had, however, brought a side of considerable all-round strength, and of the players new to England, V. S. Ransford nearly always made runs and Warren Bardsley and Charles Macartney did well. Brilliant fielding, and the astute leadership of Noble, finally saw them to victory.

The turning point came at Lord's in the second Test, when Australia won comfortably by 9 wickets. England did well to total 269 after being put in, but no fast bowler had been chosen and Australia, helped by dropped catches, gained a lead of 81, after which England collapsed. England made six changes for the third Test at Headingley, and this proved the decisive game. The wicket gave the bowlers a chance, and England began confidently, getting Australia out for 188 and reaching 137-2. Then Macartney (7-58) ran through the side. The struggle proved completely absorbing as Australia fought to set England a formidable fourth-innings target, and it was Macartney who provided the stability when Australia were in trouble at 127-7. Set 214 to win, England reached 56-2 overnight, but then collapsed before Cotter and Macartney.

One up in the series, Australia concentrated on avoiding defeat at Old Trafford and the Oval, where Bardsley scored a hundred in both innings.

*Right,* **The 1911-12 MCC side that recovered the Ashes so convincingly.** *Standing,* l-r; **S. P. Kinneir, E. J. Smith, F. E. Woolley, S. F. Barnes, J. Iremonger, R. C. Campbell, J. Vine, H. Strudwick.** *Seated;* **W. Rhodes, J. W. H. T. Douglas, P. F. Warner, F. R. Foster, T. Pawley (manager), J. B. Hobbs, G. Gunn;** *front;* **J. W. Hearne, J. W. Hitch;** *inset;* **C. P. Mead.**

**1** England's only victory of the 1909 series came in the first Test at Edgbaston where George Hirst (bowling) took 4-28 and 5-58. Colin Blythe got the other wickets. **2** Jack Hobbs and his captain Archie MacLaren go out to open England's innings.

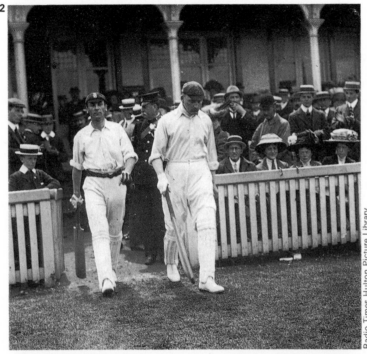

### 1911-12 in Australia
Australia 1  England 4
This series will always be remembered for the great bowling of Frank Foster and Barnes; but a decisive battle had to be fought by the England batsmen before these two bowlers could triumph. The danger came from the Australian googly bowler H. V. Hordern, who took 12 for 175 in the first Test, which Australia won by 146 runs. Only J. W. Hearne (76 and 43) played him safely, and it was Hearne (114) who played the innings of the series in the second Test, after Australia had collapsed to Barnes on the first morning. At lunch Australia were 32-4, all to Barnes, and soon afterwards they were 38-6. They fought back but never really recovered, and a century by Jack Hobbs in the England second innings helped to settle the issue.

The third and fourth Tests had many similarities. Australia batted first in each and were shot out cheaply by Foster and Barnes; in the fourth Test they were actually put in. Hobbs and Rhodes passed the Australian score each time before being parted, putting on 147 at Adelaide and 323 at Melbourne. Australia fought back magnificently at Adelaide to total 476 in their second innings, but England knocked off the runs easily, and there was no fight back at Melbourne, where England won by an innings and 225 runs.

The final Test at Sydney, although interrupted by rain, proved the most even contest. Hordern worried all the England batsmen, but a century from Frank Woolley ensured a fair total. The Australian batting again failed, but Hordern's googlies gave them a chance, and with 363 wanted they reached 193-3 on the fifth day. Then came more rain, and England won by 70 runs.

### 1912 in England
England 1  Australia 0  Drawn 2
The experiment of running a triangular tournament between England, Australia, and South Africa proved a failure, partly because of a disastrously wet summer. The first Test at Lord's was so curtailed by rain that each side batted only once, and at Old Trafford only the England first innings was completed. It was, therefore, decided to play the Oval Test to a finish but showers before the game and a huge storm after England had batted made Australia's task impossible. The features of the series were the batting of Rhodes, who at times outshone even Hobbs, and a great innings of 99 by Macartney at Lord's when England for a time scented victory.

Australia's supremacy in the early part of the new century had brought them level with England in number of victories in 1911, but England had reasserted themselves and now led by 40 wins to 35, with 19 matches drawn.

## 1920-21 in Australia

**Australia 5 England 0**

Australia cleared the board, the only time this has been done in a five-match series, and even this margin did not flatter them. Their victories were by 377 runs, an innings and 91 runs, 119 runs, eight wickets, and nine wickets, and only in the third match did England get the merest glimpse of a win. The England batting, apart from Hobbs and the dour Johnny Douglas, was barely adequate, and a weak attack was quickly disheartened by dropped catches. No England bowler approached the penetration of Jack Gregory, and the Australian batsmen scored so heavily that there were always plenty of runs in hand to give Arthur Mailey a long bowl. By taking 36 wickets, Mailey beat the previous England v Australia record of 34 set up by S. F. Barnes in 1911-12.

Only twice was the Australian first innings score kept within reasonable bounds—at Sydney in the first Test, where they were dismissed for 267, and at Adelaide in the third, where they made 354 and were led for once on first innings. But each time they came back with a record second innings score—581 at Sydney and 582 at Adelaide. England fought hard to make the 490 they needed for victory at Adelaide (Hobbs 123), but they failed.

## 1921 in England

**England 0 Australia 3 Drawn 2**

Australia extended their unbroken run of victories by winning the first three Tests, and the margins were again nearer to routs—10 wickets, 9 wickets, and 219 runs. Few England batsmen could cope with the lifting ball as propelled by Gregory, while the pace and accuracy of Ted Macdonald proved the perfect foil. Hobbs, although fielding briefly at Headingley, otherwise missed the entire series through illness, and the England selectors rang the changes on 30 players in all. England had no bowler of pace and no class spinner, and the Australians made what runs they needed and then bowled England out.

In such an uneven contest it was inevitable that peripheral matters should command more than average attention. At Trent Bridge during the first Test the crowd roared their disapproval of Gregory's bumpers. At Headingley for the third Test, Douglas was replaced as captain, after seven successive defeats, by the Hon Lionel Tennyson, although he held his place in the side. He then found himself in charge again soon after the start when Tennyson injured his hand. Although severely handicapped Tennyson made 99 runs in the match. And at Old Trafford, with the rubber and the Ashes safe and the Australians easing the pressure, Tennyson made his famous blunder of

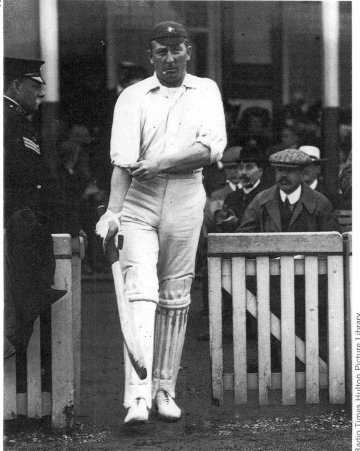

**1 Warren Bardsley is caught at slip by Frank Woolley off the bowling of Johnny Douglas at Headingley in 1921. The Australians, having already won the first two Tests, won this one by 219 runs to take a 3-0 lead in the series. The England side was changed constantly in an effort to find a winning formula, but the Australians, under W. W. Armstrong (2), were not to be beaten during the series.**

declaring too late after what had become the first day of a two-day match following rain. Warwick Armstrong, who bowled the last over before the argument, then bowled the first afterwards, so adding more confusion to the incident. At the Oval, Armstrong read a newspaper in the outfield to indicate his boredom.

## 1924-25 in Australia

**Australia 4 England 1**

The graph of the series faithfully records England's progress. Beaten by 193 runs in the first Test and 81 in the second, they lost by only 11 runs at Adelaide and would almost certainly have won but for an injury to Maurice Tate. They went on to win the fourth Test by an innings and 29 runs. A heavy defeat in the last match rightly emphasized the solidity of the Australian batting, but the decisive factor was the introduction of a new bowler named Clarrie Grimmett.

A second-wicket partnership of 190 between Herbert Collins (114) and Bill Ponsford (110) formed the basis of Australia's first innings 450 at Sydney, and although Hobbs and Herbert Sutcliffe replied with 157 (Hobbs 115), England were all out for 298. Another century opening partnership in the England second innings and a century from Woolley still left England a long way short. In the second Test, Hobbs and Sutcliffe put on 283 after Australia had amassed a record 600 (Ponsford 128, Victor Richardson 138), but the later batting failed, and a second hundred by Sutcliffe could not save England. The third Test ended after many fluctuations in a narrow Australian victory, and England won the fourth Test easily after winning the toss for the only time. Then came Grimmett, taking 5-45 and 6-37 in Australia's 307-run victory.

Sutcliffe's aggregate of 734 runs was a record, as was Tate's bag of 38 wickets.

## 1926 in England

**England 1 Australia 0 Drawn 4**

Going to the Oval after four drawn games with all to play for in a 'timeless' Test, England dropped their captain Arthur Carr for Percy Chapman. They also restored Harold Larwood and the 48-year-old Wilfred Rhodes.

They won the toss but frittered the advantage away, and Australia led on the first innings by 22. Hobbs and Sutcliffe put England in front again before the close on the second day, and then came the storm.

The story of how Hobbs and Sutcliffe defied the Australian spinners on a 'sticky dog' has become legendary. The bowlers best suited to the conditions were A. J. Richardson, off-spin round the wicket, and Macartney, left-arm over, and they spun and kicked viciously from an impeccable length. But somehow Hobbs and Sutcliffe came through. Hobbs made 100 out of 172, by which time the match was virtually won; the wicket would never be 'plumb' again. Sutcliffe went on to make 161. The Australian second innings was then broken by Larwood and Rhodes.

The earlier matches in this series had underlined the frustrations of three-day Tests, and the clamour for a fourth day became insistent (Tests in Australia had been played to a finish almost from the beginning). The four drawn matches were remarkable for the aggressive batting of Macartney, who made hundreds in the three middle Tests, including a century before lunch at Leeds, and the consistency as a pair of Hobbs and Sutcliffe.

### 1928-29 in Australia
**Australia 1 England 4**
The series was dominated by the monolithic batting of Walter Hammond. After a moderate first Test (44 and 28), he made 251 in the second, 200 and 32 (run out) in the third, and 119 not out and 177 in the fourth. A disappointing final match (38 and 16) left him 95

*Right,* **Tom Webster has a look at one of the problems that beset England in 1924-25.** *Below,* **Hobbs defies Australia on a 'sticky dog' at the Oval in 1926 to set England on the road to a Test victory that also won them the series.**

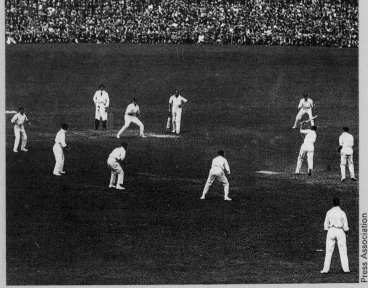

runs short of a thousand for the series. Three other England batsmen, Patsy Hendren, Sutcliffe, and Hobbs, averaged over 50, and it was Hendren (169) who played the innings that turned the opening Test England's way. This was the match in which Chapman batted again although leading by 399 on first innings. With two players indisposed, and with a final stab in the back from the weather, Australia were sunk without trace.

England had gone into the first Test with three bowlers plus Hammond, but they did not take this risk again. George Geary, who played in the remaining four Tests, topped the bowling averages, and 'Farmer' White, Larwood, and Tate completed the main attack. For the second Test Australia made the mistake of dropping Bradman, playing in his first series, and England crushed them with a record 636.

England won the third and fourth Tests narrowly, by three wickets and 12 runs respectively. The third Test, after Hammond's 200, was remarkable for a superb stand in the second innings by Hobbs and Sutcliffe on a sticky wicket when England were set 332 to win. The fourth Test, which introduced the 19-year-old Archie Jackson (164) to Test cricket, was saved for England by a stand of 262 between Hammond and Douglas Jardine in the England second innings, but the decisive moment was the running out of Bradman by Hobbs when Australia seemed set for victory. Australia won the fifth Test by consistent batting after England had begun with 519.

## 1930 in England

**England 1 Australia 2 Drawn 2**

If the 1928-29 series was dominated by Hammond, still more will that of 1930 be remembered for England's first sight of Don Bradman. Eight and 131; 254 and 1; 334; 14; and 232—those were his scores in the five Tests, totalling 974 runs and averaging 139. It was an avalanche that would have overwhelmed most sides, and England did well to go into the final Test all square. Hobbs at the age of 47 began the series well but faded, Hammond could not reproduce his Australian form, and only Sutcliffe, who missed the second Test through injury, batted up to his reputation. Grimmett harassed the England batsmen throughout.

England won the first Test by 93 runs, but they had the best of the conditions, and there was a point when Australia seemed likely to get the 429 they needed to win. Winning the toss again at Lord's, England made enough runs to have ensured a draw in normal circumstances; but they reckoned without the astonishing speed and certainty of Bradman's run-getting, and Australia replied to their first innings 425 with 729-6 (Bradman 254). The Headingley Test, in which a cloudburst saved England, will always be remembered for Bradman's 334, of which 309 came on the first day (105 before lunch, 115 in the afternoon, and 89 after tea). The Old Trafford Test was spoiled by rain.

R. E. S. Wyatt replaced Chapman as captain at the Oval, and, thanks largely to a sixth-wicket stand of 170 between Sutcliffe (161) and his new captain, England totalled 405. In any normal series this would have ensured a fight; but Australia now demonstrated their batting superiority beyond all doubt in a total of 695, and England lost by an innings.

## 1932-33 in Australia

**Australia 1 England 4**

Faith in fast bowling as the only form of attack likely to subdue Bradman was triumphantly vindicated in this series. But the manner in which it was deployed was bitterly resented throughout Australia. Fast leg-theory as conceived by Jardine, or bodyline as it was dubbed by the Australians, took on a different connotation when projected by bowlers of the pace and accuracy of Harold Larwood and Bill Voce, and the batsmen felt themselves under continual physical attack. Nevertheless Jardine persisted with his policy throughout an explosive series, which at one point seemed likely to be abandoned. When the full facts were known the method was generally condemned, and legislation to outlaw this type of bowling was eventually passed. What Bradman might have achieved without bodyline can never be known, but the likelihood is that England

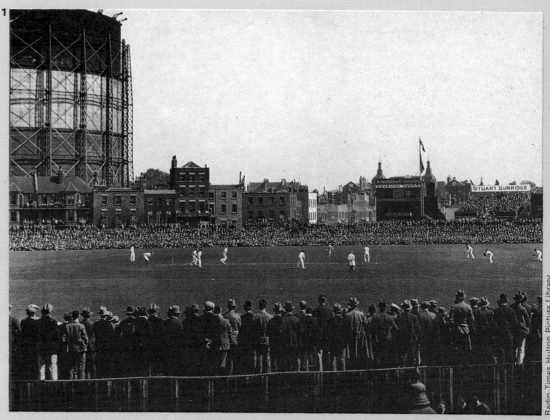

**1** England scored 405 in their first innings at the Oval in 1930, but Australia, with Don Bradman amassing 232, replied with 695 and then dismissed England again to win by an innings and 39 runs. **2** But in 1932-33, England countered Bradman with bodyline, and the policy enjoyed instant success when Bowes bowled The Don for 0 in his first innings of the series. **3** On the third day of that Melbourne Test, a record 68,188 watched as Australia gained ascendancy.

would still have won. Although outclassed in wrist-spin, they were in other respects the better side.

Australia went into the first Test without Bradman, who was unfit, and were saved on the first day by a superb innings from McCabe, whose 187 not out was the greatest innings played against bodyline. Nevertheless centuries from Sutcliffe, Hammond, and Pataudi gave England a long lead, and then the Australians crumpled before Larwood. In the second Test on a slow wicket, bodyline was less successful, and O'Reilly (10 for 129) and Bradman (0 and 103 not out) got Australia home in a low-scoring match. The genius of Bill O'Reilly (27 wickets in the series) ensured that England did not have matters all their own way in the remaining matches, but they won them all. Larwood broke all records for a fast bowler by taking 33 wickets, but Gubby Allen, who avoided bodyline throughout, took 21, seeming to underline what Larwood might have achieved by orthodox methods.

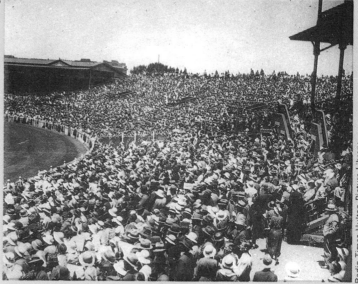

## 1934 in England

England 1 Australia 2 Drawn 2
Partly as a result of the controversy that followed the 'bodyline' series, England were without Jardine, Larwood, and Voce, and injuries to other key players continually weakened the team. A wicket that took spin helped Australia to a thrilling victory in the first Test with only 10 minutes to spare, but luck went England's way at Lord's, where they made 440 (Ames 120, Leyland 109) and then caught Australia on a rain-affected wicket. Wyatt, the England captain, was criticized for batting on into the second afternoon, but England would never have won had he not done so. As it was, the Australians nearly saved the follow on, when England would have had to bat on the worst of the wicket. Verity took 14 wickets in a single day and 15 in the match.

At Old Trafford came the famous O'Reilly over after the ball was changed. England slumped from 68-0 to 72-3, but Hendren (132) and Maurice Leyland (153) then led a recovery and England totalled 627. The wicket was over-prepared, and Australia saved the follow-on, but the honours went to England. The pendulum swung back at Headingley, where England collapsed unaccountably. Bradman made 304, putting on a record 388 with Ponsford (181), but again a draw resulted, this time through rain. At the Oval, where Australia won the toss, Bradman (244) and Ponsford (266) broke their own record with a partnership of 451 on the first day, and England were overwhelmed.

The bowling of O'Reilly and Grimmett was also a vital factor in the Australian victory.

## 1936-37 in Australia

Australia 3 England 2
After a moderate start to the tour, England surprised everyone by winning the first two Tests. After being 20-3 at Brisbane they made 358, thanks chiefly to Leyland (126), and then Voce and Allen bowled them to a substantial first innings lead despite a hundred from Jack Fingleton. Australia, set 381 to win, found their task eventually made impossible by rain. The second Test brought a double century from Hammond (231 not out), and then, after rain stopped play on the second day, an overnight thunderstorm compounded England's advantage. Only a pronounced change of luck, or massive scoring by Bradman, seemed likely to save the series for Australia. As it happened both were forthcoming.

Yet the Ashes seemed almost won on the first afternoon of the third Test, when Australia had fallen to 130-6 on a good wicket. Soon afterwards came the rain, Australia declared at 200-9, and England were shot out for 76 (M. W. Sievers 5-21, O'Reilly 3-28). Bradman then changed his

batting order, holding Fingleton and himself back to No. 6 and No. 7, by which time the wicket had recovered. Bradman (270) and Fingleton (136) then put on 346 together, and not even another Leyland hundred could save England.

Neither side could establish a commanding first-innings position at Adelaide, but 212 from Bradman at the second attempt and fine bowling by Fleetwood-Smith and O'Reilly were instrumental in levelling the series. Bradman (169) and the two spin bowlers also dominated the final Test, and Australia came from behind to retain the Ashes.

## 1938 in England

England 1 Australia 1 Drawn 2
In a series of generally over-prepared wickets, it was ironic that a dusty pitch at Headingley should decide the fate of the Ashes. Taken all round England were the stronger side, but they did not help their chances by

**Herbert Sutcliffe, though not as prolific as of yore, gave the England innings a steady start in the 1934 series.**

playing only one fast bowler in the first Test and failing to reconstruct their side at Headingley when three key players reported unfit. The entire Old Trafford match was abandoned through rain.

Three England batsmen—Charles Barnett, Len Hutton, and Denis Compton—made centuries at Trent Bridge and one, Eddie Paynter, a double-century, and England totalled 658-8. Yet the innings of the match was played by McCabe. Faced with impending disaster at 194-6, McCabe put on 69 with B. A. Barnett, then dominated the strike so successfully that he made 127 out of the last 148 in 80 minutes after Barnett was out. Australia followed on, but Brown (133) and Bradman (144 not out) saved the match. At Lord's it was England's

turn to scent defeat, despite a great 240 in their first innings by Hammond, but they closed their ranks and a draw resulted. Then came the dusty wicket at Headingley, a great century by Bradman in appalling light, and magnificent bowling by O'Reilly, who took 10 for 122 in the match.

Thus England could only square the series at the Oval, but this they proceeded to do. Hutton made a record 364, Leyland 187, and Joe Hardstaff 169 not out, and Hammond declared at 903-7. This crushing weight of runs, and injuries to Bradman and Fingleton, made the rest of the match a formality.

The position of the two countries at this stage was Australia 57, England 55, with 31 Tests drawn.

**With Len Hutton batting in a masterly manner for a record 364 at the Oval, England were able to declare at 903-7 and won to square the 1938 series.**

*Central Press*

## 1946-47 in Australia

Australia 3 England 0 Drawn 2
The last pre-war Test had ended
in England's biggest-ever victory;
the first post-war Test brought a
record victory for Australia. Yet
England might have come much
closer to recovering the Ashes but
for Bradman. And even Bradman
needed a slice of luck to re-estab-
lish himself in Test cricket at the
age of 38. After an uncertain
beginning at Brisbane he had
made 28 when he gave what
seemed a perfectly clean catch to
Ikin in the gully, only to be given
not out. He went on to make 187
in that match and 234 in the next,
both of which Australia won by
an innings.

At Brisbane England had cruel
luck with the weather, but they
could offer no such excuse at
Sydney, where Sid Barnes and

**Denis Compton's centuries in
each innings at Adelaide were
brighter moments for England
in the somewhat Australian-
dominated series of 1946-47.**

Bradman put on 405 for the
Australian fifth wicket. For the
remainder of the series Bradman's
scores were kept within reasonable limits, and with Cyril Washbrook, Hutton, and Compton
finding their form England put
up a much better show. The third
Test was drawn after an even
fight (Tests in Australia were now
limited to 30 hours' playing time,
as in England), England saved
the fourth after Compton had
made a hundred in each innings,
and England were going reasonably well in the final Test when
Hutton (122) had to retire with
tonsilitis. England actually gained

a first-innings lead, but Hutton's
illness and the spin of Colin
McCool redressed the balance
and Australia, although pressed
all the way, won by five wickets.

Hammond at 43 failed tragically, and the successes of the
tour were Bill Edrich, who proved
the most consistent batsman, and
Norman Yardley, whose all-round
form was a surprise. Alec Bedser
and Doug Wright carried the
bowling, but the support was
weak. Ray Lindwall and Keith
Miller led a strong Australian
attack.

## 1948 in England

England 0 Australia 4 Drawn 1
With Lindwall and Miller reaching their peak, ably backed up by
Bill Johnston, with Arthur Morris
emerging as a left-hander in the
great Australian tradition, and

with Bradman, Barnes, and Lindsay Hassett as effective as ever,
this was a great Australian side,
lacking only a top-class spinner.
The experimental rule that allowed
a new ball every 55 overs, however, enabled Bradman to shrug
off this weakness. England were
unlucky at Trent Bridge to bat
first on a wicket enlivened by
rain, and Australia led on the
first innings by 344, Bradman and
Hassett making centuries. England fought back well, and not
until Compton fell on his wicket
after making 184 did England's
chance of saving the match dis-
appear. At Lord's England were
again facing defeat at the end of
the second day (Australia 350,
England 207-9) and they never
recovered.

England hit back at Old Trafford to total 363 after being 119-5.
Compton, struck on the head by
a Lindwall bouncer, returned to
make 145 not out. Bedser and
Dick Pollard bowled Australia
out for 221 (Barnes was absent
injured), and England lost a
great chance of victory when the
fourth day was washed out.

The Headingley Test is of
particularly poignant memory for
England. Centuries from Washbrook and Edrich took them to
496, Australia replied with 458
and when England declared on
the last morning Australia wanted
404 in 344 minutes to win. England muffed their chances, Morris
and Bradman put on 301, and
Australia won by 7 wickets.

At the Oval England were dismissed for 52 (Hutton 30), and
Australia never relaxed their grip
on the game.

**Australian 'keeper Don Tallon
makes sure he has souvenirs
of Australia's triumphant
series under Bradman in 1948.**

*Fox Photos*

## 1950-51 in Australia

Australia 4  England 1

England included several young and inexperienced players, and Australia introduced a new and unorthodox spin bowler named Jack Iverson, who topped their averages. Miller, Hassett, and Harvey scored consistently for Australia, but Washbrook and Compton failed, and none of the new England batsmen prospered. Hutton was magnificent, but until

1 Harvey catches Dewes off the bowling of Jack Iverson in the second Test of 1950-51. 2 Frank Tyson wraps up the Australian innings at Sydney in 1954-55. It was his 10th wicket of the match and he gave England a vital victory. 3 Peter May falls victim to Gordon Rorke at Adelaide in 1958-59, when there was some controversy over the action of some Australian bowlers.

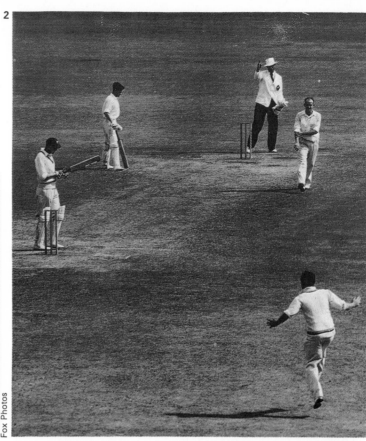

the last Test the next most successful batsman was Freddie Brown. Brown also took more wickets (18) than any previous England captain, but Bedser (30 wickets) was the outstanding bowler.

After dismissing Australia for 228 on the first day at Brisbane England were caught on a rain-affected wicket and declared at 68-7. Australia in turn declared at 32-7, setting England 193 to win. They slumped to 30-6, and on the last day a great innings by Hutton (62 not out) could not save them. Fine bowling by Bedser and Trevor Bailey and a rousing 62 from Brown gave England a narrow advantage at Melbourne, but the varied Australian attack eventually achieved a narrow victory. In the third Test, Bedser, J. J. Warr, and Brown strove heroically after Bailey and Wright were hurt, but they could not prevent an Australian first innings lead of 136 (Miller 145) and England collapsed to Iverson (6-27) to lose by an innings.

A fine 206 by Arthur Morris was matched by 156 not out from Hutton at Adelaide, possibly his greatest innings, but the remaining England batsmen could muster only 95 between them, and England lost a match they should have saved. Consolation came in the final Test when England, thanks largely to Simpson (156 not out) and Hutton, won their first Test against Australia since the war.

## 1953 in England

England 1  Australia 0  Drawn 4

Four draws and a victory at the Oval to England, who thus

regained the Ashes after losing three post-war series, was history repeating itself. But there comparisons ended. The four drawn games were packed with drama. First the Australians were dismissed for 249 at Trent Bridge (Hassett 115) and then England collapsed to Lindwall and lagged by 105. Great bowling by Alec Bedser (14 for 99 in the match) brought England right back into the game, the target needed being 229, but rain spoilt the match with England 42-1.

The Lord's Test was remarkable for the great match-saving stand between Willie Watson (109) and Bailey (71), after England had begun the final day facing almost certain defeat. Australia made 346 (Hassett 104), England replied with 372 (Hutton 145), and then Australia, helped by 109 from Miller, set England 343 to win and had them 20-3 before nightfall. There were still five hours left when Bailey joined Watson next morning, and they were not parted until 5.30.

Rain ruined the Old Trafford Test, but England got a horrible fright on the last day at Headingley, where Australia, wanting 177 in 115 minutes, set off at a gallop. The gate was closed by Bailey, bowling wide of the leg stump off a long run, but his tactics were not widely approved.

On a typical Oval wicket of the period, Australia had no answers to Jim Laker and Tony Lock in the deciding Test. But the bowler of the series was Bedser, who took a record 39 wickets.

**1954-55 in Australia**
Australia 1  England 3  Drawn 1
After a wretched start at Brisbane, England turned the tables and won the next three Tests. The chief destroyer was Frank Tyson, splendidly partnered by Brian Statham, but there were many significant performances in support. Bob Appleyard, Johnny Wardle, and Trevor Bailey completed a varied attack, while Peter May, Colin Cowdrey, Denis Compton, and Len Hutton all played important innings in the matches that were won. The Australian batting was vulnerable, but England always had to fight for their runs.

Put in at Brisbane on what proved to be a lifeless wicket, Australia made 601-8 declared (Harvey 162, Morris 153). Then Lindwall and Miller demonstrated that they were still great bowlers, and England followed on and were easily beaten. In the second Test England were themselves put in, and after lagging on the first innings by 74 they were 55-3 and in an apparently hopeless position when May and Cowdrey put on 116. Australia were set 223 to win, and Tyson, despite a huge bump on the head from a Lindwall bouncer, took 6-85 and got England home.

Early life in the wicket had

England in trouble at Melbourne, but Cowdrey (102) and Bailey pulled the game round, May made 91 in the second innings, and Tyson (9-95) and Statham (7-98) did the rest, England winning by 128. At Adelaide the wicket was more suited to spin, and Australia made 323, England replied with 341, and then great bowling by Tyson and Statham after Appleyard had made the breakthrough left England wanting only 94, which they got for five wickets. The first three days of the final Test were lost through rain, but there was time for a superb hundred from Tom Graveney and for some inept Australian batting that left England pressing for victory.

**1956 in England**
England 2  Australia 1  Drawn 2
With Hutton retired, Compton crippled, and Tyson, Statham,

and Trueman injured, England had to rebuild their side for Trent Bridge. They reached a commanding position on the last day despite interruptions by rain, but could not seal their advantage. The Lord's Test saw the return of Statham and Fred Trueman, but good Australian teamwork, highlighted by an audacious 97 from Richie Benaud in the Australian second innings and 10 for 152 in the match by Miller,

Cartoonist Roy Ullyett sums up the Manchester Test of 1956 when Jim Laker took an unprecedented 19 wickets in the match: 9-37 in Australia's first innings, 10-53 in their second.

left Australia the winners by 185 runs.

Only May (63 and 53) had made runs for England at Lords, and the selectors recalled Cyril Washbrook at Headingley. Joining May when England were 17-3, he helped to add 187 for the fourth wicket, and the partnership proved decisive. The wicket began to help the spinners, and a great 69 from Harvey only delayed the end.

David Sheppard (113) was the

man recalled at Old Trafford, Peter Richardson made 104, and Cowdrey 80, and as at Headingley the ball began to turn. But the Australian collapse (84 all out) was difficult to account for. Rain allowed only short periods of play on the next two days, but it deadened the wicket, and Australia put up a terrific fight. Colin McDonald and Ian Craig were together for more than four hours, but in the final session the ball turned again and Jim Laker completed his great feat of taking all 10 wickets and 19 in the match to put England one up, so retaining the Ashes. Lock in 55 overs in the second innings failed to take a wicket.

Compton was the man resurrected for the final Test, and he and May (94 and 83 not out respectively) retrieved a bad start. But the match was spoilt by rain. Laker took a record 46 wickets in the series.

**1958-59 in Australia**
Australia 4  England 0  Drawn 1
After a long apprenticeship, Alan Davidson and Richie Benaud had developed into great bowlers, McDonald's application brought him 520 runs, and a new batsman of Test class emerged in Norman O'Neill. The England bowlers could never quite get on top, and of the batsmen only Cowdrey and May showed anything like their true form; but they had to contend with much bowling of dubious legality.

At Brisbane on a green wicket, it was not until O'Neill got going in the Australian second innings that bat was put to ball, and then Australia ran out easy winners. At Melbourne there were centuries from May (113) and Harvey (167), and the match looked evenly poised when England batted a second time. They collapsed to the jerky, erratic Meckiff (6-38), and Australia went on to win, as at Brisbane, by eight wickets.

The England batting failed again at Sydney, and although their bowlers hit back Australia recovered to lead by 138 on first innings, and the rubber seemed decided when England slid to 64-3. Then May (92) and Cowdrey (100 not out) put on 182 and the match was saved. At Adelaide Laker reported unfit, England were forced to rely on pace, and the issue was settled as McDonald and Burke put on 171 for the first wicket after being put in. England lost this time by 10 wickets.

Meckiff, whose action was generally conceded to constitute a throw, missed this match through injury, and the man who took the eye was the giant Rorke, whose drag was unprecedented. Put in to bat in the final Test, England lost by nine wickets, and Lindwall, recalled for the fourth Test, broke Grimmett's Australian record of 216 wickets in Test cricket.

## 1961 in England

England 1 Australia 2 Drawn 2
When the two sides went to Old Trafford for the fourth Test, they had won one match each with one game drawn. The scene was set for one of the greatest of all Test matches. Australia won the toss and thanks to fine bowling on a green wicket by Statham (5-53) they were dismissed for 190. With the wicket easier, England then made 367 (May 95, Barrington 78). Then Bill Lawry and Bobby Simpson put on 113, and O'Neill made 67, but at 334-9 Australia were only 157 ahead. Soon afterwards Davidson suddenly hit Allen for 20 in one over, and 98 runs were made for the last wicket.

With 256 wanted at 67 an hour, the game was brought to a thrilling climax by a magnificent 76 in 84 minutes by Ted Dexter. Then Benaud went round the wicket and aimed at the bowler's footmarks, and after getting rid of Dexter he bowled May second ball. Australia won by 54 runs with 20 minutes to spare. Whatever happened at the Oval, they would retain the Ashes.

Led by 321 on the first innings at Edgbaston, England saved the game through Dexter (180) and Ramon Subba Row (112), but they lost the Lord's Test by five wickets through a faulty appreciation of the wicket. England played two spinners, whereas Australia turned the absence of the injured Benaud to fortuitous account by playing three fast bowlers plus Mackay. Lawry (130) was the rock on which victory was built. The third Test at Headingley was a triumph for Trueman (11 for 88), but in a low-scoring match on a patchy wicket England owed much to Cowdrey (93) for their eight-wicket victory. Cowdrey then missed the vital Old Trafford match through illness.

Australia did much to confirm their superiority at the Oval by scoring 494 in the best batting of the series (Peter Burge 181, O'Neill 117). But against a depleted Australian attack England held on for a draw.

## 1962-63 in Australia

Australia 1 England 1 Drawn 3
England ruined their chances by dropping too many catches, and they never mastered Davidson, who took 24 wickets in his last series. The Australian batting was always solid, with Brian Booth and Simpson the most consistent. By drawing the series Australia retained the Ashes.

At Brisbane Australia recovered from 194-6 to make 404 (Booth 112). England in turn were precariously placed at 169-4, but long defensive innings by Ken Barrington and Peter Parfitt helped them to 389. England could make no headway when Australia batted again, and on the last day they needed 378 to win at 63 an hour. That an England win still looked

possible in mid-afternoon was due to Dexter (99), but the game ended with England staving off defeat. At Melbourne Australia again recovered from a moderate start, but England gained a narrow first innings lead thanks to Cowdrey (113) and Dexter (93), and a chanceless century from Booth did not wholly counterbalance inspired bowling by Trueman. Sheppard (113) redeemed himself for two vital dropped catches and a duck in the first innings in England's seven-wicket win.

When Cowdrey (85) was out in the third Test, England were 201-4. They were all out for 279, Davidson and Simpson causing the damage. Australia were 174-1 in reply when Titmus got four wickets in 58 balls for 5 runs, and the Australian lead was kept to 40. But Davidson destroyed England's second innings and Australia won by eight wickets. More dropped catches helped Australia to 393 (Harvey 154, O'Neill 100) at Adelaide, and England sur-

*Left,* **An expensive miss by Colin Cowdrey in the final Test of 1962-63: Peter Burge went on to a century that helped Australia to a first innings lead.** *Below,* **Burge, who at Leeds played the innings that won the 1964 series, falls to Titmus in the fifth Test at the Oval.**

Keystone

Central Press

vived to draw thanks largely to Barrington (63 and 132 not out) and a pulled Davidson hamstring. Barrington (101 and 94) and Burge (103 and 52) dominated the final Test, which ended, like the series, in stalemate.

### 1964 in England

England 0 Australia 1 Drawn 4
England could justly claim some deprivation by the weather in this series. Half the playing time was lost at Trent Bridge, but England still had a chance of victory when the rain returned on the final day. The first two days were lost at Lord's, and then Dexter put Australia in. They recovered from 88-6 to 176 all out, and John Edrich (120) was chiefly responsible for England's lead of 70. Australia batted more solidly at the second attempt, and they were safe from defeat when the rain came again.

Great catching by Australia held England to 268 at Headingley, and Australia were 187-7 when Dexter took the second new ball. Subsequent events did not endorse his decision, Burge (160) proceeded to play the innings that won the series, and Australia led by 121. England could do no better than 229 (Barrington 85), and Australia won by seven wickets. Thus fortified they went on to Old Trafford and won the toss. Lawry (106) and Simpson (311) put on 201, Booth made 98, and on the best wicket seen for many years Australia declared at 656-8. England soon lost Edrich, but Geoff Boycott and Dexter put on 111, and then came the great stand of 246 between Dexter (174) and Barrington (256), which eclipsed the partnership of Lawry and Simpson and lifted England to within 45 of the mammoth Australian total. It was a spirited reply that captured the imagination, but the inevitable draw meant that the Ashes stayed with Australia.

At the Oval England batted first in unfavourable conditions and were led on first innings by 197. But Geoff Boycott (113) and Cowdrey (93 not out) had more than restored the balance when rain washed out the final day.

Central Press

### 1965-66 in Australia

Australia 1 England 1 Drawn 3
At Brisbane, Australia made 443-6 declared (Lawry 166, Doug Walters 155 in his first Test), and interruptions for rain left Australia only 11 hours to bowl England out twice, which they failed to do. At Melbourne England overhauled the Australian score of 358 and led by 200 (Edrich 109, Cowdrey 104), but a missed stumping chance let Australia off the hook and Burge (120) and Walters (115) forced a draw. England's best match was at Sydney, where Boycott (84), and Bob Barber (185) put on 234 for the first wicket and Edrich made 103. On a wicket known to favour spin

after a day or so, Australia lost by an innings.

At Adelaide it was Australia's turn. Boldly changing their side, but lucky in restoring Graham McKenzie because of an injury to the man chosen to replace him, they lost the toss and in a humid atmosphere soon had England 33-3. A shout from the wicket-keeper misled Cowdrey into thinking he had been called for a run and he was run out. England did well to total 241. Simpson (225) and Lawry (119) then emulated the opening stand of Boycott and Barber at Sydney, and they actually put Australia in front before they were parted. Australia led by 275, and despite

**Colin Cowdrey reflects on the state of the Oval pitch in 1968, when it seemed that the weather would rob England of victory. But the crowd helped, Underwood was devastating, and England drew the series.**

102 from Barrington, England were a beaten side.

For the second series in succession in Australia the two sides went into the final Test all square, but although Barrington made 115 and England totalled 485, their attack simply was not good enough to force a result and Australia passed their score with five wickets down (Bob Cowper 307, Lawry 108).

### 1968 in England

England 1 Australia 1 Drawn 3
After Australia had made 357 at Old Trafford and Boycott and Edrich had put on 86 for the first wicket, England collapsed unaccountably and Australia led by 192. Although England fought commendably, they never looked like saving the game. Their fielding in the series was on the whole lamentable, but they excelled at Lord's, where they hung on to some incredible catches after declaring at 351-7, made in three rainaffected days. With conditions helping the quicker bowlers Australia were dismissed for 78, and they began the final day needing 273 to avoid an innings defeat,

began well for England. Boycott and Edrich put on 107, and Fletcher (80) played his best innings, but most memorable was the running out of Boycott. His display of petulance was forgiveable; his reported refusal to apologize to the umpires, however, was inflammatory. Unmoved by criticism, he made 119 not out in the second innings, after Ray Illingworth, with good precedent, had foreborne to enforce the follow on. Stackpole (136) and Ian Chappell (104) dominated Australia's escape. Lawry was then relieved of the captaincy and dropped from the Australian side, Ian Chappell taking charge.

A great final conflict at Sydney was overshadowed by a long-threatened confrontation between Illingworth and the umpires. Jenner was hit by a Snow bouncer; Snow, as had happened several

**The batting of Geoff Boycott (1) and the bowling of John Snow (2) played their part in England's winning the 1970-71 series. Yet their absence from the field when victory was finally achieved helps to illustrate that England's win was basically a team effort.**

*Sport & General*

**Alan Knott stumps Bob Cowper off the bowling of Ray Illingworth at Leeds in 1968. Illingworth, who won back the Ashes in 1970-71, took 6-87 in Australia's second innings.**

but the rain returned to save them. And again at Edgbaston in the third Test England dominated the game but were frustrated by the weather. After making 409 (Cowdrey 104, Graveney 96), England dismissed Australia for 222, then pressed for runs and declared. Australia needed 321 to win in six hours, but what might have been a great finish was again spoilt by rain.

Australia needed only to draw the fourth Test to retain the Ashes, and they were helped by more dropped catches and further periods of rain. England eventually needed 326 at 66 an hour, and with Australia concentrating on a draw the task proved beyond them.

Few more dramatic denouements have occurred on a cricket field than the final scenes at the Oval, in the last Test. After England had made 494 (John Edrich 164, Basil d'Oliveira, dropped after the first Test and now recalled for the injured Prideaux, 158), Australia were dismissed for 324 (Lawry 135). England then went for quick runs and left Australia 352 to win at 54 an hour. Eighty-five for 5 at lunch on the final day, Australia were a beaten side when a storm flooded the playing area. With the crowd willingly helping, the deluge was mopped up just in time, and England achieved victory with six minutes to spare.

### 1970-71 in Australia

Australia 0 England 2 Drawn 4

Keith Stackpole's 207 at Brisbane, supported by Walter's 112, ensured a sizeable Australian score to open the series, but John Snow and Derek Underwood came back to dismiss Australia for 433. England got a first innings lead of 31, then bowled Australia into trouble, but Lawry (84) led a dour recovery and the game was drawn. The second Test at Perth saw England surrender a strong position to a great Test debut by Greg Chappell (102). Australia were 107-5 against England's 397 (Brian Luckhurst 131) when Chappell went in. Redpath made 171, and it was England who had to steer clear of defeat (Edrich 115 not out). After this match D. G. Clark, the MCC tour manager, criticized both sides for undue caution in the opening Tests.

The third Test was abandoned without a ball being bowled and replaced by another, six having been originally arranged. On a wicket of uncertain bounce England won a great victory in the fourth Test at Sydney. Gaining a first-innings lead of 96, they consolidated through 142 not out from Boycott; Snow (7-40) then blasted Australia out for 116, though Lawry carried his bat for 60. Helped by dropped catches, Australia came back to score 493 in the fifth Test at Melbourne (Ian Chappell 111), and England were in trouble at 88 for 3. But d'Oliveira (117) and Luckhurst (109) resisted, and with two cautious captains in charge a draw resulted.

The sixth Test at Adelaide

*Patrick Eagar*

times previously in the series, was warned for intimidation; the crowd demonstrated, a spectator manhandled Snow, and Illingworth led his team off the field. England, 80 behind on the first innings, held together to make 302, and 223 to win proved beyond Australia, despite an injury to Snow. The Australians were never happy against the fast rising deliveries of this bowler, who took 31 wickets in the series.

## England v South Africa

In 1970, South African cricket was at its peak, and had a series been played between England and South Africa that year, it would have been between the world's strongest countries. Unhappily, any chance of such a clash was bedevilled by political intrusions.

The early days of England-South Africa meetings were not at all significant as trials of strength between the two countries. Many of the South African players were not long out from England, and the England sides that went to South Africa were at best second XIs. Though four Test series were played in South Africa before the South African

Sport & General

**2**

Patrick Eagar

War broke out in 1899, no Test matches were played in that period whenever South African sides toured England. Indeed, although the first Test between these two countries was played in Port Elizabeth in 1889, the first in England did not take place until 1907.

Curiously, the war strengthened rather than weakened South African cricket, a great number of young Englishmen settling there after the hostilities. Almost immediately South Africa entered one of its more successful eras, with its googly quartet of R. O. Schwarz, G. A. Faulkner, G. C. White, and A. E. Vogler. P. F. Warner's team to South Africa in 1905-06 lost four Tests, and the Springboks were not easily beaten in England in 1907. But thereafter their strength faded, and it was 1935 before H. F. Wade's team won the first Test (and with it the series) in England. Twenty years later, Jack Cheetham's team was narrowly beaten 3-2 in perhaps the best Test series ever played in England, and in 1965 Peter van der Merwe's side repeated the 1935 feat of winning one match and so the series.

In between these Springbok successes, the series had usually gone England's way, although South Africa have had their successes at home, where they have won 13 of their 18 Test victories against England. The modern tragedy of South African cricket is that, when it reached the highest pinnacle of all and was in a position to make a stimulating contribution to world cricket, it has not been able to play its oldest adversary, England.

**Cricket was the loser when politics and sport clashed head on over the 1970 South African tour of England. The barbed wire protecting the pitch at Lord's was just one defensive measure taken by cricket authorities against a campaign that eventually saw cancelled what might have been one of the great Test series.**

### ENGLAND v SOUTH AFRICA

Tests won by England:  46
Tests won by South Africa: 18
Tests drawn:  38

**Highest team innings**
England:  654-5, Durban, 1938-39
South Africa:  538, Headingley, 1951

**Highest individual innings**
England:  243 by E. Paynter, Durban, 1938-39
South Africa:  236 by E. A. B. Rowan, Headingley, 1951

**Most runs in the matches**
England:  2,205 (*average* 53.78) by D. C. S. Compton
South Africa:  2,732 (*average* 54.64) by B. Mitchell

**Most runs in a series**
England:  753 (*average* 94.12) by D. C. S. Compton, 1947
South Africa:  621 (*average* 69.00) by A. D. Nourse Jr, 1947

**Most wickets in the matches**
England:  83 (*average* 9.85) by S. F. Barnes
South Africa:  75 (*average* 22.10) by H. J. Tayfield

**Most wickets in a series**
England:  49 (*average* 10.93) by S. F. Barnes, 1913-14
South Africa:  37 (*average* 17.18) by H. J. Tayfield, 1956-57

**Best bowling in an innings:**
England:  9-28 by G. A. Lohmann, Johannesburg, 1895-96
South Africa:  9-113 by H. J. Tayfield, Johannesburg, 1956-57

Figures up to and including the 1965 series

**1** Lord Hawke, who took two sides to South Africa at the end of the 19th century. His first side of 1895-96 had among its members C. B. Fry (**2**), and Surrey players George Lohmann (**3**), who captured 35 wickets in the three Tests, and Tom Hayward (**4**), who hit 122 in the Johannesburg Test. The 1898-99 side included Albert Trott (**5**), who played for Australia in 1894-95.

**Series of the 19th century**
(all in South Africa)
**1888-89**
South Africa 0   England 2
**1891-92**
South Africa 0   England 1
**1895-96**
South Africa 0   England 3
**1898-99**
South Africa 0   England 2

The first four England sides to South Africa were led by C. Aubrey Smith, W. W. Read, and Lord Hawke, who took the last two. Smith, many years later to be knighted as a world famous Hollywood film actor, was the captain when the first Test was played in March 1889. Bobby Abel made 46 and 23 not out in that match, and 120 in the second Test at Cape Town, where Johnny Briggs, who had taken six wickets at Port Elizabeth, had the astonishing figures of 7-17 and 8-11. Briggs hit the stumps 14 times and had one man lbw—an achievement unlikely to be equalled for individual devastation in Test cricket.

The somewhat casual rules of qualification in use at the time are illustrated by the inclusion in W. W. Read's touring side three years later of W. L. Murdoch and J. J. Ferris, who had previously played for Australia against England. F. Hearne, who opened the innings for South Africa, with J. T. Hearne in opposition, had played for Aubrey Smith's side on the first tour.

Lord Hawke's first team included C. B. Fry and S. M. J. Woods, but its most successful player was the Surrey bowler George Lohmann, who took 7-38 and 8-7 at Port Elizabeth—so redeeming himself for his 'pair' as opening batsman. At Johannesburg he took the last 9 wickets for 28 in South Africa's first innings, and in all three Tests he took 35 wickets.

The last England team before the outbreak of war also contained names that appeared in other ranks. Albert Trott had played for Australia, and Frank Mitchell, who opened the innings with 'Plum' Warner, was to captain South Africa in the triangular tournament of 1912. J. H. Sinclair, now the mainstay of South Africa's batting, made their first Test hundred, in Cape Town, but in the second innings the home side were dismissed for only 35 by Trott (4-19) and Schofield

Haigh (6-11).

When war broke out several weeks later, South Africa could not be said to have made much advance as a force in Test cricket. But a visit from Darling's Australians on their way home from England in 1902 did much to restore cricket and raise standards, and the next England team to South Africa had a rude shock.

### 1905-06 in South Africa
South Africa 4   England 1
South Africa's first ever victory, when it came in the first Test of the series in Johannesburg, was a thrilling affair by one wicket. Plum Warner's team included some famous names, J. N. Crawford, David Denton, A. E. Relf, Haigh, and Colin Blythe, but like all visiting teams up to World War II, it was well below full England strength. South Africa, needing 284 to win after being bowled out for 91 in the first innings, made the runs largely through an unbroken last-wicket stand of 48 between the left-handed Dave Nourse and his captain P. W. Sherwell.

In this series the South African selectors took the probably unique step of picking the same side for all five Tests, and their confidence was confirmed when Sherwell's side won all but the fourth Test—and most of the others by big margins. They had a highly effective opening bowler in S. J. Snooke, and the spinners Schwarz, Faulkner, and Vogler, were beginning to make a big impact. The batting was consistent and had depth.

### 1907 in England
England 1   South Africa 0
Drawn 2
After their success against Plum Warner's team, South Africa were accorded full Test status when they went to England a year later.

They met the full-strength England side, most of whom had helped beat Australia 2-0 two years before. Of those who played for England in the first Test, only Crawford and Blythe had been on the tour to South Africa. Rain spared South Africa in this match, in which their captain Sherwell, promoted from the depths of the order to open the innings, made a second innings of 115. In the second Test, however, England were bowled out after rain for 76, Faulkner taking 6-17. South Africa led on the first innings and needed only 129 to win in the last innings, but after more rain Blythe (7-40) had the last word, and England won by 53 runs.

The last of the three Tests was drawn, with honours even, and so South Africa had emerged with credit from their first overseas series.

### 1909-10 in South Africa
South Africa 3   England 2
H. D. G. Leveson Gower's

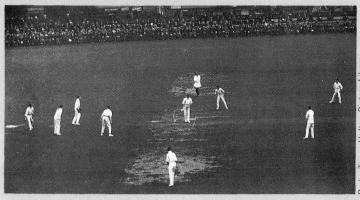

English touring team was stronger in its early batting than some of its predecessors, boasting an order that went Jack Hobbs, Wilfred Rhodes, Denton, F. L. Fane, and Frank Woolley. But its bowling was less menacing for South African batting, which had grown in confidence. Faulkner was now a world class all-rounder, and in the first Test, which South Africa won by 19 runs, he made 78 and 123, as well as taking 8 wickets. South Africa clinched the series in the fourth Test, and when Hobbs made 187 in the last Test it was too late for England to save the series.

### 1912 in England
England 3   South Africa 0
For some years South African cricket had been riding high, but now it declined with a bump and stayed down for many years. In the very wet summer of the triangular tournament, South Africa found their great spinners of other years less effective, and they lost even more easily to England than they did to Australia. In particular, they fell foul of Sydney Barnes, who took 34 wickets in the three matches and, as it proved, had worse in store for South Africa.

### 1913-14 in South Africa
South Africa 0   England 4
Drawn 1
If ever one man dominated a series, Sydney Barnes dominated the last Test series before World War I. He did not play in the last Test in Port Elizabeth, yet in the first four he captured 49 wickets. South Africa had a high-class opening batsman in Herbie Taylor, their captain, but an England side including Hobbs, Rhodes, Philip Mead, J. W. Hearne, and Woolley made plenty of runs, and Barnes did the rest. In the second Test at Johannesburg he took 17 wickets, a feat not exceeded until Jim Laker's historic 19 in 1956.

### 1922-23 in South Africa
South Africa 1   England 2
Drawn 2
Though ill health kept Hobbs out, the England team that F. T. Mann took was not far below the best, and South Africa did well to run them to a close series. Taylor, still the outstanding player

**L. A. Stricker is clean bowled by Sydney Barnes at the Oval during the triangular tournament of 1912, when the South Africans fell foul of Barnes and an extremely wet summer.**

in the country, made 176 in the first Test, enabling South Africa to win by 168 runs. England won the second in a thrilling match at Cape Town, but only by one wicket. A left-arm bowler, A. E. Hall took 11 wickets for South Africa, but George Macaulay, playing in his first Test, joined Alec Kennedy for the last wicket when England needed five runs to win, and his first scoring stroke in Test cricket won the match. Phil Mead made 181 in a rain-ruined third Test in Durban, and Frank Woolley 115 not out in another draw at Johannesburg, which left all depending on the final Test in Durban.

A hundred in each innings by England opener Jack Russell was the deciding factor. Taylor, with R. H. Catterall and Dave Nourse, were formidable opponents for the England bowling of A. E. R. Gilligan, Alec Kennedy, George Macaulay, Percy Fender, and Woolley, but though Taylor made 102 in the last innings South Africa went down by 109 runs.

**A Test win in England still eluded the South Africans in 1929, when Walter Hammond was just one England batsman they found in run-getting mood.**

### 1924 in England
England 3   South Africa 0
Drawn 2
Arthur Gilligan was the England captain when Herbie Taylor took the 1924 Springboks to England, and he played a major part in the sensational events of the first Test at Edgbaston. Put in by Taylor, England made 438, G. M. Parker, who had been brought in from the Bradford League to strengthen the touring side's bowling, taking 6-152. South Africa were then bowled out for 30 by Gilligan (6-7) and Maurice Tate (4-12). They made 390 in the second innings, but had suffered a severe blow from which they never recovered. Catterall made 120 in the second innings at Edgbaston, and the same score in the first innings of the Lord's Test, which by another coincidence was lost by the identical margin of an innings and 18 runs. At Lord's England made a mammoth 531-2 declared, Hobbs (211) and Sutcliffe making 268 for the first wicket before Woolley (134 not out) and Patsy Hendren (50 not out) added to the agony. Catterall played another fine innings of 95 in two hours in the last Test, which was spoiled by rain, but the tour overall was a disappointment.

### 1927-28 in South Africa
South Africa 2   England 2
Drawn 1
When Captain R. T. Stanyforth took a reasonably strong English team to South Africa, Herbie Taylor's long tenure of captaincy had ended, though at 38 he was to play in several more Test series before he retired. Dave Nourse had gone and his son Dudley had not yet appeared on the first-class scene, but some promising cricketers, including the wicket-keeper-batsman H. B. Cameron, were coming to the fore.

The new captain H. G. Deane did well to bring South Africa from being two down after two Tests to halve the series. Hundreds by Herbert Sutcliffe and Ernest Tyldesley and 12 wickets by

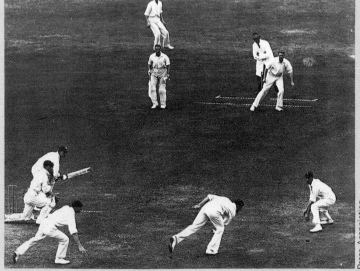

George Geary won England the first Test, and Sutcliffe, Percy Holmes, and Tyldesley won them the second after South Africa had held a first innings lead of 117. George Geary, who had promised to be a formidable opponent on the matting, did not play after the second Test, and after an even draw at Durban in the third Test South Africa came back boldly. The pace bowling of A. E. Hall and G. F. Bissett took 17 wickets to defeat an England side that began Holmes, Sutcliffe, Tyldesley, Hammond, Wyatt. Taylor made a hundred in this match, and that other pillar of Springbok batting, Catterall, made 119 at Durban, where Bissett took 7-29 in the second innings and England were beaten by 8 wickets.

### 1929 in England
England 2   South Africa 0
Drawn 3
South Africa had given an excellent performance to halve the previous series in South Africa, but once again, in 1929, they could not win a Test in England. On four occasions they led England on the first innings, without being able to press home their advantage, and England won at Leeds and Manchester, R. E. S. Wyatt and Frank Woolley making hundreds at Old Trafford, where Tich Freeman's leg-spin took 12 wickets. At the Oval, Sutcliffe made two hundreds and with Walter Hammond (101 not out) prevented South Africa from winning after they led by 234 runs on the first innings. Tests were still of three days then.

It had long been realized that the disparity between South Africa's performances at home, where they had won 10 Tests by now, and in England, where they had not won any, was largely connected with the matting pitches used in South Africa. The transformation to turf had been gradually coming, however, and the fruits of it were not long in being realized.

### 1930-31 in South Africa
South Africa 1   England 0
Drawn 4
The first Test match on grass in South Africa was played in Cape Town when Percy Chapman's team went there. One of the strongest English sides to visit the country so far, they had lost the first Test in Johannesburg by 28 runs and had only narrowly avoided an innings defeat at Newlands, where Bruce Mitchell, I. J. Siedle, and the indestructible Herbie Taylor made hundreds in the South African score of 513-8. Three more draws followed, South Africa having slightly the better of them, so that their victory in the series by the first Test win, was well deserved. Against an England team including Wyatt, Hammond, Maurice Leyland, Hendren, Andy Sandham, Tate, Bill Voce, and J. C. White, it was no mean feat.

### 1935 in England
England 0   South Africa 1
Drawn 4
Tests were still of only three days when H. F. Wade's team went to England in 1935, though it was for the last time in a series between the two countries. In the four drawn Tests England were a shade superior, though South Africa were never near defeat in any of them. At Lord's, however, the match was finished, and South Africa won their first-ever victory in England by 157 runs. They were not to know then that it would also decide the series. England were in a period of transition—the Lord's Test was the last of Herbert Sutcliffe's 54 Tests—and the fast bowling did not mount the same menace as that of a few years before. Yet only 18 months later England were making a bold effort to recover the Ashes in Australia.

Oddly, when the great Springbok victory was at last won, only three batsmen made any big contribution to it. In the first innings a total of 228 was reached through a magnificent 90 out of 126 in 105 minutes by Jock Cameron, who was to die so sadly within a few weeks of the end of the tour. When South Africa went in a second time with a lead of 30, Bruce Mitchell batted for 5½ hours to make 164 not out, supported by Eric Rowan, who made his second 40 of the match. England were left to make 309 to win in 4¾ hours, but were easily dismissed, the Greek leg-spin bowler Xenophon Balaskas adding four wickets to his five of the first innings.

### 1938-39 in South Africa
South Africa 0   England 1
Drawn 4
By now it was clear that England sides visiting South Africa must

be nearly the strongest available, and the one Walter Hammond took in the last pre-war season lacked few of the best players. Numerous runs were scored on what were by now turf pitches, and England took the series by winning the third Test, in Durban, where Eddie Paynter made 243 and Hammond 120. Seven wickets by giant fast bowler Ken Farnes helped to complete the job.

But it was the last Test, one of the four draws, that has gone down in history as the breaker of many records. Scheduled to be played to a finish, it was given up after 10 days, when the MCC team had to leave Durban to catch their ship home. They were then 42 runs short of victory with 5 wickets in hand, a remarkable state of affairs for they had needed 696 runs to win when they began their last innings late on the sixth day. South Africa opened by making 530, Peter van der Byl 125 in 7¼ hours and Dudley Nourse 103. England were bowled out for 316, but South Africa

batted again with van der Byl (97) and Alan Melville (103) making 191 together in their second opening stand of more than 100, and this time the South African score reached 481. Thereafter the pitch was frequently restored by rain, which also took away the eighth day's play, and England batted steadily on. Paul Gibb, who opened the innings with Len Hutton, made 120, Bill Edrich 219, and Walter Hammond 140. On the 10th day England needed only 200 runs, but rain further interrupted play and eventually the match was abandoned. It was the last 'timeless' Test.

### 1947 in England
England 3   South Africa 0
Drawn 2
When Alan Melville, the 1938-39 captain, took the Springboks to England in 1947, South African cricket was suffering from much the same post-war ailments as English cricket. Their players had mostly been away in the Middle East, few young ones had

Sport & General

tour, England, with Len Hutton, Cyril Washbrook, and Denis Compton leading the batting, and Alec Bedser, Cliff Gladwin, and the leg-spinner R. O. Jenkins taking most of the wickets, were just the better side, but not by much. Dudley Nourse had a fine series for South Africa, Eric Rowan was as obdurate as ever, and his brother Athol was by now a world-class off-spinner.

England won two narrow victories in the first and last Tests to clinch the series. The first, by two wickets, came in one of the most exciting finishes in Test history. England, needing 128 to win on an unpredictable pitch, got home when Cliff Gladwin and Alec Bedser ran a desperate leg-bye off the last ball of the match. The second Test in Johannesburg was notable for an opening stand of 359 between Hutton and Washbrook that lasted throughout the first day.

The last Test was also unusual, for England won after a declaration by Dudley Nourse, made, as it were, in desperation because his side were one down on the last day of the series. It asked for 172 runs in 95 minutes, and though there scarcely seemed time for England to be bowled out, they did in fact lose seven wickets before they won with a minute to spare. It remains a splendid example of a challenge thrown out boldly and taken up in the same spirit.

**1951 in England**
England 3   South Africa 1
Drawn 1
It was a younger team that Dudley Nourse took to England in 1951, and though well beaten it contained much promise for the future. Nourse and Eric Rowan were still the mainstays of the batting, but Jackie McGlew,

1 I. J. Siedle was opening bat when South Africa won their first victory in England.
2 Denis Compton (208) and 3 Alan Melville (117) were among the runs in the Lord's Test of 1947. 4 Hutton and Washbrook formed the basis of England's 1948-49 series win.
5 Injury to Nourse dampened South African hopes in 1951.

developed and so it was a fairly senior team, short of top-class experience, that went on tour. Especially it was short of penetrative bowling, and it coincided with a glorious English summer, splendid pitches, and Denis Compton and Bill Edrich in full spate.

The Springboks, notably Dudley Nourse, Alan Melville, and Bruce Mitchell, made a lot of runs and could take satisfaction from their contribution to a spectacular series that was a great advertisement for cricket. But they were well beaten in a series remembered for the superb batting

of Compton and Edrich. Compton made 753 in the series at 94.12 and scored six hundreds against the Springboks, four in Tests. Edrich played in only four Tests but made 552 runs and averaged 110.40. South Africa could look back with frustration on the first Test, which they only drew after leading by 325 runs on the first innings and making England follow-on. Alan Melville made a hundred in each innings, a feat Bruce Mitchell repeated in the last Test. Mitchell batted nearly 8 hours in a grim struggle against defeat, and eventually South Africa, at 423-7 finished only 28 runs short of an unconsidered victory.

**1948-49 in South Africa**
South Africa 0   England 2
Drawn 3
If the previous series did much to restore cricket in England after the war, the visit of George Mann's MCC side to South Africa 18 months later did the same there. In a notably happy

Roy McLean, John Waite, and Russell Endean were clearly on the way up. Athol Rowan was still a fine off-spinner, but Hugh Tayfield, who came during the tour as a reinforcement, was a worthy successor to him and Clive van Ryneveld was a valuable all-rounder.

This young team began by winning the first Test at Trent Bridge, where Nourse made 208 despite a broken thumb. Though Reg Simpson and Denis Compton made first innings hundreds for England, the pitch took some spin later and Athol Rowan (5-68) and N. B. F. 'Tufty' Mann (4-24) ran through the England second innings. At Lord's, however, the rain helped England, and the Lancashire off-spinner Roy Tattersall took 12 wickets for 101 to enable them to win by 10 wickets. Twelve wickets by Alec Bedser in wet conditions at Old Trafford brought England a nine-wicket victory there.

The fourth Test was drawn at Leeds, where Eric Rowan made 236 and 60 not out and Peter May scored a hundred in his first Test. England won the last, however, in three days, though only after some moments of doubts as to whether the last innings target of 163 was within their range.

### 1955 in England
England 3   South Africa 2
The Springbok promise of four years earlier was handsomely fulfilled when Jack Cheetham took his side to England in 1955 and played what many people

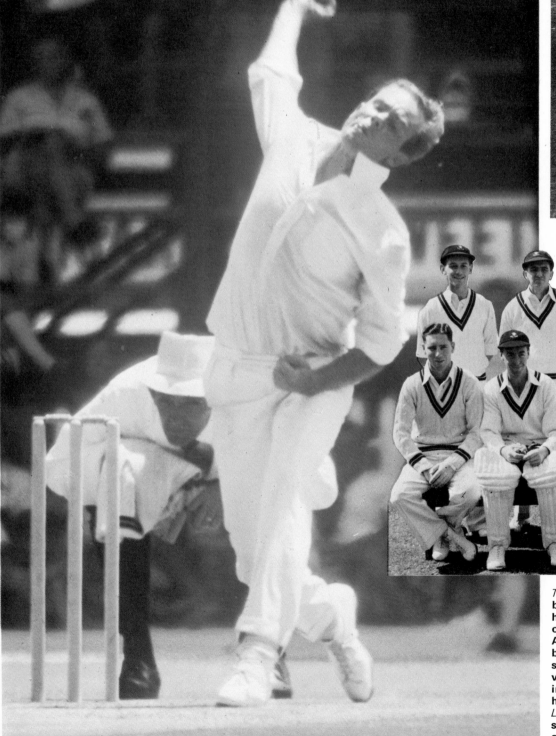

*Top,* **Jubilation at Johannesburg in 1956-57. Neil Adcock hugs Hugh Tayfield after the off-spinner had bowled South Africa to a fourth Test win by taking 9-113 in England's second innings. Their 17-run victory put South Africa back into the series after they had been two Tests down.** *Left,* **Paceman Peter Pollock spearheaded the Springbok emergence of the 1960s.**

consider the best post-war Test series. In mostly fine weather England won the first two Tests, South Africa the next two, and all depended on the last at the Oval. At that time, England's batting relied to an enormous extent on Peter May, and it is widely acknowledged that if a very close lbw decision at the Oval had not been given in his favour, South Africa would have won the rubber. May, in his first series as England captain, averaged 72, Denis Compton 54; no one else exceeded 25.

One of the Springboks' strengths was the combination of two fine fast bowlers, Peter Heine and Neil Adcock, but Tayfield was also at his best, taking 26 wickets in the series and Trevor Goddard, left-arm medium pace, took 25. McGlew was steady and averaged 52, but the other batting was not prolific, although some brilliant innings were played on occasions—the 142 of McLean at Lord's and the 108 of the tall, hard-driving Paul Winslow at Old Trafford. The Springboks' fielding

was superb and they were excellently led.

The result of the first Test was deceptive, England winning by an innings. Frank Tyson, fresh from his triumphs in Australia, took 6-28 in the second innings. At Lord's, however, England were bowled out on a fast, grassy pitch for 133 on the first day, and McLean's dazzling innings helped give South Africa a 171-run lead. But May made a spectacular 112 in the second innings, and Brian Statham (7-39), helped by a

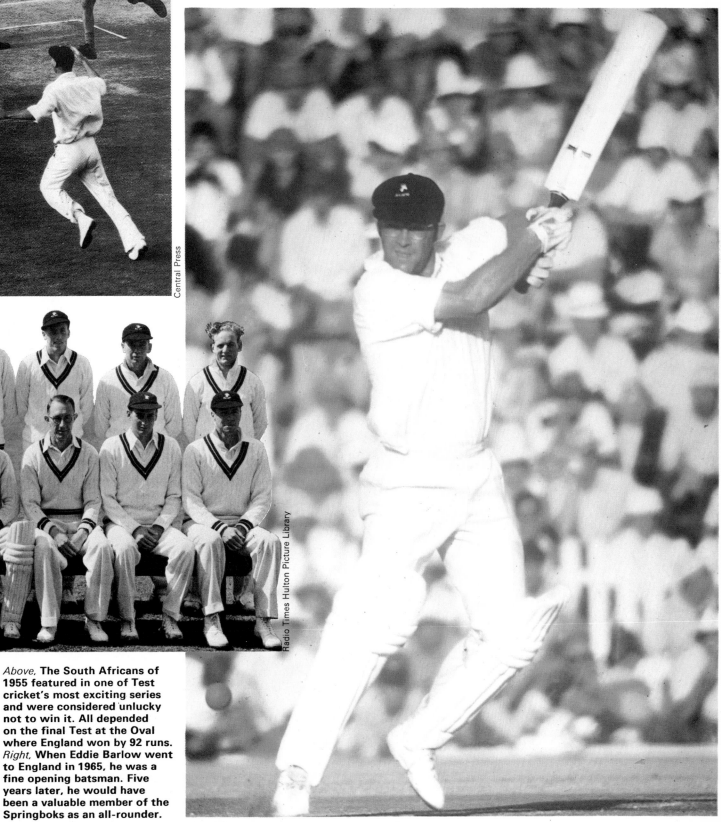

*Above,* **The South Africans of 1955 featured in one of Test cricket's most exciting series and were considered unlucky not to win it. All depended on the final Test at the Oval where England won by 92 runs.** *Right,* **When Eddie Barlow went to England in 1965, he was a fine opening batsman. Five years later, he would have been a valuable member of the Springboks as an all-rounder.**

deteriorating light that gave him time to rest, bowled South Africa out. Cheetham chipped a bone in the elbow in the second innings and did not play in either of the next two Tests, which South Africa won.

The Manchester victory was an especially fine one. Compton made 158 for England in the first innings and May 117 in the second, but in between, South Africa, batting with great dash, scored 521-8—McGlew 104, Waite 113, and Winslow who reached his only Test 100 with an enormous straight six over the sightscreen, 108. In the second innings they needed 145 to win in 2¼ hours against Bedser, Tyson, and Lock, and lost two wickets for 23. But McLean and McGlew added 72 in 50 minutes and the Springboks eventually won a historic match by three wickets with a few minutes to spare.

They won more easily at Leeds, where Tayfield (5-94) and Goddard (5-69) shared the wickets in the last innings, but could not quite hold Laker and Lock in the last Test on a typical Oval pitch of the day. But if Peter May had been given out lbw when on 4, instead of going on to make 89 not out, the series must have had another ending.

**1956-57 in South Africa**
South Africa 2   England 2
Drawn 1
Another fine series in South Africa saw the luck reversed in some ways. Peter May, though making hundreds of runs in other matches, failed in test matches, often through brilliant catching, and South Africa won a vital toss in the last Test to help them to halve the series. The cricket was less spectacular than that of the previous series, and England began with dourly earned victories at Durban and Cape Town, the latter pressed home by Johnny Wardle (7-36) on a pitch taking some spin.

England were not far off winning the third Test and the rubber, but they stuck there. South Africa won an exciting victory by 17 runs at Johannesburg, one notable as their first win over England at home on a turf pitch. Hugh Tayfield (9-113) bowled them to success in the second innings. The last Test at Port Elizabeth was played on a pitch of impossibly low bounce. Van Ryneveld won the toss, and Endean's first-innings 70 took South Africa to 164, which was a winning score in the conditions.

**1960 in England**
England 3   South Africa 0
Drawn 2
The 1960 tour was one of the most disappointing ever undertaken by South Africa. McGlew's side contained many young players of less obvious promise than those of nine years before, and they met a damp and miserable English summer that gave them no chance to settle in. The tour was further marred by the inclusion of the young fast bowler Geoff Griffin, who was frequently no-balled for throwing and did not bowl in the second half of the tour.

England, captained by Cowdrey, won the first three Tests, and though the Springboks led by 264 runs in the fifth Test at the Oval, a second innings opening stand of 290 between Geoff Pullar (175) and Colin Cowdrey (155) prevented them from coming anywhere near victory.

**1964-65 in South Africa**
South Africa 0   England 1
Drawn 4
When Mike Smith's team went to South Africa, the Springboks were approaching, but were not yet quite at, the stage of positive and commanding cricket they were to reach later. However, they were by the end the better side, and England were lucky to win the series.

England won the first Test at Durban, where the pitch deteriorated after hundreds by Ken Barrington (148) and Jim Parks (108), and the England spinners Fred Titmus and David Allen bowled South Africa out twice. In the second Test England were within sight of what would have been a dashing and worthy win at the start of the last day, for Bob Barber (97) and Ted Dexter (172) had played superbly at the start. But one of many fine innings by Colin Bland (144 not out) thwarted them, and thereafter, increasingly hampered by injuries, they hung on to their lead against strengthening opposition.

**1965 in England**
England 0   South Africa 1
Drawn 2
The last series between England and South Africa before politics intruded was in the second half of the 1965 summer. It produced three thrilling matches; two draws with close finishes and one easier win for Peter van der Merwe's Springboks at Trent Bridge. In the first Test at Lord's, England's eighth-wicket pair were defending grimly when the end came. In the second, South Africa were always in control after Graeme Pollock

had played an incredible innings of 125 in discouragingly damp, typically English conditions on the first day. He batted only 2 hours 20 minutes, and in 70 minutes after lunch made 91 out of 102.

The last Test at the Oval was drawn in an atmosphere of frustration that was symbolic of the years to come. England needed 399 to win in the last innings on a pitch becoming ever easier. They reached 308-4 (Cowdrey 78 not out) and needed another 91 in 70 minutes when a thunderstorm finished the match.

The weather had prevented a tremendous climax, just as politicians and agitators were to prevent the playing of some almost certainly tremendous cricket in the series of 1968-69 and 1970 that never took place.

**1** Play in the first Test at Lord's in 1965 was held up while the bowler's run up was dug out and then relaid.
**2** Ali Bacher was third in the Springbok Test averages in 1965 and was to have captained the South Africans in 1970.

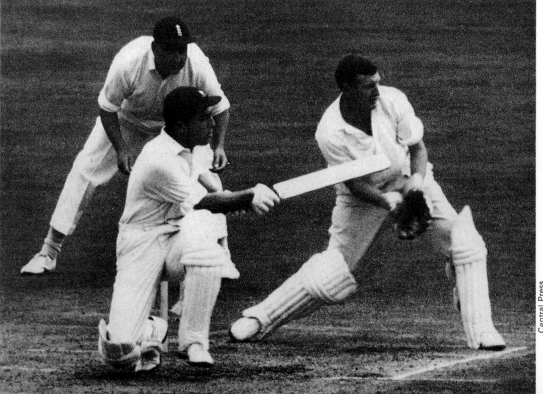

Sport & General

Central Press

## England v West Indies

Though West Indies have made many exciting contributions to cricket, they did not erupt suddenly and brilliantly on the Test scene. As far back as 1900 a West Indian team had toured England, and English teams had visited the Caribbean for many years before West Indies were considered strong enough to be given Test status, in 1928. In 1923, the West Indians had won 12 matches on their tour of England, which featured a stronger fixture list than previous visits, and it was on the results of this tour and that made to the Caribbean in 1925-26 by the Hon F. S. G. Calthorpe's team that the decision was made.

The 1928 tour overall was a success, but the Test rubber was disappointing, and until World War I West Indies generally failed to do themselves full justice in Test matches in England, though they built up a reputation for colourful cricket. In the same period, on their own pitches, however, they were more than good enough for the below-strength England teams that were sent out.

During World War II, cricketing careers were less disrupted in the West Indies than elsewhere, and some great players, notably the three 'Ws'—Everton Weekes, Clyde Walcott, and Frank Worrell—amassed hundreds of runs. The first England team to tour the West Indies after the war lost two Tests and failed to win any in the four-match series, but it really needed the triumphs by the 1950 side in England to establish West Indies as a cricketing nation that could hold its own with the best. There was a slight recession in the late 1950s, when England were able to recover the mastery at home. But under Frank Worrell and Gary Sobers in the 1960s, West Indies went on to even greater triumphs.

**During the 1960s, the all-round genius of Gary Sobers helped West Indies to two convincing series victories over England. His batting was often brilliant, and with his varied bowling he was able to exploit most conditions.**

There is always the feeling in West Indian cricket that some new prodigy may burst forth dramatically from an obscure plantation. Powerful batting and the spin of Sonny Ramadhin and Alf Valentine won the 1950 successes. A decade later it was batting and the fast bowling of Wes Hall and Charlie Griffith. But as the fast bowling strength began to fade, West Indies were kept going mainly by the genius of Gary Sobers, who in an all-round capacity did the work of three or four players. By the end of the 1960s, England were in command again—but only after many ups and downs.

### ENGLAND v WEST INDIES

Tests won by England: 20
Tests won by West Indies: 16
Tests drawn: 22

**Highest team innings**
England: 849, Kingston, 1929-30
West Indies: 681-8 dec, Port of Spain, 1953-54

**Highest individual innings**
England: 325 by A. Sandham, Kingston, 1929-30
West Indies: 261 by F. M. Worrell, Trent Bridge, 1950

**Most runs in a series**
England: 693 (*average* 115.50) by E. H. Hendren, 1929-30
West Indies: 722 (*average* 103.14) by G. S. Sobers, 1966

**Most wickets in a series**
England: 34 (*average* 17.47) by F. S. Trueman, 1963
West Indies: 33 (*average* 20.42) by A. L. Valentine, 1950

**Best bowling in an innings**
England: 7-34 by T. E. Bailey, Kingston, 1953-54
West Indies: 8-104 by A. L. Valentine, Old Trafford, 1950

Figures up to and including the 1969 series

to win. The score had reached 408-5 when the match was abandoned. George Headley's contribution to this was 223, and in the series he scored 703 runs at an average of 87.

## 1933 in England

**England 2  West Indies 0  Drawn 1**

West Indies' share in the previous colourful series in the Caribbean had roused hopes that they would show great improvement when they went to England in 1933. But it was only slight improvement.

They were blessed by a fine summer, and they had in G. C. Grant a captain who knew English cricket well. But Constantine, playing in the Lancashire League at this time, was released for only one Test, and could not form the fast bowling partnership with Martindale that might have influenced events strongly. Thus too much rested on George Headley, who averaged 55 against the 23 of the next batsman.

Of the three Tests only the second was not one-sided. England won the other two by an innings, Walter Robins taking 6-32 with leg-spin at Lord's, and Charles Marriott taking 11 wickets at the Oval. At Old Trafford West Indies led by one run on the first innings in a draw famous for the bodyline bowling of Constantine and Martindale to the England captain Douglas Jardine. Jardine met it with characteristic courage and skill and scored 127.

several ways. As the series was level it was decided to play it to a finish, but rain prevented play on the eighth and ninth days and it was given up. England began by making 849, with Andy Sandham's 325 then the highest Test score. They led by no less than 563 runs, but did not enforce the follow-on and eventually declared, setting West Indies to make 836

**1** Ames, Hendren, and Sandham (1st, 2nd, and 3rd from left) enjoyed remarkable personal success in the 1929-30 series against West Indies—the first held in the Caribbean.
**2** George Headley run-getter extraordinary, shows other talents to remove Bakewell at the Oval in 1933. The series was notable for some bodyline bowling from Emmanuel Martindale (**3**) to England captain Jardine at Old Trafford.

## 1928 in England

**England 3  West Indies 0**

For many years West Indian batting had been dependent on George Challenor, a great player when West Indies had gone to England in 1923. But by the time the first Test was played at Lord's in June 1928, he was 40 and not enjoying anything like the success of former days. Disappointingly, too, the exciting all-rounder Learie Constantine, who was producing electrifying feats against the counties, did little in the Tests.

The Tests were played over three days, and England won all three by an innings. Ernest Tyldesley (122) made the first hundred in the series at Lord's. Tich Freeman took five wickets in each innings at Old Trafford, and Jack Hobbs scored 159 at the Oval.

## 1929-30 in West Indies

**West Indies 1  England I  Drawn 2**

The first Test series in England may have been disappointing to West Indies, but the first series at home showed how difficult they would be to beat in the Caribbean. The side that the Hon F. S. G. Calthorpe led to West Indies contained some distinguished players, among them Wilfred Rhodes, George Gunn, Leslie

Ames, Bill Voce, and, above all, Patsy Hendren. Hendren was 40 at the time but his record has seldom been exceeded on any tour: 223 not out, 211 not out, 80 and 36 not out in the first Test, 40 and 96, 30 and 12, 77 and 205 not out in the second Test, 254 not out, 171, 56 and 123 in third Test, 1, 10 and 25, 61 and 55 in the fourth Test. He averaged 126 in all matches and 115 in the Tests, in which he scored 693 runs.

Tests were played over five days, but England, though they had the better of the match, could not force a win in the first Test, a second innings of 176 by the great George Headley holding them up. At Port of Spain in the second Test, however, Hendren and Ames (105) added 237 for the fourth wicket, and Voce took 7-70 to bring England victory after West Indies had led on the first innings. At Georgetown West Indies gained their first win over England. Victory was never really in doubt as long as England could be bowled out in time, which was done with 15 minutes and 289 runs to spare. George Headley made a hundred in each innings, and West Indies seized the initiative on the first day when C. A. Roach made 209 and England dropped catches.

The final Test at Kingston, though drawn, was remarkable in

## 1934-35 in West Indies

**West Indies 2 England 1**
**Drawn 1**

Though it was clear by now that England had to be near their best to win in the Caribbean, the team that R. E. S. Wyatt took was not within six or seven players of their strongest, and it was soundly beaten. Hendren, now 45, could not be expected to be the force of the previous tour, and an early injury to Ken Farnes weakened the English fast bowling. West Indies, with Constantine, Martindale, and L. G. Hylton, outgunned them in fast bowling and won two handsome victories, in the second of which Headley made 270 not out.

England's only success was at Bridgetown in a unique first Test of only 309 runs. The pitch began wet, and rain intervened later so that both sides manoeuvred to get the other in when the pitch was at its worst. England declared their first innings at 81-7, 21 runs behind. West Indies then declared their second innings at 51-6, leaving England to score 73 runs on what appeared to be an impossible pitch. But Wyatt reversed his batting order, and though England were at one time 48-6, Wyatt himself and Walter Hammond were there to steer England home by four wickets.

## 1939 in England

**England 1 West Indies 0**
**Drawn 2**

However convincing their cricket at home, West Indies were still immature in the Test sense overseas. They would assemble less as a team than as a group of individuals from different parts of the world, needing to be knit into a team. Not everyone was happy about the selection of the side in those days, either, although this is always a likely situation in a team representing numerous well separated islands.

In the last pre-war season, England, who with such gifted young players as Len Hutton and Denis Compton were on a rising tide of strength, won their victory at Lord's in the first of three Tests. Hutton made 196 and Compton 120, sharing in a stand of 248 in 140 minutes. For West Indies, George Headley made a hundred in each innings, by 1970 still the only time this feat had been performed in a Lord's Test. But he had little support, and West Indies did not reach 300 in either innings.

## 1947-48 in West Indies

**West Indies 2 England 0**
**Drawn 2**

The England team that made the first post-war visit to the West Indies was even more below strength than its predecessors. In those days, English cricket rested heavily on a few great players, notably Compton, Edrich, Hutton, Bedser, and, on overseas tours, Doug Wright. None went

*Popperfoto*

**A defiant 104 from Godfrey Evans brought England their only victory of the 1950 Test series against West Indies.**

on this tour, though when the side was beset by injuries Len Hutton joined it later.

England succeeded in drawing the first two Tests. In the second, wicket-keeper Billy Griffith was brought in as a deputy opening batsman and, playing in his first Test, made his maiden first-class hundred. Generally, however, the cricket was unexceptional, and West Indies comfortably won the last two Tests, Frank Worrell making 131 not out in one and Everton Weekes 141 in the other.

## 1950 in England

**England 1 West Indies 3**

The 1947-48 tour, easily though it had been won by West Indies, had not given any idea of how they would, for the first time, dominate a series in England. They themselves were surprised, for the completeness of the victory owed much to the success of unknown players—of London club cricketer Alan Rae, who proved a wonderfully consistent opening partner for Jeff Stollmeyer, and of Sonny Ramadhin and Alf Valentine, two untried 20-year-old spin bowlers. The three 'Ws' made a lot of runs, but that had been expected, and so talented a player as Roy Marshall

was not required in a Test.

The series did not have an especially promising start for John Goddard's side. At Old Trafford they met a bad pitch for which England, with the advantage of winning the toss, were better equipped. But from the second Test at Lord's, which West Indies won by 326 runs to record their first win in England, there was only one side in it. England were without Denis Compton for most of that season, and when he was fit again and

**Peter May's 285 not out at Edgbaston in 1957 brought an end to a period of dominance by West Indies' spinners.**

*Central Press*

33

able to play in the fourth and last Test he was needlessly run out for 44 in England's first innings, through which Len Hutton played undefeated for 202 out of 344.

The number of sparkling innings on the other side was ever growing—Clyde Walcott's 168 not out in the second innings at Lord's, the memorable 261 of Frank Worrell and the 129 of Everton Weekes at Trent Bridge, and Worrell's 138 that accompanied Alan Rae's second hundred of the series, at the Oval.

In the field, though the side had no great strength in fast bowling, it did not need it. Valentine, slow left arm, took 33 wickets and Ramadhin, with off-breaks and well disguised leg-breaks, 26. West Indies had arrived.

**1** Cowdrey catches Walcott to give Laker a wicket in the Headingley Test of 1957.
**2** But on the same ground six years later, West Indies won convincingly by 221 runs.

## 1953-54 in West Indies

**West Indies 2   England 2**
**Drawn 1**

When Len Hutton went to the Caribbean early in 1954, he had with him a team that could at last be considered representative of the best of English cricket. The English weakness, though, was that too much was apt to depend on the first few batsmen, on Hutton and Compton and on Peter May, who was about to take on the burden, and consequently the batting could not conquer the West Indian bowling, especially that of Ramadhin, in the first two Tests. But in the third England for the first time batted first. Len Hutton made 169, West Indies followed on, and were beaten. A match of huge scores in Port of Spain was drawn after all three 'Ws' had made hundreds for West Indies, and May and Compton had replied for England. But in Kingston England won a remarkable victory in the last Test to square the series. Catching West Indies on a lively pitch on the first day, Trevor Bailey took 7-34 and bowled them out for 139. Hutton then made 205 of an England score of 414, and West Indies were eventually bowled out in time for England to win by nine wickets.

## 1957 in England

**England 3   West Indies 0   Drawn 2**

The post-war hey-day of West Indian cricket was over by the time John Goddard took his second side to England in 1957. There were some brilliant young players, such as Gary Sobers and Collie Smith, in the making. Wes Hall was still only a boy with a lovely action, and though Gilchrist was very fast, he was erratic. But there was still Ramadhin, whom English batsmen had never really sorted out, and it was the wearing down of him by the England captain Peter May, supported by Colin Cowdrey, that, in the first Test at Edgbaston, turned the series conclusively to England.

In the first innings of this match England were bowled out for 186, Ramadhin taking 7-49. To this West Indies replied with 474, Collie Smith 161. When England lost Peter Richardson, Brian Close, and Doug Insole for 113 by early morning of the fourth day, they seemed certain to lose. But Peter May stood firm, for nearly 10 hours in all, to make 285 not out. Cowdrey made 154 in a record-breaking stand of 411, and England were eventually able to declare. West Indies, weary and disillusioned, then lost 7-68 and it needed a desperate stand by Goddard and D. Atkinson to halt the slide to defeat. Ramadhin in the second innings had bowled 98 overs for 179 runs and only two early wickets. He was never the same force again, and England went on to win three Tests by an

innings. Cowdrey made 152 at Lord's, and Peter Richardson 107 and Tom Graveney 164 on a pinkish-coloured pitch at the Oval, where West Indies subsequently were bowled out for 89 and 86 by Lock and Laker.

## 1959-60 in West Indies

**West Indies 0 England 1 Drawn 4**

The last series in England, for all its ultimate one-sidedness, had left no doubts about the potential of some of West Indies' young players, and by the time Peter May's team arrived early in 1960 Wes Hall headed a formidable battery of fast bowlers. May, fighting against an illness that caused his return home before the last Test, was inevitably not at his best, but Cowdrey, opening the innings, was in fine form and Ted Dexter fulfilled the highest hopes of him on hard pitches.

The series was decided in a dramatic second Test in Trinidad. Ken Barrington (121) and Mike Smith (108) made hundreds in England's first innings of 382,

and on the third day the West Indies batting broke down against the accurate fast bowling of Trueman (5-35) and Statham (3-42). The match had been tensely fought with much hostile fast bowling by both sides, and there was greater tension elsewhere. The crowd, for the varying reasons that cause a West Indian crowd to riot, stopped the match with a storm of bottle-throwing and an invasion of the playing area. The last three days of the match were peaceful, however, and England went on to win by 256 runs. They held their lead without much difficulty in the last three matches.

## 1963 in England

**England 1 West Indies 3 Drawn 1**

The West Indies tour of 1963 had much in common with that of 1950. Though it was acknowledged at the outset that West Indian strength had been growing, nobody quite expected the scintillating victory that was won. England were unlucky to lose

Colin Cowdrey with a broken arm in the famous second Test at Lord's, but their batting at this time could not cope with the formidable fast bowling of Hall, Griffith, and Sobers. And Frank Worrell could also call on a high class off-spinner in Lance Gibbs to support them. Though Fred Trueman took 34 wickets, England's bowling was ageing, and batsmen of the class of Sobers, Conrad Hunte, Rohan Kanhai, Seymour Nurse, and Basil Butcher could make plenty of runs.

Worrell won the toss on a deteriorating Old Trafford pitch and West Indies, making England follow on, spun them out a second time and won the first Test by 10 wickets. At Lord's, after an even first innings, England were thwarted of victory by Basil Butcher (133), the rain, the injury to Cowdrey, and the fast bowling

**In 1963, and again to some extent in 1966, big, fearsome Charlie Griffith tore into the England batting.**

marathon of Hall and Griffith that led to one of the most pulsating finishes in Test cricket. In the end Cowdrey, with broken arm, had to return to partner the last man for the last two balls when England were only six runs short of victory.

England levelled the series by winning the third Test at Edgbaston on a pitch that retained moisture throughout and gave the seam bowling of Trueman, Derek Shackleton, and Dexter skilfully exploited assistance. However, West Indies won the last two Tests with an exhibition that warmed the heart of a public already stimulated by the excitement of the Lord's finish.

### 1966 in England
England 1 West Indies 3 Drawn 1
The West Indies team under Gary Sobers three years later showed marked signs of decline and inevitably had a difficult job matching the exhilarating feats of 1963. That it triumphed again was due to Sobers himself who made 722 runs, took 20 wickets, and held the weakening giant together well enough to beat a troubled England side captained by Mike Smith at the start, Colin Cowdrey in the

middle, and Brian Close at the end.

Like Worrell, Sobers was fortunate in winning the toss at Old Trafford on a pitch that took spin increasingly. This time the victory was by an innings. At Lord's West Indies were within sight of defeat on the fourth day, but an unbroken sixth wicket stand of 274 between cousins Sobers and David Holford saved them. They won the next two Tests, and the series was settled by the time England, against relatively light-hearted opposition, won at the Oval.

### 1967-68 in West Indies
West Indies 0 England 1 Drawn 4
Though there had been signs of cracks in West Indies' citadel in 1966, few expected England to beat them two years later on their own hard pitches. But under Colin Cowdrey, who batted superbly

**The off-spin bowling of Lance Gibbs was a major factor in the Test victories of the great West Indies side of the 1960s. Against England in 1963 he took 26 wickets—only Griffith took more—and in 1966 headed the list with 21.**

Patrick Eagar

himself, England did it by winning the fourth Test. John Snow, who did not play in the first Test, which England were near to winning, developed as a menacing fast bowler at least as formidable as the ageing Hall and Griffith.

England nearly won the second Test as well, when a riot interrupted them in Jamaica. When they did win, it was through a remarkable declaration by Sobers, who set England to make 215 in 2¾ hours. Cowdrey followed up his first innings 148 with 71, Boycott acted as the anchor man with 80 not out, and with three minutes to spare England won by seven wickets. They were perilously near losing the last Test in Georgetown, but a four-hour stand between Cowdrey and Alan Knott held West Indies up, and England's last pair earned the vital draw.

### 1969 in England
England 2 West Indies 0 Drawn 1
A much weakened and less experienced West Indies, whom not even Gary Sobers could hold together, were beaten in a short half-season series early in 1969. This time England, captained by Ray Illingworth, won the toss and the match at Old Trafford. An even second Test was drawn, and England clinched the rubber with an exciting win by 30 runs in the third Test at Leeds. They batted slowly in a low-scoring match, but the pitch eased on the last two days and at one time West Indies, needing 303 to win, were 219-3 with Sobers to come. But when a brilliant innings of 91 by Basil Butcher ended, Sobers played on for 0 and the effort died away.

## England v New Zealand

Though it was not until 1929-30 that New Zealand played their first Test match, there has always been an especially close relationship between English and New Zealand cricket, with a special feeling of responsibility on the English side. This has been accentuated by the relative lack of interest shown by Australia in New Zealand cricket, but it also has deep roots, going back perhaps to the first visit of an English team in 1864, when George Parr's side moved on to New Zealand from Australia.

One thorny problem since New Zealand entered the Test arena has been whether or not it was a good thing for England teams to visit New Zealand only on brief visits at the end of a long Australian tour. The England players are by then tired and the extra month is an anti-climax. On the other hand, it costs little to take the team on to New Zealand, and a series there at that time has the advantage of months of advance publicity while MCC tour Australia.

There has, however, been a significant change in the arrange-

ments for New Zealand visits to England. Whereas the period between visits of New Zealand teams once ranged from six to nine years, under the half-season touring system now employed by England there is a visit roughly every four years. This gives New Zealand greater continuity, and, so more players can use the experience of one tour on another. As a result, there was a noticeable improvement in New Zealand cricket and in 1973 they twice came close to beating England, being in the end unfortunate to lose the series 2-0.

### 1929-30 in New Zealand
New Zealand 0 England 1 Drawn 3
When they played their very first Test against New Zealand, England had another team currently playing a series in West Indies, so they were by no means at full strength. A. H. H. Gilligan had taken over the captaincy when his brother Arthur was taken ill, and he had under him a side that was approximately half-amateur and had Duleepsinhji and Frank Woolley as its stars. England won the first match at Christchurch by eight wickets when Maurice Allom took 5-38 as part of a destructive opening fast bowling partnership with Maurice Nichols.

But they could only draw the other three matches. At that time C. S. Dempster, who opened the innings for New Zealand, was one of the most prolific scorers in the world, and he made 136 and 80 not out in a drawn second Test, sharing in an opening stand of 276 with J. W. E. Mills (117). New Zealand had the better of this match, but as on other occasions in later years, when they were in a good position they were not vigorous enough to press home their advantage.

## 1931 in England
England 1  New Zealand 0
Drawn 2

When Tom Lowry took the first Test-playing New Zealand side to England in 1931—another had done well on a visit in 1927 but had not played Tests—it was intended that the only Test should be at Lord's. But in a wet summer the New Zealanders did so well in the preliminary matches, and in the Test, that two other Tests were arranged at Old Trafford and the Oval.

At Lord's, they were thwarted in the first innings by an eighth-wicket stand of 246 between Leslie Ames (137) and Gubby Allen (122)—in 1970 still a record—but made 469-9 in their second innings, Dempster 120, M. L. 'Curly' Page 104. They were not out of the reckoning when the match was left drawn. England, needing 240 to win, were then 146-5. At the Oval, Herbert Sutcliffe, Duleepsinhji, and Walter Hammond made hundreds for England in a score of 416-4, and after some rain New Zealand were beaten by an innings, Allen taking 5-14 in the first innings. Rain almost completely washed out the Manchester Test.

## 1932-33 in New Zealand
New Zealand 0  England 0
Drawn 2

The two matches played at the end of the 'Bodyline' tour produced two scores of over 500 by England, but no result. Rain affected both matches, which were notable mainly for two enormous innings by Walter Hammond—227 in Christchurch after being missed in the slips early on, and 336 not out in Auckland out of a total of 548-7 declared. This innings lasted 5¼ hours, a historic piece of hitting including 10 sixes and 33 fours, and by passing Bradman's 334 made at Leeds in 1930, it became the highest Test innings to date.

## 1937 in England
England 1  New Zealand 0
Drawn 2

The three-match Test series in 1937 introduced Len Hutton to Test cricket in the first Test and Denis Compton in the third. Hutton was out for 0 and 1 in the first, which was drawn with England comfortably on top, but made 100 in the second Test at Manchester, which England won by 130 runs after Tom Goddard had taken 6-29 in the second innings. One significant feature of this match was the isolated resistance in the last innings of 19-year-old Martin Donnelly. Test matches played by New Zealand in this era were of only three days, and the third was also drawn. Joe Hardstaff made his second hundred of the series, and Compton scored 65 before being run out by a deflection off the bowler.

## 1946-47 in New Zealand
New Zealand 0  England 0
Drawn 1

Only one Test, at Christchurch, was played by Walter Hammond's team immediately after the war, and it was drawn after Walter

**1 Ken James whips the bails off, but Hammond was given the decision and went on to score 100 not out against the New Zealanders at the Oval in 1931. 2 England won the match by an innings and 26 runs. 3 In 1949, Bert Sutcliffe's batting delighted all who saw it. The Kiwis had perhaps their finest ever side, but a three-day Test was not long enough for either side to get a result. 4 New Zealand bat at Wellington in the second Test of the 1950-51 series.**

Hadlee had made 116 for New Zealand and Hammond, in his last Test, had made 79. The match suffered badly from the weather, and for the first time in history an extra day was added when rain prevented play on the third day.

## 1949 in England
England 0  New Zealand 0
Drawn 4

The visit of Walter Hadlee's team to England in 1949 was both a success and a failure. It was a success from the New Zealand point of view because they had a strong side, especially rich in batting, and in a glorious summer of hard pitches made many runs. But the Test matches, still of only three days, were all drawn and are remembered as monuments of stalemate and frustration.

New Zealand shared the advantage in the first Test at Leeds, and led by 171 runs on the first innings at Lord's, where Martin Donnelly made 206. Donnelly made 75 and 80 at Old Trafford, where Bert Sutcliffe scored 101 in the second innings, and though Reg Simpson's 103 helped England to a first innings lead of 147, there was still no sign of a result.

In the last Test, at the Oval,

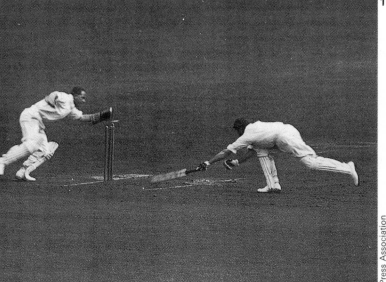

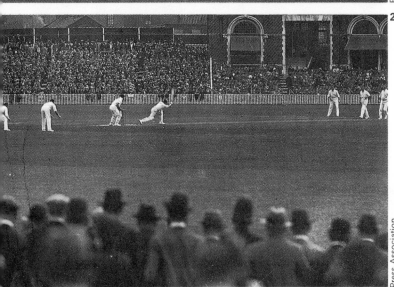

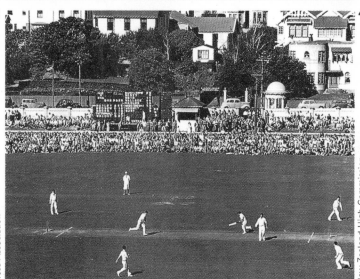

New Zealand were at one time within sight of defeat, for though they made 345 in the first innings, England replied with 482, Len Hutton 206 and Bill Edrich 100, and took five wickets for 188 in the second innings. But two resolute innings by W. M. Wallace and John Reid steered New Zealand safely out of danger, and the series ended on the same note of batting mastery as had existed throughout.

## 1950-51 in New Zealand
New Zealand 0   England 1
Drawn 1
The note was maintained at Christchurch 19 months later when Sutcliffe made 116 for New Zealand and Trevor Bailey 134 not out for England in another high-scoring draw. But England won the other Test by six wickets, after being made to work hard on a deteriorating pitch, New Zealand were still a formidable batting side in this era, though Donnelly had settled in Australia and was no longer available.

## 1954-55 in New Zealand
New Zealand 0   England 2
When Len Hutton's team went to New Zealand after retaining the Ashes in Australia, New Zealand standards had declined. The first match was interrupted by rain and the third and fourth days of what, unusually, was a five-day match were lost through rain. However, the English bowlers finished off the earlier work of Tyson and Statham, and England won by eight wickets.

The second, which England won by an innings with a score of only 246 and a first innings lead of only 46, was remarkable for New Zealand's melancholy achievement of the lowest score in Test history. On a pitch of varying bounce that took some spin, Frank Tyson (2-10) and Brian Statham (3-9) made the initial breakthrough and Bob Appleyard, (4-7) and Johnny Wardle (1-0) carried on. The innings of 26 lasted only 27 overs.

## 1958 in England
England 4   New Zealand 0
Drawn 1
If the collapse of March 1955 had been a bitter moment in New Zealand's cricket history, there was not much to relieve the memory in the next tour of England in 1958. The summer was extremely wet, which always tends to give England an extra advantage, and though New Zealand had capable fast bowlers in Bob Blair, John Hayes, and Tony MacGibbon, they were short of orthodox spin and experienced batting. Reid had a good all-round tour, but Bert Sutcliffe, past his best perhaps, was haunted by injury.

England, with Peter May playing some magnificent innings, were far too good. They began by bowling New Zealand out for 94

1 New Zealand sides of the 1950s and early 1960s relied heavily on John Reid (being caught by Parks off Snow in 1965), and with his dismissal came frequent collapses.
2 Brian Hastings defends at Lord's in the 1969 series.

at Edgbaston, Trueman 5-31, and in a calamitous match at Lord's, which was over by 3.30 p.m. on the third day, New Zealand made 47 and 74. England made only 269, but after heavy rain the pitch gave a lot of help to the redoubtable Laker and Lock, who took 4-13 and 5-17 respectively. In the second innings, these two, with Trueman, Peter Loader, and Bailey, were almost as devastating.

New Zealand's torment at the hands of Laker and Lock continued at Headingley, where they were bowled out for 67, and England needed to make only 267-2, Arthur Milton 104 not out and Peter May 113 not out, to win easily by an innings. They won by an innings again in Manchester, where May made another 100, but the almost incessant rain came to their aid in the last Test.

### 1958-59 in New Zealand
New Zealand 0   England 1
Drawn 1
Another innings defeat followed in Christchurch seven months later when Lock took 11 wickets and Ted Dexter made 141. But rain interrupted the second Test when May (124 not out) had taken England to a big lead.

### 1962-63 in New Zealand
New Zealand 0   England 3
Three years later Ted Dexter's England side won all three Tests, Ken Barrington (126), Peter Parfitt (131), and Barry Knight (125) making hundreds in the first, which was won by an innings, as was the second. A hundred by John Reid kept the margin in the third to seven wickets.

### 1965 in England
England 3   New Zealand 0
Throughout the lean years, John Reid was often fighting a lone battle, supported by players of considerably less ability and experience than himself. When he took the 1965 side to England for the first half-season tour, the weaknesses in batting and spin still remained, and wet weather and bad pitches did not help. England, captained by Mike Smith, made big scores, culminating in the 546-4 at Leeds where John Edrich (310 not out) and Ken Barrington (163) put on 369 for the second wicket.

### 1965-66 in New Zealand
New Zealand 0   England 0
Drawn 3
Although the run of defeats ended in this series, New Zealand were within a fraction of defeat in the first two matches and their failings, as well as one cause of them, were painfully obvious. The low bounce of pitches prepared on rugby grounds discouraged strokeplay and this, plus the long years of struggle, especially against England, produced a negative approach to the game. Such negativity robbed New Zealand of the elusive first victory when they had England in difficulties in the final Test. With a first innings lead of 74, they took six hours to make 129 in the second innings, and then they bowled defensively in the last innings. It seemed a sadly significant performance.

### 1969 in England
England 2   New Zealand 0
Drawn 1
Though the 2-0 defeat does not suggest it, there was heartening improvement in New Zealand's performance on the 1969 tour. A promising left-arm spinner, Hedley Howarth, was an encouraging find, and there were more signs of belligerence in the batting. They were unlucky to play the first Test on a bad pitch at Lord's, where John Edrich made the first of two hundreds, and to play the last amid showers at the Oval, where Derek Underwood took 12 wickets for 101.

### 1970-71 in New Zealand
New Zealand 0   England 1
Drawn 1
New Zealand's rising standards were confirmed 18 months later when Ray Illingworth's side arrived after winning in Australia. England won the first Test in Christchurch after bowling New Zealand out for 65 on a damp pitch on the first day. But New Zealand came back remarkably well later as the pitch dried. In the second Test, on a splendid pitch in Auckland, they came as near to winning as they have done in the long history of the series. After some rousing batting by Mark Burgess and Mike Shrimpton had enlarged on a sticky start and enabled Graham Dowling to declare only a few runs behind, England lost four cheap wickets and had Cowdrey and d'Oliveira injured. However, Cowdrey, with a runner, batted well and Alan Knott followed up a dashing first-innings century with a dogged 96 in the second to delay New Zealand's first win for yet another series.

In 1965 John Edrich took a triple century off the New Zealanders at Headingley as England amassed 546-4.

Patrick Eagar

## England v India

Though Test matches between England and India date from only 1932, cricketing relations between the two countries can be traced back to the 19th century. G. F. Vernon took an English side to India in 1888-89, and another side, under Lord Hawke, went there in 1892-93. Since 1932, England have dominated the series, although from the 1950s India have shown themselves much stronger opposition, especially on their own wickets.

### ENGLAND v INDIA

| | |
|---|---|
| Tests won by England: | 19 |
| Tests won by India: | 6 |
| Tests drawn: | 20 |

**Highest team innings**

| | |
|---|---|
| England: | 571-8 dec, Old Trafford, 1936 |
| India: | 510, Headingley, 1967 |

**Highest individual innings**

| | |
|---|---|
| England: | 246* by G. Boycott, Headingley, 1967 |
| India: | 203* by the Nawab of Pataudi, Delhi, 1963-64 |

**Most runs in a series**

| | |
|---|---|
| England: | 594 (avge 99.00) by K. F. Barrington, 1961-62 |
| India: | 586 (avge 83.71) by V. L. Manjrekar, 1961-62 |

**Most wickets in a series**

| | |
|---|---|
| England: | 29 (avge 13.31) by F. S. Trueman, 1952 |
| India: | 35 (avge 18.91) by B. S. Chandrasekhar 1972-73 |

**Best bowling in an innings**

| | |
|---|---|
| England: | 8-31 by F. S. Trueman, Old Trafford, 1952 |
| India: | 8-55 by V. M. Mankad, Madras, 1951-52 |

*Not out.
Figures up to and including the 1972-73 series

### 1932 in England
England 1   India 0
The batting of Duleepsinhji in the county championship was still to the fore of English cricket, perhaps promising great things from his countrymen when they toured England in 1932 and played the first Test match between the two countries. In the event, England won without too much trouble, although they lost Percy Holmes, Herbert Sutcliffe, and Frank Woolley for 19 runs in the first 20 minutes. Douglass, Jardine, and Les Ames led a recovery to 259, but India were unable to consolidate their advantage and found the task of scoring 346 to win in the second innings too much.

### 1933-34 in India
India 0   England 2   Drawn 1
England sent a comparatively strong team for the first series in India, and proved too good all round. India found the bowling of Nobby Clarke, Maurice Nichols, Hedley Verity, and James Langridge a difficult proposition, and were unable to total more than 258. England, on the other hand, twice made over 400. At Bombay Brian Valentine (136) helped England to 438, and des-

pite 118 by Lala Amarnath in India's second innings, England won by nine wickets. India followed on at Calcutta, only to save the match, but England clinched the series in the last Test, winning by 202 runs. Amar Singh took 7-86 in England's first innings, and Verity replied with 7-49 when the Indians batted.

### 1936 in England
England 2   India 0   Drawn 1
India's chances of winning their first Test were upset when Amarnath, their leading all-rounder, was sent home for disciplinary reasons before the Lord's Test. England won two of the matches handsomely, but India had their moment of glory in the drawn second Test at Old Trafford. Facing a first-innings arrears of 368, India were given a great start by Vijay Merchant (114) and Mushtaq Ali (112) who shared a stand of 203. For England, Walter Hammond made 167 in a total of 571-8 declared.

England won the first Test at Lord's by 9 wickets, Gubby Allen taking 5-35 and 5-43 in the match. Hammond was again in fine form at the Oval, where England once more won by 9 wickets. He scored 217 and with Stan Worthington (128) put on 266 for the fourth wicket. India, following on 249 behind, scored 312 with Allen taking 7-80.

### 1946 in England
England 1   India 0   Drawn 2
In the only match finished, England won at Lord's by 10 wickets, but later India only just escaped defeat at Old Trafford. The Oval Test was ruined by the weather. The series was notable for the introduction to Test cricket of Alec Bedser, who took 11 wickets in each of the first two games. He claimed 7-49 and 4-96 at Lord's where Joe Hardstaff hit a magnificent 205 not out in a total of 428. At Old Trafford, India, facing England's first innings of 294, began with an opening stand of 124 from Merchant and Mushtaq Ali, but were out for another 46. They saved the game when their last pair, Sohoni and Hindlekar stayed together for the last 13 minutes. Bedser's figures were 4-41 and 7-52. Merchant scored 128 at the Oval where India totalled 331, but England managed only 95-3 before the game was abandoned.

### 1951-52 in India
India 1   England 1   Drawn 3
India made history by recording their first victory over England, winning by an innings and 8 runs in the final game at Madras, and so sharing the series. The first three matches were drawn. At New Delhi, England had a hard fight after being dismissed for 203. India ran up 418-6 with Merchant (154) and Vijay Hazare (164 not out) adding 211 for the third wicket, but a determined 138 not

out by Alan Watkins saved England. Hazare hit another century at Bombay, Pankaj Roy made 140 and Tom Graveney replied with 175; and as in the next Test at Calcutta there was never much chance of a finish. England won the fourth Test by 8 wickets on a Kanpur pitch taking spin, but at Madras they had no answer to 'Vinoo' Mankad, who took 8-55 and 4-53, Roy (111) and 'Polly' Umrigar (130) led the Indian batting.

### 1952 in England
England 3   India 0   Drawn 1
After their promising performances in the previous series, India went to England minus Merchant, Mankad (who later played in three Tests), Amarnath, and Mushtaq Ali, played defensively too often, and were outclassed. Only rain saved them from overwhelming defeat in all

**Though a useful bowler, Vijay Hazare presented England with more problems as a prolific batsman in India in 1951-52.**

four games. The first match, at Headingley, was notable for the worst start to an innings in Test history. Facing arrears of 41, India lost their first four second-innings wickets without a run being scored and England won by 7 wickets.

A magnificent all-round effort by Mankad made the Lord's match. He scored 72 and 184, and bowled 73 overs for 5-196 in England's first innings. Despite this, England won easily by 8 wickets, Len Hutton making 150 and Godfrey Evans 104 in a total

**Ted Dexter captained England in 1961-62, when India won their first ever series over England by two Tests to none.**

of 537. Fred Trueman demoralized India at Old Trafford, taking 8-31 in a first innings total of 58. They did little better when they followed on, being out for 82 and so were dismissed twice in a day. Hutton made 104 in the England innings of 347-9 declared.

### 1959 in England
England 5   India 0

For the first time ever England won all five Tests in a series, India's contribution to this feat being a somewhat dubious distinction. The negativity that had beset the 1952 side seemed amplified, and few of the batsmen seemed prepared to take advantage of one of England's finest summers.

Three of England's victories came with an innings to spare, and the other two were won with plenty in hand. Brian Statham and Fred Trueman consistently upset the Indian batting, and the bowlers encountered Peter May, Colin Cowdrey, Ken Barrington, and Geoff Pullar full of runs.

Only the fourth Test provided any real interest, and it was the only one that went into the fifth day. Geoff Pullar (131) and Mike Smith (100) scored centuries for England, and when India batted a second time wanting 548 to win A. A. Baig, an Oxford freshman recruited during the tour, made 112 and Umrigar 118 before they went down by 171 runs.

### 1961-62 in India
India 2   England 0   Drawn 3

For the first time India won a series against England, their success being well deserved. The England batting was unreliable and the bowling lacking in penetration, and the absence of players such as Cowdrey, Statham, and Trueman should not detract from the Indian victory.

At Bombay, England reached 500-8, Barrington 151 not out, but India saved the game comfortably. England were made to follow on for the first time against India at Kanpur, but with Pullar (119), Barrington (172), and Ted Dexter (126 not out) showing a return of form they reached 497-5 without inviting India to bat again.

After rain had washed out the last two days at New Delhi, the teams met in Calcutta, where India won by 187 runs, C. G. Borde and S. Durani doing most damage. Durani (6-105 and 4-72) was again a problem for the England batsmen at Madras, and with the Nawab of Pataudi scoring 103 in their first innings India took the match by 128 runs and the series by two Tests.

### 1963-64 in India
India 0   England 0   Drawn 5

Though five draws in a five-Test series was not a novel experience for India, who had achieved it twice before with Pakistan, it was for England. Not that it affected attendances, for the

**1** India's first victory in 1961-62 came at Calcutta where Salim Durani (batting) enjoyed a fine match, scoring 43 and taking 5-47 and 3-66 when England batted. **2** India's captain, the Nawab of Pataudi, looks ruefully at his stumps at the end of an innings of 148 in 1967.

might have been.

Solid batting from Hanif (187 not out) and Asif enabled the tourists to open the series with a draw. Barrington scored 148 in England's first innings. Rain interfered with the second Test at Trent Bridge, where England won by 10 wickets after Pakistan had been dismissed for 140, and England, with Barrington batting nearly seven hours for his 109 not out, led by 112. The conditions were tailor-made for Derek Underwood when the tourists batted again, and he finished with 5-52.

Geoff Arnold (5-58) was mainly responsible for Pakistan's dismissal for 216 at the Oval, and after Barrington had hit his third century in three games, Pakistan batted again 224 in arrears. At 65-8 they looked doomed to an innings defeat. Then Asif came to the wicket, and with Intikhab Alam increased the Test record for the 9th wicket to 190. Unprecedented scenes greeted his century in 2 hours 19 minutes. Hundreds of Pakistanis raced on to the field and hoisted him shoulder high until the police rescued him. Revived with a drink from the team manager, he then continued the entertainment until stumped by Alan Knott for 146. Barrington fittingly hit the winning runs for

grounds were packed to capacity for the run-glut encouraged by the easy pitches. England suffered heavily from injury and sickness, and Cowdrey and Peter Parfitt flew out later to strengthen the side.

Cowdrey's arrival brought England their first century in the series, when he scored 107 in the third Test at Calcutta. B. K. Kunderam (192) and Manjrekar (108) had opened India's century account in the first Test at Madras. Cowdrey followed with 151 at New Dehli, but Hanumant Singh (105), Kunderam (100), and Pataudi (203 not out) gave India a century advantage of six to two. M. L. Jaisimha had scored 129 at Calcutta.

With Barry Knight (127) and Parfitt (121) to the fore, England made 559-8 at Kanpur, and Fred Titmus then took 6-73 to make India follow on. But a century from R. G. Nadkarni (122 not out) ensured the stalemate would not be broken.

### 1967 in England
England 3   India 0
Upset by terrible weather and injuries, India gave a dismal display in the first half of a shared tour with Pakistan. Only in the second innings of the first Test at Headingley, where they followed on and made 510, did they distinguish themselves. Pataudi's 148 proved to be their only Test century. Not even that score could stop England winning by 6 wickets, and Close's men found less resistance in the other two Tests.

## England v Pakistan

Pakistan achieved the unexpected and the unprecedented on their first tour of England by winning one Test and so drawing the series. No other touring side had managed to win a Test on their first visit, but as they embarked on a half-tour in 1971 it was still their only success on English soil. Although they had produced a number of good individual efforts, too often their sides have lacked depth in English conditions. On their own pitches, however, they have proved much sterner opposition.

England's fielders find themselves in some danger as 'The Noob' pulls a short ball to leg in the third Test of 1967. There was never any danger for England in the series, though, and they won all three tests comfortably.

### ENGLAND v PAKISTAN

| | |
|---|---|
| Tests won by England: | 9 |
| Tests won by Pakistan: | 1 |
| Tests drawn: | 14 |
| **Highest team innings** | |
| England: | 558-6 dec, Trent Bridge, 1954 |
| Pakistan: | 608-7 dec, Edgbaston, 1971 |
| **Highest individual innings** | |
| England: | 278 by D. C. S. Compton, Trent Bridge, 1954 |
| Pakistan: | 274 by Zahir Abbas, Edgbaston, 1971 |
| **Most runs in a series** | |
| England: | 453 (*avge* 90.60) by D. C. S. Compton, 1954 |
| Pakistan: | 407 (*avge* 67.83) by Hanif Mohammad, 1961-62 |
| **Most wickets in a series** | |
| England: | 22 (*avge* 19.69) by F. S. Trueman, 1962 |
| Pakistan: | 20 (*avge* 20.40) by Fazal Mahmood, 1954 |
| **Best bowling in an innings** | |
| England: | 7-56 by J. H. Wardle, Oval, 1954 |
| Pakistan: | 6-46 by Fazal Mahmood, Oval, 1954 |

*Not out. Figures up to and including the 1972-73 series

### 1954 in England
England 1   Pakistan 1   Drawn 2
A series that was to have such a satisfying climax for the tourists began in a depressing manner, rain preventing play until mid-afternoon on the fourth day of the first Test. Further frustration followed at Trent Bridge, this time in the batting of Denis Compton (278) and Reg Simpson (101), and England won by an innings and 129 runs. Rain proved their saviour at Old Trafford, when they were 25-4 in the second innings, having made only 90 in reply to England's 359-8.

Then came the thrilling last Test at the Oval, where Pakistan won by 24 runs. England, needing 168 to win, were 109-2 at one stage, but collapsed completely and were out for 143. Fazal Mahmood took 6-53 and 6-46 to offset Johnny Wardle's 7-56 in Pakistan's second innings.

### 1961-62 in Pakistan
Pakistan 0   England 1   Drawn 2
England's first-Test victory at Lahore by 5 wickets with 35 minutes to spare proved decisive. Pakistan began strongly, but slumped from 315-3 to 387-9, Javed Burki 138, and 139 from Ken Barrington kept England within striking distance. MCC then went on to India, where they played five Tests, before the second and third Tests were played at Dacca and Karachi. Hanif Mohammad scored a century in each innings of a dull draw at Dacca, and Dexter's double century (205) and Parfitt's 111 in England's 507 in the last Test gave Pakistan no hope of squaring the series.

### 1962 in England
England 4   Pakistan 0   Drawn 1
Hopes that the Pakistanis would do well again in England were not fulfilled, and only the weather saved them from defeat in all five Tests. Their leading batsman Hanif Mohammad was far from fit and never struck form, although his younger brother Mushtaq was a success. Bowling was the tourist's main weakness, and only once could they dismiss England for less than 400. Both Parfitt and Graveney enjoyed averages of a hundred or more, and no Pakistan bowler averaged less than 30 in the Tests.

This was a young, inexperienced touring side, and it found the English conditions vastly different from those at home. Pakistan had only recently been changing from matting wickets to lifeless turf that allowed little movement of the pitch. Consequently, they were at a loss against the seam bowling of Len Coldwell, Statham, and Trueman.

### 1967 in England
England 2   Pakistan 0   Drawn 1
As on the previous tour, Pakistan's main problem was their bowling, for although they had a capable spin attack, there was no penetrating fast bowling. The batting had more depth, but, like the Indians earlier in the season, the Pakistanis seemed reluctant to throw caution to the winds. Only when Asif Iqbal launched his unexpected attack at the Oval was there any indication of what

England, whose 8-wicket victory with a day to spare was something of an anticlimax.

**1968-69 in Pakistan**
Pakistan 0   England 0   Drawn 3
Internal political riots ruined the series and finally caused the abandonment of the third Test. The unrest was apparent from the first Test, in which Cowdrey scored 100 and Asif (70) and Majid Jahangir (68) batted well and entertainingly for Pakistan. D'Oliveira's unbeaten 114 was the outstanding innings of a dull game at Dacca. At Karachi, Colin Milburn enlivened the proceedings with a quick-fire 139, Graveney scored 105, and Alan Knott was within four runs of his maiden Test century when rioting stopped play.

**1** Asif Iqbal enlivened the last Test of the 1967 series between England and Pakistan with a magnificent 146.
**2** Alan Knott, batting for Kent against the Pakistanis of 1971, made up for his lost century at Karachi in 1968-69 with a match-saving 116 in the Edgbaston Test of 1971. It was in this match that the Pakistan opener Zahir Abbas (**3**) batted more than 9 hours for his mammoth 274.

Sportography

Patrick Eagar

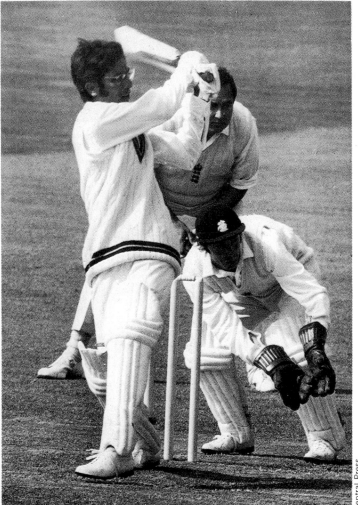

Central Press

**1971 in England**
England 1   Pakistan 0   Drawn 2
An England side still flushed from success in Australia found themselves brought back to reality in the first Test as Pakistan kept them in the field for more than two days as they amassed 608-7. Young Zahir Abbas batted just over 9 hours for a magnificent 274 and shared a stand of 291 with Mushtaq Mohammed (100). Asif Iqbal also reached his century, and it needed a fighting 73 by D'Oliveira and 116 from Knott to give the England innings respectability after Asif Masood had shown the England bowlers up. England followed on 255 behind, but rain on the final day cost Pakistan almost certain victory. Luckhurst scored 108 not out in England's 229-5 and Asif Masood finished with match figures of 8 for 147.

Rain for most of the second Test meant that all depended on Headingley, where England won an exciting victory by 25 runs. Boycott followed his second-Test 121 not out with 112, but Pakistan passed England's 316 by 34 and then dismissed England for 264, Salim Altaf taking 4-11. The tourists needed 231 for victory with more than a day to play, but on the final day Illingworth made the initial breakthrough on a wicket that had threatened to take spin throughout, and though the youngest Mohammed, Sadiq, scored 91, the series, somewhat unjustly, eluded Pakistan.

43

*Radio Times Hulton Picture Library*

# Australia v South Africa

In a series of much excitement and memorable cricket, the pendulum has swung noticeably from one country to the other. In the first 50 years of Australia-South Africa encounters, South Africa won only one Test, but then in the next 20 years they won 13 to Australia's 8. There were two extraordinary series, in 1952-53 and again 11 years later, when South Africa, against all expectations, earned a draw. The Test ban on South Africa has prevented any series since 1969-70.

| AUSTRALIA v SOUTH AFRICA | | |
| --- | --- | --- |
| Tests won by Australia: | 29 | |
| Tests won by South Africa: | 11 | |
| Tests drawn: | 13 | |
| **Highest team innings** | | |
| Australia: | 578, Melbourne, 1910-11 | |
| South Africa: | 622-9 dec, Durban, 1969-70 | |
| **Highest individual innings** | | |
| Australia: | 299* by D. G. Bradman, Adelaide, 1931-32 | |
| South Africa: | 274 by R. G. Pollock, Durban, 1969-70 | |
| **Most runs in a series** | | |
| Australia: | 834 (avge 92.66) by R. N. Harvey, 1952-53 | |
| South Africa: | 732 (avge 73.20) by G. A. Faulkner, 1910-11 | |
| **Most wickets in a series** | | |
| Australia: | 44 (avge 14.59) by C. V. Grimmett, 1935-36 | |
| South Africa: | 30 (avge 28.10) by H. J. Tayfield, 1952-53 | |
| **Best bowling in an innings** | | |
| Australia: | 7-34 by J. V. Saunders, Johannesburg, 1902-03 | |
| South Africa: | 7-23 by H. J. Tayfield, Durban, 1949-50 | |

*Not out. Figures up to and including the 1969-70 series

## 1902-03 in South Africa
South Africa 0  Australia 2
Drawn 1
The outbreak of war in South Africa in 1899 could scarcely have been expected to raise standards, but though hostilities dragged on into 1902, there was plenty of evidence of the keenness of the English-speaking population to restart and improve their cricket. It was then that the South African cricket authorities issued an invitation of great boldness and farsightedness. They invited Joe Darling's Australian side, then touring England, to return home by way of South Africa. The invitation was accepted, South African cricket surged forward from that time, and though well beaten in two of the three Test matches, the home side had their moments.

Australia, transplanted to matting from the turf pitches of England, where they had won the series, found themselves fielding while South Africa made 454 in the first Test in Johannesburg. L. J. Tancred made 97 and C. G. B. Llewellyn followed up an innings of 90 by taking 6-92. Australia, amazingly, had to follow on, but they had no trouble in saving the three-day match, and twice in the other two Tests bowled South Africa out for 85. South Africa's defeat in the last Test was delayed by a spectacular innings of 104 in 80 minutes by J. H. Sinclair, which included six sixes, but Australia won by 10 wickets and Darling took his side home having made a lasting contribution to South African cricket.

## 1910-11 in Australia
Australia 4  South Africa 1
When P. W. Sherwell took the first South African side to Australia in 1910, South Africa had enjoyed some years of success founded largely on the googly bowling of Ernest Vogler, Reginald Schwarz, and Aubrey Faulkner. But they proved less effective on Australian turf than they had at home on matting and in England. In addition, there was no genuine fast bowler, and the others could not stop Australia making hundreds of runs. In the first Test Warren Bardsley made 132 and Clem Hill 191. In the second Victor Trumper made 159, in the third 214 not out. Hill (100) and Warwick Armstrong (132) made hundreds in the fourth Test, and Macartney 137 in the fifth.

South Africa were not entirely eclipsed, for an innings of 204 by Faulkner kept the losing margin to 89 runs in the second Test (South Africa's innings were 506 and 80!) and they actually won the third in Adelaide. J. W. Zulch (105) and S. J. Snooke (103) made hundreds in the first innings, Faulkner made 115 in the second and on a deteriorating pitch on the sixth day Australia went down by 38 runs. It was the last time for nearly 42 years that South Africa were to win a Test match against Australia.

## 1912 in England
Australia 2  South Africa 0
Drawn 1
The Triangular Tournament of 1912 has gone done in cricket history as a major disaster, but no one had a more disastrous season on the playing side than the South Africans, who lost all three Tests to England and the first two to Australia. They were still passing through a recession after the decline of the googly bowlers, and Australia outplayed them in the first Test at Old Trafford, winning by an innings. C. Kelleway (114) and Bardsley (121) made hundreds, and though Faulkner scored 122 not out for South Africa, T. J. Matthews performed the feat, by 1971 achieved only four times in first-class cricket history, of taking a hat-trick in each innings. Oddly he took no other wickets in the match.

In the second Test at Lord's, Kelleway (102) and Bardsley (164) again made hundreds and South Africa lost by 10 wickets.

**Australia and South Africa meet at Old Trafford in the first Test of the ill-fated triangular tournament of 1912.**

It was only in the third at Nottingham that they had any relief. The match was drawn after they had led by 110 runs on first innings.

## 1921-22 in South Africa
South Africa 0  Australia 1
Drawn 2
Once again South Africa was visited after a war by an Australian side that helped boost its cricket. But the Australian Imperial Forces side led by H. L. Collins did not, of course, play official Tests on its way home from England. Two years later, however, the triumphant Australians of 1921 also called on their way home and played three Tests. Warwick Armstrong had sustained an injury on the sea voyage, and so the side was again captained by Collins, who made 203 in the second Test in Johannesburg.

The first two matches were drawn in Australia's favour, though C. N. Frank made 152 and the left-handed Dave Nourse 111 after South Africa had followed on in the second. Australia won the third in Cape Town by 10 wickets, Arthur Mailey taking 4-40 in the first innings and Charlie Macartney 5-44 in the second. Previously much of the damage had been done, as in England, by Jack Gregory and Ted McDonald.

## 1931-32 in Australia
Australia 5  South Africa 0
The 1930s were not an easy decade for South African cricket, which was slowly negotiating the change from matting to turf pitches at home. When they went to Australia in 1931, under the dashing wicket-keeper-batsman Jock Cameron, they were in no

state to resist the genius of Don Bradman in his prime, and lost all five Tests by big margins—three by an innings, one by 10 wickets, and one by 169 runs.

Having begun by being caught on a bad pitch at Brisbane, a fate wont to befall weak sides, they finished on the worst of Melbourne sticky pitches, which reports say had been turned into a 'surface of treacle'. On the first day at Melbourne, South Africa were bowled out for 36 in less than 90 minutes, the slow left-arm bowler Bert Ironmonger taking 5-6. In fact, 10 batsmen contributed 17 runs between them, for Cameron made 11 and extras came to 8. Australia made only 153, but it was easily enough to give them victory by an innings. After a blank second day and a late start on the third, Ironmonger (6-18) and Bill O'Reilly (3-19) bowled South Africa out again in less than 90 minutes for 45. The whole match was over in 109 overs.

Bradman, injured in the field, did not bat in this match, but his previous scores—226, 112, 2 and 167, and 299 not out—gave him an average of 201.50.

## 1935-36 in South Africa
South Africa 0   Australia 4
Drawn 1
When the next Australian team went to South Africa, under Vic Richardson, the Springboks had every reason to hope they would do better, for they had just returned from winning their first series in England. But within a few days 'Jock' Cameron, a tower of strength in England, had died suddenly, and this melancholy event seemed to set the tone for what followed. Had it not rained during the second Test in Johannesburg, South Africa would have lost all five Tests. As it was, they lost three by an innings and one by nine wickets.

Australia seemed, by now, to have some jinx over South African cricket, which they had done much to foster. In particular, Australian spinners feasted on the South African bastmen—in this series Clarrie Grimmett took 44 wickets at 14 apiece and O'Reilly 27 at 17 each. With the bat Stan McCabe averaged 84 and Jack Fingleton 79. Dudley Nourse played a fine innings of 231 in the second innings of the drawn Test, but otherwise the encounter was a bitter disappointment for South Africans.

## 1949-50 in South Africa
South Africa 0   Australia 4
Drawn 1
The immediate post-war period was not the time to expect the balance to change, and Lindsay Hassett's Australian team had almost as easy a passage as its predecessor. The South African bowling was exceptionally thin, and the Australian batsmen Arthur Morris, Neil Harvey, Hassett, and others made hundreds of easy runs. In the drawn Test in Johannesburg J. A. R. Moroney made a hundred in each innings.

There was only one rough patch in Australia's triumphant passage—when they found themselves in danger of following on 236 runs behind in the third Test at Durban. After making 311 themselves, Eric Rowan 143, the Springboks had incredibly removed Australia for 75, thanks to a magnificent piece of off-spin bowling by Hugh Tayfield (7-23 in 8.4 overs). Dudley Nourse, the Springbok captain, had the weekend to decide whether to enforce the follow-on, and eventually he decided against it. South Africa were then bowled out for 99 by Bill Johnston (4-39) and Ian Johnson (5-34). Australia, needing 336 on a pitch not entirely reliable, made them with 25 minutes and five wickets to spare, Neil Harvey playing a superb innings of 151 not out. The Springboks must have wondered then if they would ever beat Australia again.

## 1952-53 in Australia
Australia 2   South Africa 2
Drawn 1
A defeat in England in 1951 did little to raise South African spirits, although there were promising young cricketers in Jackie McGlew, Roy McLean, John Waite, and Russell Endean. Yet they actually won two Tests and squared the series in Australia. Under the inspiring captaincy of Jack Cheetham, the young and athletic Springboks achieved a standard of fielding seldom seen before or since. They caught everything, and Hugh Tayfield emerged as a great off-spinner in Australian conditions.

The first Test went to Australia, though the Springboks, who had not won a state match and had lost to New South Wales, did better than most people expected, and lost by only 96 runs. They then staggered the cricket world by winning the second Test, in Melbourne, their first victory over Australia for 42 years. They were slightly behind on the first innings, but Endean made 162 not out in the second innings and Tayfield (7-81) completed the triumph. Within a fortnight Australia had won the third Test by an innings, Neil Harvey (190) making the third of his four hundreds in the series, and when Australia had much the better of a draw in Adelaide, there was inevitably a tendency to write off South Africa's second-Test success as a flash in the pan.

But back at Melbourne they won one of the most glorious victories in Test history, for it was achieved after Australia, batting first, had made 520 in their first innings, Harvey 205. The Springboks scored consistently to reach 435, and then the fast bowler Eddie Fuller, with help from Tayfield and P. N. F. Mansell, dismissed Australia for 209. The Springboks still had to score 295 to win, and at 191-4 the match was in the balance. Then Roy McLean came in to make 76 out of 106 in 80 minutes, the match was won, and the rubber magnificently halved.

## 1957-58 in South Africa
South Africa 0   Australia 3
Drawn 2
When Ian Craig, aged only 22, took Australia's next team to South Africa, there was roughly the same cause for hope among South Africans as there had been in the 1930s, for South Africa had met with more success in England in 1955 than Australia had in 1956. But the bogy of Australian spin was not laid. Richie Benaud took 30 wickets and Lindsey Kline 15, and with Alan Davidson's 25 this was quite enough to defeat some over-defensive South African batting. Mackay, who averaged 125, and Benaud easily covered up the moderate form of Craig and Neil Harvey.

Though South Africa began the first Test by making 470-9, they lost the second, could not press home a promising position in the third, when Neil Adcock and Peter Heine bowled Australia out in the first innings for 163, and easily lost the last two.

## 1963-64 in Australia
Australia 1   South Africa 1
Drawn 3
Once again South Africa's chances in Australia seemed hopeless and once again they amazed everybody by sharing the honours, this time through the fast bowling of Peter Pollock, the swing bowling of J. T. Partridge, and the exciting batting of their young stars, Eddie Barlow, Graeme Pollock, and Colin Bland. Only their fielding was below par.

The series began with a draw at Brisbane in a match made memorable by the calling of Ian Meckiff for throwing. Though Eddie Barlow made 109 and 54 in the second Test, Bill Lawry's 157 helped Australia win it comfortably by eight wickets. South Africa were by no means out of the running in the drawn third Test, and they followed with a magnificent 10-wicket victory won mainly by a historic third-wicket stand of 341 in 283 minutes between Barlow (201) and Graeme Pollock (175). With more enterprising captaincy by Trevor Goddard in the last Test, South Africa might have won the series, for they had much the better of the draw.

## 1966-67 in South Africa
South Africa 3   Australia 1
Drawn 1
So often had South Africa failed at home against Australia that when Bobby Simpson's team went there in 1966 many people envisaged another disappointment. But this time they picked the right teams, they were well led by Peter van der Merwe, their young batsmen destroyed the Australian spin, and Trevor Goddard, free of the captaincy, bowled magnificently to take 26 wickets.

Before the start of the Test series, excitement was kindled by Transvaal's victory over the Australians, the first ever over an Australian side in South Africa, and a series of much magnificent cricket was followed with intense enthusiasm. South Africa won a sensational first-Test victory in Johannesburg after Australia had passed their first innings total of 199 with only one wicket down. In the second innings the Springbok wicketkeeper Denis Lindsay played the first of three swashbuckling hundreds that tipped the scales at vital times—he was to score 606 runs in the series and take 24 catches. Australia won the second Test in Cape Town with 25 minutes and seven wickets to spare, in spite of Graeme Pollock's second innings 209. Of the last three, South Africa won two and would have won the other by the biggest margin of all but for rain. The scales had at last been tipped.

## 1969-70 in South Africa
South Africa 4   Australia 0
When Bill Lawry's team went to South Africa early in 1970 after a two-month tour of India, there were some who thought they would be more successful than their immediate predecessors, and that the Springboks, not having played Test cricket for three years, would be at a disadvantage. But to the heroes who had won the last series South Africa could now add Barry Richards and Mike Procter in their prime, and though Trevor Goddard was not the force of other days they won even more easily.

Australia's best chance was in the first Test at Newlands, where the pitches that season had been taking spin. But Ali Bacher won the toss, Eddie Barlow made 127, and South Africa, with more maturity of judgement than they had shown in the previous series, never lost their grip on a match they won by 170 runs. After that there seemed little hope for Australia on the other pitches, and their defeats were even more conclusive.

None was more devastating than that in the second Test in Durban. Richards, while making a superb 140, almost reached 100 before lunch on the first day, and Graeme Pollock made 274, the highest Test score by a South African. Australia were routed, and the cricket world was left regretting more than ever the factors outside cricket that prevented South Africa playing against all the other main cricketing countries in this golden era.

1 Arthur Morris still has a long way to go as John Waite runs him out during the fifth Test of the 1952-53 series. 2 The wicket-keeping of Wally Grout and the bowling of Richie Benaud (joining forces to dismiss Adcock) were features of Australia's victory in South Africa five years later. 3, 4, & 5 In 1970, South Africa, with such players as the fast bowling all-rounder Mike Procter (3), Barry Richards (4), and wicket-keeper Denis Lindsay (5) humbled the touring Australians by winning all four Tests. 6 South Africa's rise began in 1963-64, when bespectacled Eddie Barlow and Graeme Pollock set the Springboks on the way to a series-equalling victory at Adelaide with a third-wicket stand of 341. 7 Richie Benaud bowls out of Test cricket. 8 Ali Bacher, captain of the 1970 South Africans, ducks as Stackpole hooks.

## Australia v West Indies

A ticker-tape farewell to a cricket team sounds like something out of sporting fiction. But that is what was given to Frank Worrell's West Indians in Melbourne after they had played—and lost—one of the most colourful series in Test history, in 1960-61. By 1973, there had been six other series between the two sides, and though none of the others matched that one, they usually had an above-average share of incident and eventful cricket. The first was in 1930-31, less than three years after West Indies had been accorded Test status, and they were still in a largely disorganized state of development. The various islands were several days journey apart, and many members of the first side to Australia met each other for the first time on the voyage out.

| AUSTRALIA v WEST INDIES | | |
|---|---|---|
| Tests won by Australia: | | 19 |
| Tests won by West Indies: | | 6 |
| Tests tied: | | 1 |
| Tests drawn: | | 9 |
| **Highest team innings** | | |
| Australia: | 758-8 dec, Kingston, 1954-55 | |
| West Indies: | 619, Sydney, 1968-69 | |
| **Highest individual innings** | | |
| Australia: | 242 by K. D. Walters, Sydney, 1968-69 | |
| West Indies: | 219 by D. Atkinson, Bridgetown, 1954-55 | |
| **Most runs in a series** | | |
| Australia: | 699 (*avge* 116.50) by K. D. Walters, 1968-69 | |
| West Indies: | 827 (*avge* 82.70) by C. L. Walcott, 1954-55 | |
| **Most wickets in a series** | | |
| Australia: | 33 { (*avge* 17.96) by C. V. Grimmett, 1930-31 (*avge* 18.54) by A. K. Davidson, 1960-61 | |
| West Indies: | 26 (*avge* 26.76) by L. R. Gibbs 1972-73 | |
| **Best bowling in an innings** | | |
| Australia: | 8-71 by G. D. McKenzie, Melbourne, 1968-69 | |
| West Indies: | 7-55 by G. E. Gomez, Sydney, 1951-52 | |
| Figures up to and including the 1973 series | | |

### 1930-31 in Australia
Australia 4   West Indies 1
In spite of their inexperience and the renown of Bradman, just back from his first tour of England, the West Indians were far from apprehensive. They had three formidable fast bowlers in G. N. Francis, H. C. Griffith, and Learie Constantine, who was also a spectacular all-rounder, and a great batsman in George Headley. They hoped for fast pitches, improvement from their lesser known players, and that their fallible slip-catching, one of the failings of their 1928 tour of England, had been repaired.

But like their equally hopeful successors 21 years later they were in for a disappointment. Their captain G. C. Grant, a

Melbourne says farewell to Frank Worrell's West Indians, who lost the series but won a great victory for cricket.

former Cambridge blue, made 50 not out in each innings, but the fast pitches they had been expecting were not forthcoming and the leg-spin of Clarrie Grimmett proved the decisive factor in the first Test. West Indies were caught on a wet pitch at Sydney in the second Test and beaten by an innings. A second-wicket stand of 229 and an innings of 223 by Bradman started them on the road to another innings defeat at Brisbane, though Headley made 102 not out in a total of 193. At Melbourne, Bradman made 152 after Bert Ironmonger (7-23) and Grimmett had bowled West Indies out for 99 and they lost by an innings again.

At the end of this gloomy first tour there was, however, one ray of light. In the last Test, at Sydney, West Indies found a faster pitch that was affected by rain more than once. They batted first, scoring 350-6 through 123 not out by F. R. Martin and 105 by Headley. Grant was able to declare twice when it suited him, and with his fast bowlers enjoying a damp, lively pitch, West Indies won their first victory over Australia by 30 runs.

### 1951-52 in Australia
Australia 4   West Indies 1
In the 21 years between the first and second series West Indian

cricket had made big advances to the era of the three 'Ws' and of Ramadhin and Valentine. Australia were still strong, retaining the bulk of the great 1948 side, but Bradman had retired, and West Indies, still fresh from their English triumphs of 1950, travelled with some confidence. Nevertheless, the result was the same, a 4-1 defeat and a grievous disappointment. Mostly the damage was done by the Australian fast bowlers, Ray Lindwall, Keith Miller, and Bill Johnston, who were too much for the main West Indian batsmen. Sonny Ramadhin was not a force on Australian pitches, though the left-arm spinner Alf Valentine took 24 Test wickets at 28 apiece. The downfall of the three 'Ws' was complete, for Frank Worrell averaged only 33, Everton Weekes 24, and Clyde Walcott 14. Their performance was typical of the general inability of John Goddard's side to adapt themselves.

Australia won the first Test only by three wickets, but Lindsay Hassett and Miller made hundreds in the second, which was won by seven wickets. By now the West Indian batsmen were in some trouble against the bumpers of Lindwall and Miller, but their luck changed temporarily over Christmas at Adelaide. The third Test there began on a wet pitch, and Gerry Gomez, Worrell (6-38), and Goddard bowled Australia out for 82. Before the end of the first day West Indies had themselves been bowled out for 105 and Australia had lost two second innings wickets. On the third day, Christmas Day, West Indies needed 233 to win, and with Australia not holding their chances, they won by six wickets.

Australia clinched the rubber with a thrilling win by one wicket at Melbourne. No innings total exceeded 300, and Australia needed 260 to win in the last innings on a pitch taking some spin. A brilliant innings of 102 by Hassett, the Australian captain, took Australia a long way towards victory, and though the odds always seemed to be slightly on West Indies, a last-wicket stand of 38 between Doug Ring and Bill Johnston, who took advantage of questionable field-placing, won the match. After their narrow escape, Australia won the last Test easily.

### 1954-55 in West Indies
West Indies 0   Australia 3
Drawn 2
Australia's first visit to the Caribbean was made immediately after they had lost a home series against Len Hutton's England team. The tour came usually late in the West Indian season, from March to June, and the Australians were highly popular. They also made a lot of runs, Neil Harvey and Keith Miller making three Test hundreds each. For West Indies Clyde Walcott made

no less than five, including one in each innings of the second and fifth Tests. But the spin of Richie Benaud and Ian Johnson, plus the fast bowling of Lindwall and Miller, was too much for the other West Indian batsmen.

Australia easily won the first, third and fifth Tests and had the better of two draws in between. Injury prevented Jeff Stollmeyer from captaining West Indies for more than two Tests, a serious loss, though his deputy Dennis Atkinson shared in a remarkable world record for the seventh wicket, adding 347 with C. Depeiza (122) at Bridgetown in the fourth Test. They batted more than a day together, and Atkinson scored 219.

### 1960-61 in Australia
Australia 2   West Indies 1
Tie 1   Drawn 1

There was little in the early stages of the West Indies tour of 1960-61 to suggest that one of the great Test series of cricket history was about to take place. Australia, under Richie Benaud, were on the crest of a wave and West Indies were climbing back after the failure of 1957 in England. Frank Worrell had taken over the captaincy from Gerry Alexander.

The tour began with a defeat by Western Australia, and though

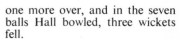

1 Guillen removes Australian captain Hassett at Melbourne in 1951-52. Australia won an exciting match by one wicket and the series by three Tests.
2 Grout is run out and the Brisbane Test of 1960-61 is one ball away from history.
3 Conrad Hunte begins West Indies first home win over Australia, in 1964-65.

one more over, and in the seven balls Hall bowled, three wickets fell.

Six runs were needed at the start of the over and Wally Grout acquired a leg-bye off the first. Off the second Benaud was caught at the wicket for 52, and off the fourth Ian Meckiff and Grout ran a bye to the wicket-keeper. Off the fifth Grout survived a high chance to the bowler and a run resulted. The sixth saw a remarkable piece of cricket. Meckiff hit the ball hard and high towards the leg boundary and was starting the third run, which would give victory to Australia, when the nimble Conrad Hunte threw in from the boundary. The throw was perfect and Grout was just run out. Lindsay Kline, the last

Victoria were beaten mainly by spin, New South Wales beat the tourists by an innings, and no one rated their chances highly in Brisbane. They began well, however, making 453, Sobers 132, but Norman O'Neill scored 181 and Australia led by 52 on the first innings. Alan Davidson, then in his prime as an all-rounder, bowled well in West Indies' second innings, and Australia eventually needed 233 to win at 45 an hour. When they were 92-6, they looked beaten but a rousing partnership developed between Davidson (80) and Benaud (52). When it had added 134 and only 7 runs were needed, the match seemed over, and in fact many people left to catch their trains or aircraft for home.

Wes Hall, with his long run, had slowed up the advance by taking the new ball when 27 were needed in 30 minutes, and with this in mind Benaud was encouraged to call for a quick single. Davidson became the first of three batsmen run out—by a throw from Joe Solomon at mid-wicket. As it proved, there was time for only

man, came in with the scores level and two balls to go. He hit the first towards square-leg and Meckiff, who had been backing up fast, seemed certain to get home. But Solomon again threw down the wicket, this time with only one stump in view, and the match went into history as the first tied Test.

This set the tone for all that followed. Public interest had been won to an unparalleled degree, and most of the cricket did not disappoint the big crowds. West Indies, not at their best in the second Test, also had the worse of the wicket, and Australia won by seven wickets. The third Test in Sydney, however, produced a complete change, for after Gary Sobers had played a brilliant innings of 168 on the first day, Lance Gibbs took the first three of his eight wickets in the match and West Indies won a substantial first innings lead. This was soon extended, thanks to wicket-keeper Gerry Alexander's 108. Gibbs, Valentine, and Sobers bowled Australia out in the last innings on a pitch taking spin and West

Indies won by 222 runs.

In the breathless later stages of the fourth Test in Adelaide, West Indies seemed certain to take the lead in the series. They had made a good start, Rohan Kanhai scoring the first of his two hundreds in the match, and when Australia batted Lance Gibbs performed the first hat-trick recorded against Australia in the 20th century. Worrell declared the second innings leaving Australia to make 460 in 6½ hours and when they soon lost 3 wickets for 31 their chances seemed slim. By tea they were slimmer still, and the ninth wicket fell with 110 minutes left. But with runs of no importance, Ken Mackay and Kline played out time and Australia earned a draw.

So, with the series level, all depended on the last Test at Melbourne. On the first day, Benaud put West Indies in, and when, on the second day, Bobby Simpson and Colin McDonald made 146 before a world record crowd of over 90,000 all appeared to be going to Australian plans. But Gibbs and Sobers worked through the batting to restore a

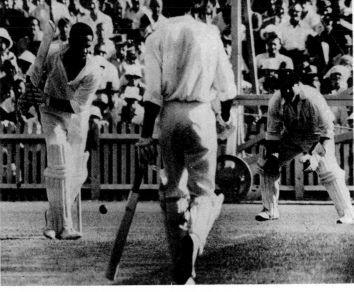

**1** West Indies wicket-keeper John Hendriks may well be offering up a prayer of thanks as Doug Walters finally goes for 242 in the last Test of 1968-69. **2** On that tour, Gary Sobers led a side no longer the force of earlier years.
**3** Lance Gibbs's hat-trick at Adelaide in 1960-61 was the first performed against Australia in the 20th century.

Bill Lawry (210) and Bobby Simpson (201) beginning the match with a stand of 382 that did not end until well into the second day. But they could not win the match, and it was in vastly different conditions that they won at Port of Spain by 10 wickets with three days to spare. Though West Indies batted first, Australia adapted themselves better by far to a pitch of eccentric bounce.

### 1968-69 in Australia
Australia 3   West Indies 1
Drawn 1
The next visit of West Indies to Australia had been eagerly awaited, but when it came their fortunes were fading. Hall and Griffith were on the wane, and history shows that ageing fast bowlers have little success in Australia. West Indies began by winning the first Test on a pitch that deteriorated, but thereafter the batting of Lawry (667 runs), Ian Chappell (548), and Doug Walters (699) was too powerful.

Australia won comfortable victories in the second and third Tests and made a bold effort to score 360 in 5¾ hours on the last day of the fourth Test. When they were 304-3 they seemed likely to do it but four run-outs upset them and they eventually survived with their last pair at the crease 21 runs short. They easily won the last Test, when their batting and fielding were even more superior to West Indies' than before, and they acquired a reputation that took a rout in South Africa and a narrower defeat at home by England to deflate.

Central Press

balance fascinatingly maintained almost throughout the match, until Australia, needing 258, got home by two wickets and won.

### 1964-65 in West Indies
West Indies 2   Australia 1
Drawn 2
After 1960-61 there was bound to be anticlimax, and the next series was a disappointment. West Indies, at the pinnacle of a golden era, were clearly the better side, winning two of the first three Tests. But the series was marred by Australian criticism of the dubious bowling action of Charlie Griffith. In the fourth Test in Barbados, Australia made 650-6,

## Australia v New Zealand

### 1945-46 in New Zealand
**New Zealand 0   Australia 1**
It is hard to credit that Australia and New Zealand, separated by just 1,400 miles of ocean, had, by the beginning of the 1970s, met in only one Test match. Yet, although plans were going ahead for an exchange of tours in 1973-74 involving three Tests in each country, the match played at Wellington in March 1946 remained the only one played to date.

It was the first Test anywhere after World War II, and it was unfortunately played on a bad pitch that tipped the scales even more heavily in favour of the more experienced Australians. Captained by W. A. Brown, they were at full strength except for Bradman, whose health and cricket future were still uncertain. New Zealand could ill afford the absence in England of the brilliant Martin Donnelly. They were bowled out for 42 and 54, Bill O'Reilly in his farewell Test taking 5-14 and 3-19. Australia, who had declared at 199-8, won in two days.

| AUSTRALIA v NEW ZEALAND | |
| --- | --- |
| Tests won by Australia: | 1 |
| Tests won by New Zealand: | 0 |
| **Highest team innings** | |
| Australia: | 199-8 dec, Wellington, 1945-46 |
| New Zealand: | 54, Wellington, 1945-46 |
| **Highest individual innings** | |
| Australia: | 67 by W. A. Brown, Wellington, 1945-46 |
| New Zealand: | 14 by V. J. Scott and W. M. Wallace, Wellington, 1945-46 |
| **Most runs in the match** | |
| Australia: | 67 (avge 67.00) by W. A. Brown |
| New Zealand: | 24 (avge 12.00) by W. M. Wallace |
| **Most wickets in the match** | |
| Australia: | 8 (avge 4.125) by W. J. O'Reilly |
| New Zealand: | 6 (avge 6.66) by J. A. Cowie |
| **Best bowling in an innings** | |
| Australia: | 5-14 by W. J. O'Reilly, Wellington, 1945-46 |
| New Zealand: | 6-40 by J. A. Cowie, Wellington, 1945-46 |

## Australia v India

Having maintained a high standard of first-class cricket throughout World War II, India went to Australia in 1947-48 for the first series between the two countries. Thus they were present during the last home season of Sir Donald Bradman, then preparing for his swansong in England in 1948. It was a tough time for them to go, and they were well beaten by powerful opposition, as they were by lesser opposition on their next visit to Australia 20 years later. Between then, however, they won two matches at home against visiting Australian sides, in 1959-60 and 1964-65.

### 1947-48 in Australia
**Australia 4   India 0   Drawn 1**
There were several players of high reputation and achievement in the team Lala Amarnath captained on the first visit to Australia. But even with 'Vinoo' Mankad, Vijay Hazare, and Gul Mahomed among them, the Indians could not prove a decisive influence in alien conditions, and unfortunately the captain himself did little in the Tests. The Indians beat an Australian XI at Sydney by 47 runs before the first Test, but they were caught on a wet pitch at Brisbane. Bradman made 185, and he was able to declare at the right moment, for Ernie Toshack, left-arm medium pace, to bowl

**1** Australian skipper Benaud is brilliantly caught by C. G. Borde in the Calcutta Test of the 1959-60 series, in which India won their first Test victory over Australia.
**2** Jaisimha hooks towards his century at Brisbane in 1968.

the Indians out for 58 and 98. Toshack took 5-2 in 19 balls in the first innings, and 6-29 in the second.

The weather was so bad in Sydney during the second Test that only 10 hours play was possible in six days, and on this occasion D. G. Phadkar and Hazare caught Australia on an evil pitch, bowling them out for

| AUSTRALIA v INDIA | | |
| --- | --- | --- |
| Tests won by Australia: | | 16 |
| Tests won by India: | | 3 |
| Tests drawn: | | 6 |
| **Highest team innings** | | |
| Australia: | | 674, Adelaide, 1947-48 |
| India: | | 381, Adelaide, 1947-48 |
| **Highest individual innings** | | |
| Australia: | | 201 by D. G. Bradman, Adelaide, 1947-48 |
| India: | | 145 by V. S. Hazare, Adelaide, 1947-48 |
| **Most runs in a series** | | |
| Australia: | | 715 (avge 178.75) by D. G. Bradman, 1947-48 |
| India: | | 438 (avge 43.80) by N. J. Contractor, 1959-60 |
| **Most wickets in a series** | | |
| Australia: | 29 | (avge 15.17) by A. K. Davidson, 1959-60 (avge 19.58) by R. Benaud, 1959-60 |
| India: | | 26 (avge 25.84) by E. A. S. Prasanna, 1969-70 |
| **Best bowling in an innings** | | |
| Australia: | | 7-38 by R. R. Lindwall, Adelaide, 1947-48 |
| India: | | 9-69 by J. S. Patel, Kanpur, 1959-60 |
| Figures up to and including the 1969-70 series | | |

107. But no play was possible on the last day, which would have started with India in the intriguing position of 142 runs on with three second-innings wickets standing.

This low-scoring match was the only one in which Bradman failed. His other scores in the series were 185, 132 and 127 not out, 201 and 57 retired hurt—in all 715 runs at 178.75. Though Mankad made two Test hundreds and Hazare two in the same match in Adelaide, where Denis Compton and Arthur Morris had performed the same feat a year before, Australia won two of the last three Tests by an innings.

### 1956-57 in India
**India 0   Australia 2   Drawn 1**
On the way home from England, Ian Johnson's Australian side played and lost the only Test in Pakistan before stopping in India for a three-match series. Lindwall took 7-43 in the second innings of the first Test in Madras, which Australia won, but though Jim Burke made 161 and Neil Harvey 140 in the second, India earned a draw with a long defensive action.

The third Test in Calcutta was played on a pitch that took spin, conditions that put India on a more even footing. Though short of pace as always, they had two fine spinners in Mankad and Ghulam Ahmed. 'Polly' Umrigar put Australia in on the first day, but later Richie Benaud's leg-spin, which accounted for 11 wickets, gave Australia the slight edge throughout and when India tried to make 231 to win in the last innings, they lost by 94 runs.

### 1959-60 in India
**India 1   Australia 2   Drawn 2**
Australian standards had risen again and the Ashes had been recovered when Richie Benaud took his side to India for a full

series three years later. But the visitors were bedevilled by illness, and after India's off-spinner J. S. Patel (9-69 and 5-55) had used a new turf pitch in Kanpur with such success that Australia lost the second Test by 119 runs, they had to work hard to clinch the series. They had won the first Test by an innings.

Neil Harvey, who with Norman O'Neill was one of the successes of the series, made a second hundred in the third Test, but the only other Australian win was in the fourth at Madras, where Les Favell made his only Test hundred and Benaud took eight wickets.

### 1964-65 in India
India 1   Australia 1   Drawn 1
The next Australian visit was by Bobby Simpson's side on its way back from England in 1964, and for the first time India halved the series. After a holiday in Europe, Australia acclimatized themselves well to win by 139 runs at Madras, although the young Nawab of Pataudi, the Indian captain, made 128 not out. In Bombay however, India made 256 in the last innings and won by two wickets. Pataudi made 86 and 53, but Australia were handicapped by the illness that prevented Norman O'Neill from batting in either innings. The series ended in anticlimax at Calcutta, for after India had led by 61 runs in a low-scoring first innings and Australia were fighting back with 143-1 in the second, rain set in and prevented any play on the last two days.

### 1967-68 in Australia
Australia 4   India 0
The Nawab of Pataudi led the second Indian tour to Australia, where his father had toured with the England team in 1932-33. India's usual lack of class fast bowling prevented them from doing themselves justice, and they were also found wanting in close catching. Nor was their later batting as obdurate as it can be in their own country.

Simpson (103) and Bob Cowper (108) made hundreds in the first Test, which Australia won by 146 runs, though India's form was an improvement on what they had shown against the states. The hundreds in the second Test at Melbourne came from Simpson (109), Bill Lawry (100), and Ian Chappell (151) and though India made 352 in the second innings, A. L. Wadekar 99, they lost by an innings. After two Tests Simpson relinquished the captaincy to Lawry, who was to take the side to England later that year on Simpson's retirement, and India gave one of their best performances of the tour. Their off-spinner Erapalli Prasanna took 6-104 on a good pitch in Australia's second innings, after which India made a wonderful attempt to score 395 to win and lost by only 39 runs, M. L. Jaisimha scoring 101, the tourists' only

hundred of the series. The last of the four-Test series was lost more easily when Bobby Simpson, playing in his last Test, took 5-59.

### 1969-70 in India
India 1   Australia 3   Drawn 1
By the time Bill Lawry took the Australians to India for the last two months of 1969, as the first half of a tour that would also take in South Africa, the spinning skill of Prasanna and B. S. Bedi was such that India were as well equipped with spin as any country in the world. But their batting collapsed in the second innings of the first Test against Alan Con-

nolly (3-20) and Johnny Gleeson (4-56). They shared an even draw in Kanpur before winning by seven wickets in New Delhi, where Bedi (5-37) and Prasanna (5-42) bowled Australia out for 107 in their second innings, and Wadekar's 91 not out ensured India reached 181 to win in the last innings.

Excitement was intense with the series thus levelled and two Tests to play, but Australia won them both, through the fast bowling of Graham McKenzie, Eric Freeman, and Connolly in Calcutta, and perhaps through winning the toss in Madras. In the final match,

**Feet in the air is Indian wicket-keeper Engineer, making a vain attempt to stump Doug Walters in 1967-68. Walters, on leave from the army, celebrated his return to the Australian side with 93 and 62 not out at Brisbane. India made a great attempt to score 395 to win but failed by 39.**

the two off-spinners Prasanna and Ashley Mallett took 10 wickets each, but Australia batted first and, though at one time they were 24-6 in their second innings, Redpath's staunch 63 restored their position.

## Australia v Pakistan

The first Test match ever played between Australia and Pakistan was historic in various ways. It was the slowest match on record by most reckoning, and its first day produced only 95 runs—in 1973 still the record low for a day's play. It also produced a Pakistan victory, but this was not repeated in the five matches played between the two countries in three other seasons.

| AUSTRALIA v PAKISTAN | |
|---|---|
| Tests won by Australia: | 5 |
| Tests won by Pakistan: | 1 |
| Tests drawn: | 3 |
| **Highest team innings** | |
| Australia: | 585, Adelaide, 1972-73 |
| Pakistan: | 574-8 dec, Melbourne, 1972-73 |
| **Highest individual innings** | |
| Australia: | 196 by I. M. Chappell, Adelaide, 1972-73 |
| Pakistan: | 166 by Saeed Ahmed, Lahore, 1959-60 and by K. Ibadulla, Karachi, 1964-65 |
| **Most runs in a series** | |
| Australia: | 341 (*avge* 68.20) by I. M. Chappell, 1972-73 |
| Pakistan: | 334 (*avge* 55.66) by Saeed Ahmed, 1959-60 |
| **Most wickets in a series** | |
| Australia: | 18 (*avge* 21.16) by R. Benaud, 1959-60 |
| Pakistan: | 13 (*avge* 8.76) by Fazal Mahmood, 1956-57 |
| **Best bowling in an innings** | |
| Australia: | 8-59 by A. A. Mallett, Adelaide, 1972-73 |
| Pakistan: | 7-80 by Fazal Mahmood, Karachi, 1956-57 |

Figures up to and including the 1972-73 series

### 1956-57 in Pakistan

Pakistan 1 Australia 0
In October 1956 Ian Johnson's Australian side was on its way back from an unsuccessful tour of England when, after a short holiday in Europe, they flew from Rome to Karachi. There they found a matting pitch and Fazal Mahmood, the greatest bowler in the world in these conditions. From the first the Australian batsmen, suddenly switched from the turf pitches of England and short of practice, were struggling against Fazal, who took the first 6 wickets for 26. At the end of the first day Australia had been bowled out for 80 and Pakistan had made 15-2, but it was said by those participating to be one of the most fascinating day's play they had ever known, such was Fazal's artistry.

The run output on subsequent days was not much higher—184, 138, and 112. Fazal took seven wickets in the second innings and 13 for 114 in the match, which ended in no less bizarre fashion than it had begun. In the last 2 hours and 40 minutes of the fourth day, Pakistan, needing 69 to win, batted so slowly that with nine wickets standing they were six runs short at the end. As the next day was one of mourning on the anniversary of the death of former

Prime Minister Liaquat Ali Khan, they had to wait until the day after to finish the match early in its fifth day.

### 1959-60 in Pakistan

Pakistan 0 Australia 2 Drawn 1
The Australians next visit to Pakistan preceded a tour of India. They arrived fresher for it, and though rain prevented a grass pitch from being used in the first match at Dacca as had been intended, Australia, under Richie Benaud, were not undone by Fazal this time. Benaud (4-69) and Alan Davidson (4-42) bowled Pakistan out in the first innings,

Benaud (4-42) and Mackay (6-42) in the second, and Australia won by eight wickets.

These were five-day Tests, and Australia won the second by seven wickets with 12 minutes to spare after Norman O'Neill had made 134 in their first innings and Saeed Ahmed had long delayed Pakistan's defeat with an innings of 166. The third Test was notable mainly for the presence of the President of the United States, Dwight D. Eisenhower.

### 1964-65 in Pakistan

Pakistan 0 Australia 0 Drawn 1
The third Australian visit to

Pakistan was paid, like the first, after a tour of England, Bobby Simpson's side playing in Karachi after three Tests in India. Pakistan made a wonderful start, with 'Billy' Ibadulla, playing in his first Test, making 166 and putting on 249 for the first wicket with Abdul Kadir (95). But Simpson made a hundred in each innings and Australia had no difficulty in earning a draw.

### 1964-65 in Australia

Australia 0 Pakistan 0 Drawn 1
Within a month of the match in Karachi, Pakistan, captained by Hanif Mohammad, had begun a tour of Australia and New Zealand. The Australian section comprised three state matches, against Queensland, New South Wales, and South Australia, and one Test

**1** Fazal Mahmood, so deadly on matting wickets, bowls to McDonald at Dacca in 1959-60. On an earlier meeting, in 1956, Fazal had bowled the Pakistanis to a surprise win.
**2** The Warwickshire batsman Billy Ibadulla returned home in 1964-65 to score 166 in his first Test, at Karachi.

match at Melbourne. In this, Pakistan gave a good account of themselves and were never in serious danger of defeat, thanks mainly to the brilliant batting of their captain, who made 104 and 93.

Associated Press

# South Africa v New Zealand

By 1973, South Africa and New Zealand had met in only five series, three of them brief ones in New Zealand after tours of Australia by South African teams. The other two rubbers were during full tours of South Africa by New Zealand and the second of these, in 1961-62, provided easily the best series. South African cricket had not yet entered its golden era of the 1960s, and New Zealand, captained by John Reid, drew the series 2-2. Previously they had lost to South Africa almost as comfortably as to England.

| SOUTH AFRICA v NEW ZEALAND | |
| --- | --- |
| Tests won by South Africa: | 9 |
| Tests won by New Zealand: | 2 |
| Tests drawn: | 6 |

**Highest team innings**
South Africa: 524-8 dec, Wellington, 1952-53
New Zealand: 505, Cape Town, 1953-54

**Highest individual innings**
South Africa: 255* by D. J. McGlew, Wellington, 1952-53
New Zealand: 142 by J. R. Reid, Johannesburg, 1961-62

**Most runs in a series**
South Africa: 426 (*avge* 60.85) by D. J. McGlew, 1961-62
New Zealand: 546 (*avge* 60.64) by J. R. Reid, 1961-62

**Most wickets in a series**
South Africa: 28 (*avge* 18.28) by G. B. Lawrence, 1961-62
New Zealand: 22 { (*avge* 20.63) by A. R. MacGibbon, 1953-54 / (*avge* 28.04) by J. C. Alabaster, 1961-62 }

**Best bowling in an innings**
South Africa: 8-53 by G. B. Lawrence, Johannesburg, 1961-62
New Zealand: 6-60 by J. R. Reid, Dunedin, 1963-64

*Not out. Figures up to and including the 1963-64 series

## 1931-32 in New Zealand
New Zealand 0   South Africa 2
South Africa arrived in New Zealand after a demoralizing tour of Australia in which they had lost the rubber 5-0. However, at Christchurch, they made 451, thanks to an opening stand of 196 between J. A. J. Christy (103) and Bruce Mitchell (113), and won the three-day match by an innings. New Zealand batted better to make 364 in the first innings of the second Test in Wellington, Giff Vivian making 100, but South Africa led them on the first innings, largely through Xenophon Balaskas's only Test century —122 not out—and bowled them out cheaply in the second innings to win by eight wickets.

## 1952-53 in New Zealand
New Zealand 0   South Africa 1
Drawn 1
It was 21 years before the next series, which came after Jack Cheetham's unheralded South Africans had amazed the cricket world by drawing 2-2 with Australia. This time the Tests were of four days duration, and in the first, which South Africa won by an innings and 180 runs, Jackie McGlew made 255 not out, then the highest by a South African in Test cricket. South Africa won the toss and batted for a long time in both Tests, and in the second could not bowl New Zealand out. It ended in a dull draw.

## 1953-54 in South Africa
South Africa 4   New Zealand 0
Drawn 1
The result of this series was a somewhat harsh reflection on the performance of a New Zealand side that was unbeaten outside Tests and was not outplayed in any Test after the first, which they lost by an innings. They had a chance in the second Test until they lost their last seven wickets for 25 runs; they made 505, John Reid 135, in the drawn third Test, and they were in with a chance in the fifth until late in the fourth and last day. But they were often in

**Jack Cheetham, catching Matt Poore off Tayfield's bowling, led South Africa to victory over New Zealand in 1953-54.**

tangles against Neil Adcock's fast bowling and the brilliant off-spin of Hugh Tayfield, then approaching his prime.

## 1961-62 in South Africa
South Africa 2   New Zealand 2
Drawn 1
South Africa were in a period of transition, but New Zealand had John Reid at the peak of his powers and he made 546 runs in the series, averaging 60. New Zealand lost the first Test in Durban by 30 runs, largely because Jackie McGlew, an old enemy, carried his bat through the first innings and Peter Pollock in his first Test took 6-38 when New Zealand batted again. The second Test was drawn, but New Zealand won the third by 72 runs, batting first to make 385 and never quite surrendering the advantage.

South Africa won the fourth Test by an innings, but New Zealand were not done yet. At Port Elizabeth Reid totalled 95 runs over the two innings and took six wickets, and in an exciting match New Zealand just held on to win by 40 runs.

## 1963-64 in New Zealand
New Zealand 0   South Africa 0
Drawn 3
Hopes were high for an exciting series after Trevor Goddard's South Africans had emulated their predecessors in Australia by drawing a rubber there—and with most dashing batting. But the New Zealand tour was an anti-climax, and all three Tests were drawn. South Africa might have won the second Test, but could not make 65 to win in 27 minutes, and New Zealand's ninth-wicket pair thwarted them in the third.

**On his Springbok debut, Peter Pollock took 6-38 in New Zealand's second innings of the first Test of the drawn series of 1961-62.**

Associated Press

54

## West Indies v New Zealand

Though matches between West Indies and New Zealand have been few and far between, and not until 1971-1972 did a New Zealand side visit the Caribbean, the series between the two countries will always have a special significance for New Zealanders. In 1956 at Auckland, West Indies became their first ever Test victims. The 1955-56 series was notable in two other respects: it was the only full tour of New Zealand by West Indies, the others following Australian visits, and the New Zealand side included S. C. Guillen, who had played for West Indies on their first tour, in 1951-52.

### 1951-52 in New Zealand
New Zealand 0  West Indies 1  Drawn 1

Despite quite a respectable performance by New Zealand when the series between the two countries began at Christchurch in February 1952, West Indies were stronger in all departments and won by five wickets. Sonny Ramadhin found something akin to his English form and took nine wickets. Bert Sutcliffe, thinking that what life there would be in the pitch would be there on the first day put West Indies in first at Auckland. But Alan Rae made 99, Jeff Stollmeyer 152, Everton Weekes 51, Frank Worrell 100, and Clyde Walcott 115, and West Indies declared at 546-6. New Zealand followed on and had lost a second-innings wicket when bad light intervened late on the third day. Rain on the fourth day prevented any play and the match was drawn.

### 1955-56 in New Zealand
New Zealand 1  West Indies 3

West Indies played four Tests on their two-month tour early in 1956 and one of them gave New Zealand their first Test victory. They had been playing Test cricket since 1930. First omens were unpropitious, for on the first day in Dunedin they were bowled out for 74, Ramadhin 6-23, and after Everton Weekes had made 123, West Indies went on to win by an innings. Weekes made 103 in Christchurch, and West Indies again won by an innings. John Goddard, the former captain who came now as player-manager, made 83 not out. When Weekes made 156 in the third Test—he made 904 on the tour, averaging 104 in first-class matches—and West Indies won by nine wickets, the fourth Test in Auckland seemed a foregone conclusion. But the luck turned.

New Zealand had mustered 203-6 with some difficulty on the first day when the light failed and a tropical cyclone broke. Next day the faster bowlers had a lively pitch and Tony MacGibbon (4-44) and Harry Cave (4-22) bowled out West Indies to give their side a lead of 110. An innings of 41 by the expatriate Guillen enabled New Zealand to set West Indies to make 268 in four hours, and Cave (4-21), Don Beard, and the leg-spinner Jack Alabaster gave them no chance of recovering from a start of 22-6. Amidst great enthusiasm New Zealand won by 190 runs.

### 1968-69 in New Zealand
New Zealand 1  West Indies 1  Drawn 1

After the historic Australian tour of 1960-61, West Indies did not go on to New Zealand, but the next team, under Gary Sobers, did, and once again New Zealand won a Test. They played with much distinction in the first, which they lost by five wickets, Bruce Taylor's 124 in 110 minutes including five sixes. Though Joey Carew made 109 and Seymour Nurse 95, West Indies were 47 behind on the first innings. New Zealand declared their second innings with eight wickets down, setting West Indies to make 345 in 5¼ hours, and largely through some magnificent batting by Seymour Nurse (168), the runs were made for the loss of five wickets.

A week later in Wellington New Zealand had their revenge. Again the winners were led on first innings, but on a lifting pitch West Indies were bowled out for 148 in the second innings. At 39-3 New Zealand were unpromisingly placed, but a priceless innings of 62 not out by Brian Hastings won them by six wickets what was now their fifth Test victory. Another mighty innings of 258 by Seymour Nurse put them in some danger of losing the last Test, but after they had followed on, a hundred by Hastings (117) easily warded off defeat. After this series, it was hoped that New Zealand would soon visit the West Indies.

*Above,* **The batting of Seymour Nurse dominated the series between West Indies and New Zealand in 1968-69. In the three Tests he totalled 558 runs at an average of 111.60, and almost swung the series West Indies' way with 258 at Christchurch.** *Below,* **The first Test of the series was memorable for Bruce Taylor's 100 in 86 minutes—the fifth-fastest Test century.**

# West Indies v India

Whereas Pakistan had had several successes against West Indies, India did not beat them until March 1971. That victory eventually brought them the series, and it was perhaps the greatest achievement in their history.

| WEST INDIES v INDIA | |
|---|---|
| Tests won by West Indies: | 12 |
| Tests won by India: | 1 |
| Tests drawn: | 15 |
| **Highest team innings** | |
| West Indies: | 644-8 dec, New Delhi, 1958-59 |
| India: | 454, New Delhi, 1948-49 |
| **Highest individual innings** | |
| West Indies: | 256 by R. B. Kanhai, Calcutta, 1958-59 |
| India: | 220 by S. M. Gavaskar, Port of Spain, 1970-71 |
| **Most runs in a series** | |
| West Indies: | 779 (*avge* 111.28) by E. D. Weekes, 1948-49 |
| India: | 774 (*avge* 154.80) by S. M. Gavaskar, 1970-71 |
| **Most wickets in a series** | |
| West Indies: | 30 (*avge* 17.66) by W. W. Hall, 1958-59 |
| India: | 27 (*avge* 29.22) by S. P. Gupte, 1952-53 |
| **Best bowling in an innings** | |
| West Indies: | 9-95 by J. Noreiga, Port of Spain, 1970-71 |
| India: | 9-102 by S. P. Gupte, Kanpur, 1958-59 |
| Figures up to and including the 1970-71 series | |

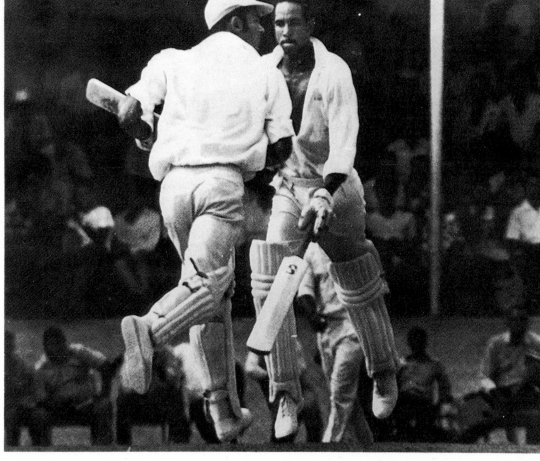

U.P.I.

## 1948-49 in India
India 0  West Indies 1  Drawn 4
John Goddard's side contained many of those players who were to triumph in England just over a year later, though Frank Worrell, for non-cricketing reasons, did not tour. This was also the last

*Above,* **Airborne runners Gary Sobers and Charlie Davis both took hundreds off the Indian attack at Port of Spain in 1970-71 but could not save the series.** *Below,* **Contractor comes under fire from Wes Hall in the 1961-62 series.**

Associated Press

tour of the great George Headley, but he was then 39 and seldom fit enough to do himself justice. Travel in post-war India was still uncomfortable, the pitches generally defied the bowlers of both sides, and West Indies had a hard job to win against an Indian side that included Lala Amarnath and Mushtaq Ali, as well as the up-and-coming Vijay Hazare, 'Vinoo' Mankad, D. G. Phadkar, and Rusi Modi.

Everton Weekes, averaging 111 with four Test centuries, dominated the batting, and in the first innings of the first Test four West Indians—Clyde Walcott, Gerry Gomez, and R. J. Christiani being the others—made centuries. But the only match finished was the fourth, at Madras, which West Indies won by an innings after an opening stand of 239 between Alan Rae (109) and Jeff Stollmeyer (160).

## 1952-53 in West Indies
West Indies 1  India 0  Drawn 4
There was a similar result when Vijay Hazare took the first Indian team to the West Indies. Both sides indulged in an orgy of run-making—Weekes this time averaging 102—and the only match finished was in Barbados, where there had been rain before the start. In a fairly low-scoring match, West Indies won by 142 runs. Subhash 'Fergie' Gupte, a leg-spinner who took 27 wickets in the series, served India well, but in the last innings Ramadhin (5-26) proved too much for India.

## 1958-59 in India
India 0  West Indies 3  Drawn 2
'Gerry' Alexander's West Indian team won an easy victory, the decisive factor being the fast bowling of Wes Hall and Roy Gilchrist who together took 56 wickets in the series. The new young batsmen such as Rohan Kanhai, Gary Sobers, and Basil Butcher made hundreds of runs, but it was not the happiest of tours. Gilchrist was prone to bowl both bumper and 'beamer' and was eventually sent home for disciplinary reasons. Without him West Indies lost their subsequent three-match rubber in Pakistan.

## 1961-62 in West Indies
West Indies 5  India 0
A year before, India had defeated Ted Dexter's England side, but they had an unhappy tour of West Indies in which almost everything went wrong. They lost their captain Nari Contractor, who suffered a serious injury from a Charlie Griffith bumper; Hall, Lance Gibbs, and Sobers bowled them out; Kanhai, Sobers, Worrell, and Easton McMorris made a lot of runs; and West Indies won all five Tests easily.

## 1966-67 in India
India 0  West Indies 2  Drawn 1
Fresh from their second triumphant tour of England in the 1960s, West Indies had little difficulty winning in India. Sobers had one of his best series, averaging 114 and taking 14 wickets. Gibbs' off-spin was another major

No matter what the bowling, runs flowed and flowed from the bat of Sunil Gavaskar when India won in 1970-71.

reason for West Indies' success and only in the last Test, where it needed stern defence by Sobers and Griffith to save the match, were India on level terms.

### 1970-71 in West Indies
West Indies 0   India 1   Drawn 4
When India's new captain A. L. Wadekar took his side to the Caribbean early in 1971, West Indies, over-reliant on Sobers, were not the force of other days and India, in Eparalli Prasanna, B. S. Bedi, and S. Venkataraghavan, had an unusually strong hand of spinners. But the memory of previous failures in West Indies, the shortage of fast bowling, and a lack of class batting led most people to discount an Indian victory. Yet though Sobers scored 594 at an average of 87, and Charlie Davis, Rohan Kanhai, and others made runs, West Indies could not bowl out India. Sunil Gavaskar, a little known 21-year-old Bombay University student, made 774 runs at an average of 154.80, and the older Dilip Sardesai averaged 80.

Despite the fact that Prasanna was not always fit, the other spinners and the medium-paced Abid Ali brought India victory in the second Test in Trinidad. India had looked like winning the first in Jamaica, but they had to fight a defensive action to save the fourth and an even longer one in the fifth when West Indies led them by 166 runs. But Gavaskar's 220, following his 124 in the first innings, warded off defeat, and in the end it was West Indies who were saving the match.

Sobers clips another four to leg against Pakistan in 1957-58, and Sabina Park, Kingston, watches as Len Hutton's world record is attacked and broken.

## West Indies v Pakistan

Though by the end of the 1960s there had been only two Test series between West Indies and Pakistan, and both of these in the late 1950s, they were full of incident and each was remarkably evenly fought.

### 1957-58 in West Indies
West Indies 3   Pakistán 1
Drawn 1
In the first Test in Barbados, West Indies scored 579-9, then dismissed Pakistan for 106. In the second innings, however, Hanif Mohammad batted for 16 hours to make 337 and save the match. More prodigious scoring followed in the third Test at Kingston; Gary Sobers made his first Test hundred and extended it to the world Test record score of 365 not out, and in the same innings of 790-3 Conrad Hunte scored 260. In the fourth Test Sobers, then only 21, made a hundred in each innings, and after that match West Indies led 3-0. But in the last Test Pakistan gave an excellent performance, bowling out West Indies through the pace of Fazal Mahmood and Khan Mohammad in the first innings and through the spin of Nasim-ul-Ghani in the second to win by an innings.

### 1958-59 in Pakistan
Pakistan 2   West Indies 1
Going on to Karachi after a three-month tour of India where they won 3-0, West Indies found the brilliant Fazal too much for them on matting and lost the first Test by 10 wickets. In Dacca, too, Fazal took 12 wickets for 100, and Pakistan won a low-scoring match by 41 runs. This match witnessed one of most remarkable collapses in Test history—in West Indies' first innings the last six batsmen failed to score and 65-3 became 76 all out. But in the last Test at Lahore Rohan Kanhai made a brilliant 217, rain interfered with both Pakistan innings, and West Indies won by an innings and 156 runs.

| WEST INDIES v PAKISTAN | |
|---|---|
| Tests won by West Indies: | 4 |
| Tests won by Pakistan: | 3 |
| Tests drawn: | 1 |
| **Highest team innings** | |
| West Indies: | 790-3 dec, Kingston, 1957-58 |
| Pakistan: | 657-8 dec, Bridgetown, 1957-58 |
| **Highest individual innings** | |
| West Indies: | 365* by G. S. Sobers, Kingston, 1957-58 |
| Pakistan: | 337 by Hanif Mohammad, Bridgetown, 1957-58 |
| **Most runs in a series** | |
| West Indies: | 824 (*avge* 137.33) by G. S. Sobers, 1957-58 |
| Pakistan: | 628 (*avge* 69.77) by Hanif Mohammad, 1957-58 |
| **Most wickets in a series** | |
| West Indies: | 21 (*avge* 30.28) by R. Gilchrist, 1957-58 |
| Pakistan: | 21 (*avge* 15.85) by Fazal Mahmood, 1958-59 |
| **Best bowling in an innings** | |
| West Indies: | 5-42 by E. Atkinson, Kingston, 1957-58 |
| Pakistan: | 6-34 by Fazal Mahmood, Dacca, 1958-59 |

*Not out. Figures up to and including the 1958-59 series

## New Zealand v India

As so many touring sides have discovered, India are notoriously hard to beat on their own pitches, and it is no surprise, therefore, that New Zealand did not win a Test there until 1970. It was their third visit to India, the first being in 1955-56, and prior to 1970 New Zealand rarely had the spin bowlers needed for victory on Indian pitches. It was significant that when they did win, at Nagpur, it was largely through the nine wickets of Hedley Howarth, whose left-arm spin bowling had been one of the successes of the tour of England from which they were returning.

**NEW ZEALAND v INDIA**

| | |
|---|---|
| Tests won by New Zealand: | 2 |
| Tests won by India: | 7 |
| Tests drawn: | 7 |

**Highest team innings**
New Zealand: 502, Christchurch, 1967-68
India: 537-3 dec, Madras, 1955-56

**Highest individual innings**
New Zealand: 239 by G. T. Dowling, Christchurch, 1967-68
India: 231 by V. Mankad, Madras, 1955-56

**Most runs in a series**
New Zealand: 611 (*avge* 87.28) by B. Sutcliffe, 1955-56
India: 526 (*avge* 105.20) by V. Mankad, 1955-56

**Most wickets in a series**
New Zealand: 15 { (*avge* 18.40) by B. R. Taylor, 1964-65 / (*avge* 28.86) by R. C. Motz, 1967-68
India: 34 (*avge* 19.67) by S. P. Gupte, 1955-56

**Best bowling in an innings**
New Zealand: 6-38 by G. R. Bartlett, Christchurch, 1967-68
India: 8-72 by S. Venkataraghavan, New Delhi, 1964-65

Figures up to and including the 1969-70 series

### 1955-56 in India
India 2    New Zealand 0
Drawn 3
The first series between the countries has been the only one of five Tests, New Zealand, under H. B. Cave, making a full 5½ month tour of Pakistan and India. Having lost 2-0 in Pakistan, they went on to India, drawing the first Test at Hyderabad. 'Polly' Umrigar (223) Vijay Manjrekar (118) and A. G. Kripal Singh (100) made hundreds for India and John Guy (102) and Bert Sutcliffe (137 not out) for New Zealand. 'Vinoo' Mankad made 223 at the start of the second Test in Bombay, and New Zealand were bowled out twice, largely by 'Fergie' Gupte, at this time one of the best leg-break bowlers in the world. In another prolific draw in New Delhi, Sutcliffe made 230 not out and John Reid 119 not out for New Zealand and Manjrekar 177 for India.

At one time during the fourth Test, New Zealand, 204 ahead on first innings, were within distant sight of victory, but in the end they had to stave off defeat after hundreds by Pankaj Roy (100) and G. S. Ramchand (106 not out) and 90 by Manjrekar had revived India. India finished with a resounding victory at Madras, where they declared at 537 for 3 after Mankad (231) and Roy (173) had put on 413 for the first wicket. Spin once again finished the match, Gupte taking nine wickets and J. S. Patel and Mankad four each.

**New Zealand century makers at Calcutta in 1964-65; Bert Sutcliffe, tucking Nadkarni away to leg, scored 151 not out and Bruce Taylor made his maiden first-class hundred.**

**In the first match played by India and New Zealand, at Hyderabad in 1955-56, 'Polly' Umrigar scored 223 and India amassed 498-4 declared.**

### 1964-65 in India
India 1    New Zealand 0
Drawn 3
Nine years passed before John Reid's team stopped in India on its way to England. The first three Tests were drawn, with New Zealand usually slightly better placed. In the second, the left-handed Bruce Taylor made his maiden first-class 100 in fast time and then took 5-86 and in the third Dilip Sardesai (200 not out) and Borde (109) revived India

after Taylor (5-26) had played a big part in bowling them out for 88. But in the last Test, another hundred by Sardesai (106) and 113 by India's captain, the Nawab of Pataudi, combined with the off-spin of S. Venkataraghavan, who took 12 wickets, to bring them down.

### 1967-68 in New Zealand
New Zealand 1    India 3
The first rubber in New Zealand between the two countries was played when Pataudi's team went there after touring Australia. They were delighted to find pitches that took spin, and with such bowlers as Eparalli Prasanna, B. S. Bedi, and R. G. Nadkarni they were greatly superior to New Zealand in this department. Consequently, they won comfortably. New Zealand did, however, have the satisfaction of winning their first ever Test against India. Batting first at Christchurch they made 502, their captain Graham Dowling scoring 239, and their fast bowlers, notably Gary Bartlett (6-38), eventually brought victory by six wickets.

### 1969-70 in India
India 1    New Zealand 1
Drawn 1
The visit of Dowling's team to India confirmed the improvement in New Zealand cricket. India won the first Test by 60 runs. Prasanna and Bedi taking 16 wickets on a sympathetic Bombay pitch. The match had been transferred there from Ahmedabad at a late hour because of riots. New Zealand's victory at Nagpur followed, Howarth taking 4-66 and 5-34, and the tourists were desperately unlucky not to win the drawn third Test at Hyderabad. Only 521 runs were scored in five days amid rain and riots, and eventually when India were being bowled out in the last innings, more rain and a marked lack of urgency to dry the ground caused a final abandonment.

**At Christchurch in 1967-68, Graham Dowling made 239 and led New Zealand to her first ever victory over India.**

## New Zealand v Pakistan

Three of New Zealand's five series with Pakistan to 1973 took place in conjunction with visits to India. The exceptions were the Pakistan tours to New Zealand in 1964-65, then again in 1973. The pattern of results was similar too, for it was not until 1969-70 that New Zealand won their first Test match against Pakistan, and the rubber it gave them was, in fact, the first they had ever won against any opponents.

### 1955-56 in Pakistan
Pakistan 2   New Zealand 0
Drawn 1
The first Test played between the two countries was at Karachi in October 1955, at the start of the lengthy tour of the Indian subcontinent by H. B. Cave's team. It was only the second match for New Zealand tourists, and they were well beaten on the matting, the off-spinner Zulfiqar Ahmed taking 11 wickets. But they did better on turf at Lahore and twice exceeded 300, Noel McGregor 111 in the first innings, only for Pakistan to muster 561—a remarkable total considering they were 111-6 at one time. A seventh-wicket stand of 308 between Waqar Hassan (189) and Imtiaz Ahmed (209) restored them, and eventually, needing 116 to win in the last innings, they won an exciting victory by four wickets. New Zealand were lucky to escape with a draw after being dismissed for 70 in the Dacca Test, which was played in a heavy atmosphere and on wet matting.

### 1964-65 in New Zealand
New Zealand 0   Pakistan 0
Drawn 3
The eight-week tour of New Zealand by Hanif Mohammad's Pakistan side of 1964-65 followed a few preliminary matches and one Test in Australia. Hanif did not reproduce his marvellous consistency of the Australian visit, though he made 100 not out in the last Test, and New Zealand, with better fast bowlers in Frank Cameron, Dick Motz, and Richard Collinge, had at least an equal share in three dull, unadventurous draws.

The spin bowling of Pervez Sajjad (*above*, bowling on the 1971 Pakistan tour of England) and the long innings by Glenn Turner (*below*) were features of the abandoned third Test in Pakistan in 1969-70.

Patrick Eagar

### 1964-65 in Pakistan
Pakistan 2   New Zealand 0
Drawn 1
Within six weeks hostilities were resumed in Pakistan. This time Pakistan won easily, beginning with a victory by an innings in the first Test at Rawalpindi, which lasted only 12 hours 40 minutes. In their second innings, New Zealand were removed for 79, the left-arm spinner Pervez Sajjad taking four wickets in each innings. In a high-scoring draw at Lahore, Hanif made 203 not out and Barry Sinclair 130, but Paki-

stan gave a purposeful performance in the last Test to win by eight wickets. Reid's 128 started New Zealand off well, but Saeed Ahmad made 172 in Pakistan's first innings and, when they batted again to score 202 to win, a rousing 126 by Mohammad Ilyas quickly finished the match off.

### 1969-70 in Pakistan
Pakistan 0   New Zealand 1
Drawn 2
It was a stronger New Zealand team, captained by Graham Dowling, that visited Pakistan on its way back from an unlucky tour of England. They drew at Karachi on a pitch that took spin throughout and then won their long-awaited first victory at Lahore in the second Test. On the first day the spinners Vic Pollard and Hedley Howarth took six wickets when Pakistan were bowled out for 114. New Zealand never relaxed their grip on the match, and won with five wickets to spare.

Earlier in 1969, England's series in Pakistan had been interrupted by public disorder, and the last Test played by the New Zealanders in Dacca had its ugly moments. A long innings of 110 by Glenn Turner set New Zealand off well, but a brilliant 92 by Asif Iqbal gave Pakistan a first innings lead, and when New Zealand declined to 101-8 in their second innings before the spin of Intikhab Alam and Pervez, it looked as if Pakistan might save the series. But the last two wickets added 99, Mark Burgess making a magnificent 119 not out, and in the end it was a Pakistan batting collapse that the final riot interrupted.

## India v Pakistan

India and Pakistan played each other in three series between 1952-53 and 1960-61 but have not met since. The political and religious differences that led to the partition of India were never far from the surface. The cricket played was wretchedly cautious, for both sides were fully aware of the damage defeat might allegedly cause to national prestige. Eventually, after 12 successive draws, the series lapsed, and the outbreak of war between the two countries in 1965 did not help to heal the breach.

### 1952-53 in India
India 2   Pakistan 1   Drawn 2
India were Pakistan's first opponents after they entered Test cricket, and it was a promising side that A. H. Kardar took to India in October 1952. Fazal Mahmood and Mahmood Hussain were the backbone of their fast-medium bowling, and they would have been an even stronger force if a third fast bowler Khan Mohammad had not been injured early in the tour. The batting was not as productive as it was to become later, however, for Hanif Mohammad was only 17 and the best of Imtiaz Ahmed was also yet to come. But what gave India the upper hand was the lack of spin on the Pakistan side. The left-arm spin of 'Vinoo' Mankad with Ghulam Ahmed in support was invaluable to India—they took 25 and 12 wickets respectively—and the batting of Vijay Hazare and 'Polly' Umrigar ensured India plenty of runs.

Mankad took 13 wickets in the first Test at New Delhi, when Pakistan followed on and lost by an innings. But at Lucknow, they themselves won by an innings. Hazare and Mankad were unable to play and Fazal was in his element on matting, taking 12 wickets for 94. For Pakistan, Nazar Mohammad carried his bat through the innings of 331, making 124 not out in over 8½ hours. The veteran Lala Amarnath was too much for Pakistan on a fresh pitch on the first morning in Bombay, and India won the third Test by 10 wickets. The last two Tests in this series began the long history of draws.

### 1954-55 in Pakistan
Pakistan 0   India 0   Drawn 5
India's only visit to Pakistan was a two-month tour two years later. The pattern was much the same. The same three Pakistan fast bowlers gave their side an advantage when the pitches helped fast bowling, and India had the leg-spin of 'Fergie' Gupte, who took 21 Test wickets, as an important weapon on their side. Mankad, the Indian captain, also played a useful part in the attack though out of form with the bat. Pakistan's first official Test match at home was played at Dacca, and it set the defensive tone. The matches were of four days duration, but it would have needed many more for them to be finished. The sides, evenly matched, were content to leave the issue undecided.

### 1960-61 in India
India 0   Pakistan 0   Drawn 5
Pakistan's second visit to India must have established in most people's mind the feeling that the meetings between the two countries were doing no good to cricket and no particular good to political relations. It is hard to apportion the blame for the deadlock other than evenly, but Pakistan, captained by Fazal, did win the toss and bat first in the first four Tests. With Hanif, Saeed, Ahmed, Javed Burki, and Imtiaz in their prime, they were rich in batting, but the great Fazal was past his best and the bowling was weaker. Nevertheless, Fazal did take 5-26 in the third Test at Calcutta, where India were bowled out for 180—the only time in the series when they made less than 400. But rain and the deadslow tempo of the game prevented a result, even though Tests in this series were played over five days. The nearest either side came to victory was in the last Test, in New Delhi. Pakistan following on, would have been bowled out in the second innings in time for India to win but for a last-wicket stand of 38 between Mahmood Hussain and Mohammad Farooq.

*Above,* **Winning the toss rarely meant much advantage to either side when India and Pakistan met in 1960-61. With national prestige at stake, neither side was prepared to take undue risks, and the draw at Madras in that series (*below*) was one of 11 in as many matches.**

Indian Embassy

Indian Embassy

# Test cricket from 1971

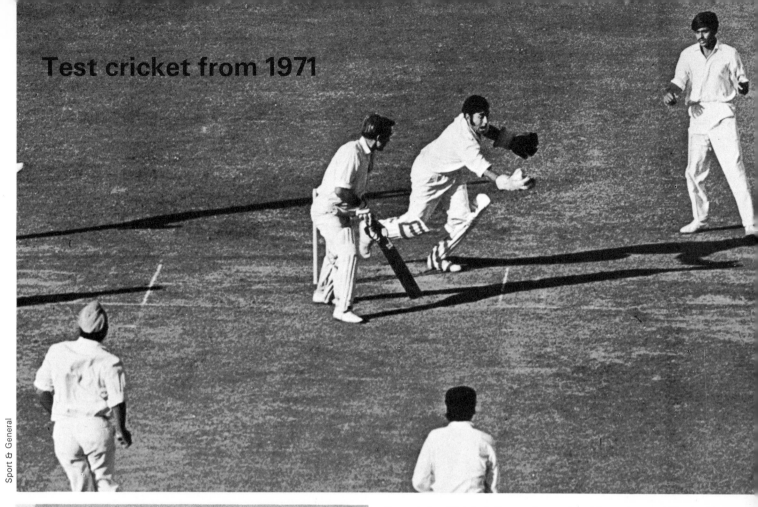

*Above* **John Edrich falls another victim to Bishen Bedi, one of the three-pronged spin attack who bowled India to a win in the three-match series in 1971** *Left* **Glenn Turner amassed 672 runs for New Zealand in eight Test innings in the West Indies.**

## 1971 England v India

England 0 India 1 Drawn 2

In the third match of this short series, an England batting collapse in the second innings at the Oval gave India their first win on English soil. Such a collapse came hardly as a surprise, because in all the Tests the home players had shown distinct vulnerability against a three-pronged spin attack of Chandrasekhar, Bishen Bedi and Venkataraghavan.

The first Test at Lords had been left ruined by rain with India 38 runs short of a target of 183 with two wickets in hand. England had been grateful for John Snow's Highest Test score of 73 in the first innings, after being 71-5 to Chadrasekhar and Bedi. Captain Wadekar, Vishwanath and Solkar made solid contributions for India, while Gavaskar's second innings 53 seemed to create a certain win, until Gifford pegged them back.

Rain saved India at Old Trafford when they were 65 for 3, needing 420 to win. Illingworth and Luckhurst made hundreds, and Peter Lever, at number 9, hit 88 not out.

But at the Oval, the visitors needed only 173 for victory, which they accomplished with six wickets down. After England had led by 71 on the first innings, they crumbled in the face of Chandrasekhar whose bounce and turn proved mesmeric. He finished with 6 for 38, a performance to win both the match and the series.

## 1971-72 W. Indies v N. Zealand

W Indies 0 N. Zealand 0 Drawn 5

The series of five drawn Tests represented a triumph for the New Zealanders, so often the poor relations at the highest level. But though no result was achieved, it was an exciting rubber.

The tenacity of the visitors was visible from the start as they extricated themselves from trouble to save the first two Tests. At Kingston, Lawrence Rowe made 214 and 100 not out on his Test debut, but Turner, 223, and Wadsworth, 78, saved the day with a sixth-wicket stand of 220. Bevan Congdon, the skipper, turned a score of 99 for ·6 into 348 all out at Port of Spain, making 166 not out.

Dropped catches cost the New Zealanders the Third Test, while the stand of 387 between Turner, 259, and Jarvis, 182, only contributed to the dullness of the Fouth Test. In the final match, rain and some brave late batting from Taylor, and Wadsworth ensured a draw.

As a series New Zealand had more to be proud of than their hosts, especially Turner's 672 runs at 96.00 and Taylor's 27 wickets at under 18 a piece.

*Above* **In the 1972 series England's bowlers tormented Doug Walters outside his off stump. Here he falls to a Parfitt catch off Underwood, the hero of the Leeds Test.**
*Left* **Bob Massie goes round the wicket at Lords, on his way to taking 16 for 137 in the match in a quite remarkable display of controlled swing bowling.**

### 1972 England v Australia
England 2 Australia 2 Drawn 1
England as expected retained the Ashes, but only after a tremendous fight against Ian Chappell's unheralded side. The performances of Stackpole and Greg Chappell with the bat and Lillee and Massie with the ball contributed to a thrilling drawn series.

The fate of the Ashes was decided in controversial circumstances in the Fourth Test at Headingly. Derek Underwood, who had been out of favour, was recalled to bowl on a turning pitch perfectly suited to his brisk left-arm spin. He returned match figures of 10 for 82 and England were home by nine wickets on the third day.

They had previously won the First Test by 89 runs in a low-scoring match in which the Australians never recovered from being bowled out by Snow and Arnold for 142 in the first innings, Lillee's magnificent 6 for 66 never quite redressing the balance.

The series was squared at Lords in a remarkable match dominated by the swing bowling of Bob Massie who took 8 wickets in each innings to finish with 16 for 137. Greg Chappell showed immense class in making 131 and Australia won by eight wickets.

Poor fielding cost England an early advantage in the Third Test, Stackpole who made 114 being particularly favoured. But after failing once more against Massie and Lillee and seeing Edwards make 170 not out, the England batsman competently saved the game in the fourth innings.

Appropriately it was Lillee's pace which brought the series level at the Oval. He took 10 for 181 for a final return of 31 wickets. Both Chappells got hundreds and Australia won a great victory by six wickets.

### 1972-3 Australia v Pakistan
Australia 3 Pakistan 0
Disturbed by off-the-field conflicts that resulted in two players being sent home, Pakistan twice played their way into winning positions only to fail badly under pressure.

A thrashing in the First Test by an innings and 114 runs—Mallett taking 8 for 59 in their second innings—led to an improvement at Melbourne. But set to make 293 on a perfect batting wicket they fell 92 short. In the Third Test, their fourth innings target was only 158, but their lack of character showed when Walker (6 for 15) bowled them out for 106.

Mushtaq Mohammed, Majid Khan, and Sadiq Mohammed all made centuries but not when the pressure was really on, and the bowlers lacked penetration.

## 1972-73 India v England

India 2 England 1 Drawn 2

Not until the end of the series did a weakened England come to grips with the spin of Chandrasekhar and Bedi, who had plagued their batsmen so much in England in 1971. Only three England wickets fell to pace in the five Tests. The visiting spinners were, however, less effective.

Nevertheless England won the First Test by six wickets, a remarkable start for captain Tony Lewis playing his first Test. Though Chandrasekhar had 8 for 79 in the first innings, Greig, 68 not out and 70 not out saw England home.

The Indian spinners held sway in Calcutta and Madras, earning wins by 28 runs and 4 wickets. But Lewis steadied his ship in the Fourth Test with a fine 125 which ensured his side would not lose.

The bat was always in command at Bombay and England could not square the series. Engineer and Vishwanath made hundreds for India while Fletcher and Greig hit their first three-figure scores for England.

Chandrasekhar finished with 35 wickets, Bedi with just 10 less. On wickets so suited to spinners, England's failure could be deduced from the fact that the top three in their bowling averages were Arnold, Greig and Old, all at fast-medium.

## 1973 New Zealand v Pakistan

N. Zealand 0 Pakistan 1 Drawn 2

Pakistan gained some consolation for their disappointments in Australia by winning the Second Test and with it the rubber. Mushtaq Mohammed was the key figure in their win. He made a majestic 201, putting on 350 with Asif Iqbal, who scored 175. Then he and his captain, Intikhab Alam spun New Zealand out with their leg-breaks and googlies for an innings victory.

The First Test had been drawn, after Sadiq Mohammed had begun the match with an excellent 166. But perhaps the most remarkable event of the series occured in the last match, after Pakistan had batted first and made a promising 402.

New Zealand had slumped in their reply to 251 for 9 when last man Richard Collinge joined Brian Hastings. The pair added 151 to beat the world record for the last wicket partnership which had stood for almost 70 years. The stand, together with 107, from Rodney Redmond in his first Test match was enough to save the game and provide some consolation for the New Zealanders in a series they had been hopeful of winning on their home soil.

## 1973 Pakistan v England

Pakistan 0 England 0 Drawn 3

Both teams arrived in Pakistan following a gruelling programme of Test cricket—Pakistan from their sojourn in Australia and New Zealand; England from the five keenly fought Tests in India.

This weariness undoubtedly contributed to three rather stagnant Tests in which the Pakistan batting held the upper hand. The England batting coped marginally more successfully than they had in India and always made enough runs to survive.

Pakistan had already sprung one bombshell in New Zealand by announcing that Intikhab Alam had been relieved of the captaincy while play was actually in progress during the final Test.

Majid Khan, his replacement, was not an immediate success as his replacement, nor did he show the same flair with the bat that he had shown in Australia.

Amiss became the fourth player on the tour to make his maiden Test century when he compiled 112 on the opening day of the First Test at Lahore. But largely through the efforts of Sadiq Mohammed, 119, and Asif Iqbal, 102, Pakistan gained a first innings lead. England batted consistently in the second innings to earn a draw.

At Hyderabad, Amiss led the way with 158 as England amassed 487. Pakistan replied with 569 for nine declared—Mushtaq Mohammed 157, Intikhab 138—and looked to be on the way to victory as England slumped to 77 for 5. But Greig and Knott added 112 and staved off the impending defeat.

The last match provided if nothing else a remarkable statistic in that three batsmen were dismissed for 99. That fate befell both Majid and Mushtaq in Pakistan's first innings of 445 for six declared. And Amiss, seeking his third hundred in successive Tests, fell at the same score as England totalled 386, Lewis making 88.

As on the previous tour, student unrest caused stoppages, both in Karachi and Hyderabad. Particularly in Karachi, where more than an hour's play was lost on one day, the play and the players were inhibited by impending invasions of the playing area.

*Top right* **Tony Greig (left) and Dennis Amiss both hit their maiden Test centuries on England's tour of India and Pakistan in 1972-3. On the same trip Keith Fletcher and Tony Lewis, the captain, also accomplished that feat.**

*Above right* **Chandrasekhar was the architect of India's win in the series, taking 35 wickets.**

*Right* **Captain in Australia and New Zealand in 1972-73, Pakistan's Intikhab Alam lost the job for the England series, but his leg-spin still gave the visitors problems. At Hyderabad he had further consolation with a highest Test score of 138.**

## 1973 West Indies v Australia

W. Indies 0 Australia 2 Drawn 2

Australia, playing positive and aggressive cricket, generally batted with more consistency than the home country. Their win in the series was some consolation for losing their main bowling weapon, Dennis Lillee, with a serious back injury after the First Test.

In that match Doug Walters recaptured some of the form that had totally deserted him in England in 1972, making 72 in 100 minutes. Foster replied with 125 and then Stackpole hit 142 in Australia's second innings to ensure a draw.

West Indies were led by Rohan Kanhai in place of the injured Garry Sobers who missed his first Test since 1955. Kanhai hit 105 in the drawn Second Test in which both Chappells and

Doug Walters all reached their centuries.

Walters also made a century in the next match, which was the West Indies' for the taking when, chasing 334, they had reached 268 for 4. But the last five wickets fell for only 21 to put Australia one up.

The Fourth Test was their's also when fast bowlers Hammond and the tall Max Walker skittled West Indies for 109 after even first innings in which Lloyd and Ian Chappell had made hundreds. Australia won this Test by 10 wickets.

Chappell understandably played safe in Port-of-Spain in the Fifth Test, in which Walker had five more victims in the first innings, finishing with 26 wickets in a tremendous personal series.

## 1973 England v New Zealand

England 2 N. Zealand 0 Drawn 1

Bevan Congdon's New Zealand team twice had chances to record their first win in England, but narrowly failed to make use of either opportunity.

Illingworth was preferred to Lewis as England's leader, and in the First Test the home country struggled to make 250 in the first innings. The pace trio of Snow, Arnold and Greig shot New Zealand out for 97. After Greig had followed that with 139 to add to Amiss's 138, England looked set for a massive win as they set the visitors a target of 479.

Four wickets fell for 130, then Congdon, 176, and Pollard, 116, masterminded such a recovery that they fell only 38 short of turning defeat into victory.

New Zealand should have won the Second Test at Lords, after Congdon, 175, Pollard, 105 not out, and Burgess, 105, had given them a first innings lead of 302. But a dropped catch behind the wicket at final phase on the last day saved England for whom Fletcher played a match-saving innings of 178.

The Third Test went more to form. Boycott made an excellent 115 and England led by 143 runs on the first innings. New Zealand failed in the face of some immaculate outswing bowling by Arnold, England's most impressive performer with the ball throughout the series. Though Turner, whose Test form had not equalled that which had brought him a 1,000 runs in May, was last out, New Zealand were still easily beaten by an innings.

1 Alvin Kallicharan is caught by Rodney Marsh in the 3rd Test at Trinidad in 1973, one of the tall Max Walker's 26 victims in the series. 2 Greg Chappell made 106 in the Bridgetown Test. 3 The middle-order batting of Vic Pollard proved a considerable thorn in England's side in 1973. Pollard's 116 took New Zealand to within 38 runs of their target of 479 in the First Test. He followed that with another impressive century at Lord's in the Second Test. 4 Bevan Congdon, the New Zealand skipper, was undetered by a painful blow on the jaw during his 176 at Nottingham. 5 Geoff Arnold, England's most penetrative bowler in the series, had Congdon's wicket more cheaply at Headingly.

# Test cricket—
# a gallery of great players

Ian Chappell and the injured Ray Illingworth toast the end of the magnificent 1972 Test series in which both led their countries to two victories.

# Barrington

## Kenneth Frank (1930-    )

Ken Barrington was one of the most prolific post-war batsmen in world cricket, until a heart attack in October 1968 ended his first-class career shortly before his 39th birthday. Over the years he had worked out a method of playing which could never be called graceful but which was highly effective, especially in conditions outside his native England. Early in his career for Surrey he had a strong off-side style, but this became less pronounced, and by the time of his test recall, in 1959, he had changed his stance to face more towards the bowler. Thus he was mainly an on-side player and a fine cutter, but could hit the ball off the front foot on the off-side if required.

His technique, though not strictly from the text-book, was less controversial than his approach to batting. It was generally thought that for a player of his run-making capacity, he scored too slowly. He was too good a batsman, it was felt, to submit to a bowler as readily as he sometimes appeared to do, and the fact that he had periods of fluency in most innings strengthened this belief. He would often come in and make 30 runs in reasonable time before slowing down. Several times in Test matches he suddenly emerged from a period of inactivity to reach his hundred with a perfectly struck six. On one famous occasion in Melbourne he made the fastest Test hundred of the year by an Englishman—in 122 balls—and played as boldly and as well as anyone could have asked. But though he was a saver of matches rather than a winner of them, he was a rare comfort to any captain as a reliable, remarkably consistent backbone to the innings. He was one player whom many Australians of his day have said they would have liked on their side, a batsman of immense patience, determination, and application.

A very competent fielder either in the slips or, in later years, away from the bat, he was also a leg-break bowler who was only just beginning to be fully appreciated when he retired. His control was good and he spun the ball more than many modern leg-spinners. And if the MCC tour of South Africa had taken place in 1968-69 and his health had been maintained, he would have been played as an all-rounder, certainly for the minor matches. In the 1964-65 tour of South Africa, his Test figures were only 3 for 33, but he took 24 wickets in all first-class matches at an average of 7.25.

It was as a leg-spinner that Barrington was recommended to Surrey in 1947. Born in Reading, he had become assistant grounds-man to the Reading club, for which he was taking many wickets, when at the age of 16 he was invited to play for the Surrey Colts. He became a professional in 1948 but had to do military service, and it was 1951 before his promise as a batsman became obvious. Under the coaching of Andrew Sandham, he soon began to make runs in the Minor Counties competition. He first played for Surrey in a first-class match in 1953, and developed so fast in 1954 that he played in his first Test match the following year.

Perhaps he had come up too swiftly. For though by then he was 24, the normal peak of the average slow-developing English batsman is around 30. After his two Tests at Lords' and Leeds against South Africa in 1955, he did not play Test cricket for four years—but 80 Tests were to follow.

Though he had poor seasons in 1956 and 1957, he had the advantage of playing in a strong, confident side—this was Surrey's seven-year reign as champions—and especially of watching at close quarters Peter May, considered the best batsman in the world at that time. By 1959, which he began by making a hundred in each innings against Warwickshire, he was a welcome sight for selectors looking for new blood after England's 4-0 defeat in Australia the previous winter.

Thus was resumed a Test career in which he made 20 hundreds, including at least two against each of England's opponents, and 6,806 runs, a number surpassed at the time of his retirement only by Hammond, Cowdrey, Bradman, and Hutton. His first two hundreds were made in the 1959-60 tour of West Indies, and for some years he made most runs on overseas wickets in India, Pakistan and Australia. Strangely, too, he developed a humorous presence on the field which communicated itself more easily to overseas crowds than it ever did in England.

It was not until 1964 that he made his first Test hundred in England, but characteristically, when it came, it was extended to 256 in the marathon innings at Old Trafford with which England answered Australia's 656 and Bobby Simpson's 311. He was dropped by the England selectors in 1965 after taking what was considered an excessive time to score 137 against New Zealand, but this was a passing interlude in a career for Surrey and England which, though seldom spectacular, was immensely productive.

*Above right* **Ken Barrington in action in the Test series against South Africa in 1965. Earlier in that season he played only two Test innings against New Zealand, scoring centuries in both. Despite his awkward and unattractive style, Barrington was a tremendous compiler of runs, particularly on tours. Abroad, too, his sense of fun made him a popular visitor.**

Barnaby's

## BARRINGTON Kenneth Frank

**Teams:** Surrey and England

| Test series | | Tests | Runs | 100s | Average |
|---|---|---|---|---|---|
| 1955 | v South Africa | 2 | 52 | – | 17.33 |
| 1959 | v India | 5 | 357 | – | 59.50 |
| 1959-60 | in West Indies | 5 | 420 | 2 | 46.66 |
| 1960 | v South Africa | 4 | 227 | – | 37.83 |
| 1961 | v Australia | 5 | 364 | – | 45.50 |
| 1961-62 | in India | 5 | 594 | 3 | 99.00 |
| 1961-62 | in Pakistan | 2 | 229 | 1 | 76.33 |
| 1962 | v Pakistan | 4 | 60 | – | 20.00 |
| 1962-63 | in Australia | 5 | 582 | 2 | 72.75 |
| 1962-63 | in New Zealand | 3 | 294 | 1 | 73.50 |
| 1963 | v West Indies | 5 | 275 | – | 27.50 |
| 1963-64 | in India | 1 | 80 | – | 80.00 |
| 1964 | v Australia | 5 | 531 | 1 | 75.85 |
| 1964-65 | in South Africa | 5 | 508 | 2 | 101.60 |
| 1965 | v New Zealand | 2 | 300 | 2 | 150.00 |
| 1965 | v South Africa | 3 | 202 | – | 33.66 |
| 1965-66 | in Australia | 5 | 464 | 2 | 66.28 |
| 1966 | v West Indies | 2 | 59 | – | 14.75 |
| 1967 | v India | 3 | 324 | – | 64.80 |
| 1967 | v Pakistan | 3 | 426 | 3 | 142.00 |
| 1967-68 | in West Indies | 5 | 288 | 1 | 41.14 |
| 1968 | v Australia | 3 | 170 | – | 56.66 |
| **Total** | | **82** | **6,806** | **20** | **58.67** |

**Career runs:** 31,714 *Average:* 45.63
**Highest Test and career score:** 256 v Australia, Old Trafford, 1964
**Career wickets:** 273 *Average:* 32.61

# Bedser
## Alec Victor (1918-    )

Alec Bedser was a model bowler and, in an age when the successful professional cricketer was often touched by controversy, had an exemplary career as a player. After his retirement, he gave cricket the same service off the field as he did on it, and he was awarded the OBE in 1964.

Tall and powerfully built, Bedser had a bowling action that was a marvel of economy. He took a relatively short run-up, but the swing of his massive body dragged the maximum bounce from the pitch while allowing him to sustain life and accuracy at a fast-medium pace over long periods.

Bedser's main delivery was the inswinger with which, during his career, he had many of his great opponents, from Don Bradman downwards, caught at backward short leg. He also bowled a slightly slower leg-cutter, which on a wet pitch could be akin to a fast, high-bouncing leg-break.

The leading English bowler of the early post-war years and an automatic selection for England until 1954-55, Bedser was unlucky that the war cut into his early career. He was born in Reading, and with his twin brother, Eric, joined the Surrey staff in 1938 after a period in a firm of solicitors. He made his first-class debut the following year against Oxford University, but it was not until 1946 that he took his first first-class wicket. He was then 28, and the intervening years had been spent in the RAF.

It was not long before English cricket realised that it possessed a potentially great fast-medium bowler. Bedser was selected to play against India in the 1946 series, and he took 7-49 and 4-96 against them in the first post-war Test at Lord's. In the next

decade, he took 236 Test wickets to surpass Clarrie Grimmett's 216 wickets—the most taken by a bowler in Test cricket to that date.

England's bowling was weak during the early part of Bedser's career, and he had to carry much of the burden on his own shoulders. Yet he carried the burden so lightly that in 1953, when England's fortunes were about to turn, he took 39 wickets in the series against Australia. In the first Test at Trent Bridge, he took 7-55 and 7-44.

He decided not to go on the 1953-54 tour of West Indies, and played in only two of the four Tests in the following summer against Pakistan. But the real turning point in his international career came in December 1954, on his third tour of Australia.

He had toiled through Australia's massive winning total of 601-8 dec in the First Test of the series. But on a grassy, damp wicket, which seemed tailor-made for his swing and cut, he was left out at Sydney for the Second Test. In that match Frank Tyson and Brian Statham bowled England to a 38-run win and, although Bedser was once again within a whisker of being picked for the Third Test, he did not return to the side again on that tour. Until the Sydney match he had played in every post-war England-Australia Test. Indeed, he played in only one more Test, against South Africa at Old Trafford in 1955—a match the Springboks won by three wickets with minutes to spare.

He was then 37, but he continued playing for Surrey through their championship-winning years and then two more years during their gradual decline. In 1960, he took on the captaincy of the county while Peter May was ill, and at the end of that season, aged 42, he retired.

A successful businessman, he still made time after his retirement as a player to serve on committees and to become an England selector from 1962. In 1962-63, he was assistant-manager to the Duke of Norfolk on the MCC tour of Australia and New Zealand, and in 1969 he became chairman of selectors.

**1 Alec Bedser as a player. Power and control combined to produce a fine bowler respected by all who faced him. Don Bradman reckoned that in certain conditions he was the most difficult bowler in the world to play. Yet he was no mean batsman—sent in as a night-watchman against Australia at Leeds in 1948 he hit 79—and he held 290 catches during his career.**
**2 Bedser as administrator, pictured on his appointment as chairman of the England Test selectors in 1969.**

| BEDSER Alec Victor | | | |
|---|---|---|---|
| **Teams:** Surrey and England | | | |
| **Test series** | **Tests** | **Wkts** | **Avge** |
| 1946      v India | 3 | 24 | 12.41 |
| 1946-47   in Australia | 5 | 16 | 54.75 |
| 1946-47   in New Zealand | 1 | 4 | 23.75 |
| 1947      v South Africa | 2 | 4 | 58.25 |
| 1948      v Australia | 5 | 18 | 38.22 |
| 1948-49   in South Africa | 5 | 16 | 34.62 |
| 1949      v New Zealand | 2 | 7 | 30.71 |
| 1950      v West Indies | 3 | 11 | 34.27 |
| 1950-51   in Australia | 5 | 30 | 16.06 |
| 1950-51   in New Zealand | 2 | 2 | 69.00 |
| 1951      v South Africa | 5 | 30 | 17.23 |
| 1952      v India | 4 | 20 | 13.95 |
| 1953      v Australia | 5 | 39 | 17.48 |
| 1954      v Pakistan | 2 | 10 | 15.80 |
| 1954-55   in Australia | 1 | 1 | 131.00 |
| 1955      v South Africa | 1 | 4 | 38.25 |
| **Total** | **51** | **236** | **24.89** |

**Career wickets:** 1,924 *Average:* 20.41
**Best Test Bowling:** 7-44 v Australia, Trent Bridge, 1953
**Best career bowling:** 8-18, Surrey v Nottingham, Oval 1952
                8-18, Surrey v Warwickshire, Oval, 1953
**Highest Test score:** 79 v Australia, Leeds, 1948
**Highest career score:** 126, Surrey v Somerset, Taunton, 1947

Fox Photos

Syndication International

Keystone

# Benaud

## Richard (Richie)
## (1930-    )

Captain of Australia from 1958 to 1963, Richie Benaud was the first player to score 2,000 runs and take 200 wickets in Test cricket. Yet for all his brilliance as an all-rounder, it is as a captain that his reputation stands highest of all.

An astute competitor, he had a flair for putting over his side's performance in the best possible light. He took more risks than most captains and was greatly respected by his own players and many others. The completeness of Australia's 4-0 victory to regain the Ashes from England in 1958-59 was a tribute to his aggressive leadership.

In one way, Benaud had an advantage over previous Australian Test captains in England. As a professional journalist, he was a frequent visitor to England, reporting tours other than those in which he was playing, and he knew English cricket unusually well.

Benaud was born in Penrith, near Sydney, the son of a successful Sydney grade-cricketer and schoolmaster. At 18, he played for New South Wales, primarily as a batsman, and his Test career began at 21 against the visiting West Indians in 1951-52. He toured England for the first time in 1953.

Few visiting leg-break bowlers have prospered in England on limited experience, and talented though Benaud was, he might not have survived the tours of 1953 and 1956 as a bowler alone.

In 1953, he took 2 Test wickets and 57 tour wickets. He was left out, perhaps injudiciously, of the side that lost the Ashes at the Oval. On the 1956 tour, he took 60 wickets including 8 in the Tests.

He was, however, an ideal batsman to have at No. 7 or 8

in a Test side, confident and full of attacking strokes. In 1953, he played an extraordinary innings of 135 at Scarborough in which he hit 11 sixes. In the Lord's Test match that same year, he made a vigorous 97. (It was in this Test that he took a brilliant catch in the gully off Cowdrey. The catch, taken from a well-timed square drive, lives in the memory of all who saw it.) He hit 100 in 78 minutes against the West Indies at Kingston in 1954-55, the third fastest hundred in Test history.

Between his visits to England, Benaud was highly successful on the harder pitches in Australia, South Africa, India, and Pakistan. He had an outstanding tour of South Africa, taking 106 wickets —a record for a visiting bowler —and scoring four centuries, including two in Test matches. His aggressive and positive play in South Africa helped the Australian selectors choose him for the captaincy against England in 1958-59. In that series, he claimed 31 wickets, and on the 1959-60 tour of India and Pakistan took another 47 in the Tests. In all, he bagged 248 Test wickets, a number exceeded only by Fred Trueman and Brian Statham of England.

The spectacular series with the West Indies in 1960-61, beginning with the famous tie at Brisbane, set the seal on Benaud's captaincy. Not only had he regained the Ashes from England, but his policy of attacking cricket recaptured much of the waning enthusiasm for cricket in Australia.

His most memorable bowling feat followed in July 1961 when, in the fourth Test at Old Trafford, England needed 256 runs to win. Benaud, troubled with a persistent shoulder condition since the initial first-class match of the tour, had bowled himself sparingly. But with England advancing to 150 for one, he bowled round the wicket into the rough and suddenly broke the back of the England innings. He had Dexter caught at the wicket, bowled May round his legs, had Close caught at square leg, and bowled Subba Row. Australia won the match by 54 runs with 20 minutes to spare, and kept the Ashes. In 32 overs, Benaud had taken 6 for 70.

In 1962, Benaud was awarded the OBE. His reign as captain lasted through a halved series with Ted Dexter's England team in 1962-63 until a year later when he handed over the captaincy to Bobby Simpson during the series with South Africa. He continued to play for New South Wales until 1964 when, although still batting well, he retired.

After his retirement, he reported Australian tours in the West Indies, South Africa, and England, where he became a regular television commentator every summer.

Keystone

## BENAUD Richard

**Teams:** New South Wales and Australia

| Test series | | Tests | Runs | 100s | Avge | Wkts | Avge |
|---|---|---|---|---|---|---|---|
| 1951-52 | v West Indies | 1 | 22 | — | 11.00 | 1 | 14.00 |
| 1952-53 | v South Africa | 4 | 124 | — | 20.66 | 10 | 30.60 |
| 1953 | in England | 3 | 15 | — | 3.00 | 2 | 87.00 |
| 1954-55 | v England | 5 | 148 | — | 16.44 | 10 | 37.70 |
| 1954-55 | in West Indies | 5 | 246 | 1 | 41.00 | 18 | 27.00 |
| 1956 | in England | 5 | 200 | — | 25.00 | 8 | 41.25 |
| 1956-57 | in Pakistan | 1 | 60 | — | 30.00 | 1 | 36.00 |
| 1956-57 | in India | 3 | 53 | — | 13.25 | 23 | 16.86 |
| 1957-58 | in South Africa | 5 | 329 | 2 | 54.83 | 30 | 21.93 |
| 1958-59 | v England | 5* | 132 | — | 26.40 | 31 | 18.83 |
| 1959-60 | in Pakistan | 3* | 84 | — | 28.00 | 18 | 21.16 |
| 1959-60 | in India | 5* | 91 | — | 15.16 | 29 | 19.58 |
| 1960-61 | v West Indies | 5* | 194 | — | 21.55 | 23 | 33.86 |
| 1961 | in England | 4* | 45 | — | 9.00 | 15 | 32.53 |
| 1962-63 | v England | 5* | 227 | — | 32.42 | 17 | 40.47 |
| 1963-64 | v South Africa | 4*† | 231 | — | 33.00 | 12 | 37.41 |
| **Total** | | **63** | **2,201** | **3** | **24.45** | **248** | **27.04** |

**Career runs:** 11,720 *Average:* 36.51
**Highest Test score:** 122 v South Africa, Johannesburg, 1957-58
**Highest career score:** 187, Australians v Natal, Pietermaritzburg, 1957-58
**Career wickets:** 945 *Average:* 24.73
**Best Test bowling:** 7-72 v India, Madras, 1956-57
**Best career bowling:** 7-18, New South Wales v MCC, Sydney, 1962-63

*Captain.  †After the first Test of this series, Benaud handed the captaincy over to Bobby Simpson.

At times exhilarating, at times a bore—that's Geoff Boycott. **1** The Yorkshire and England opener drives a ball through the covers. **2** Boycott pictured in July 1969, after the substitution of contact lenses for the familiar spectacles. His loss of form in the 1969 season, despite his normal meticulous attention to practice, was considered to be in no small part due to the change in optical aids. **3** In action against New Zealand at Lord's —scene of four painful Test innings in 1969.

*Central Press*

*Syndication International*

*Sport and General*

# Boycott
## Geoff (1940-    )

Geoff Boycott is widely acknowledged as the most accomplished and most prolific opening batsman in the world. But his career at both Test and county level has sometimes been tarnished by criticisms of selfish play in which the needs of his side have been placed second to his own interests.

Yet both for country and county the responsibility on his shoulders has been frequently so great that his ability to play one long innings after another has been desperately needed—particularly for the weak-batting Yorkshire side whose captaincy he took over in 1971. It was no coincidence that in his first year in charge he averaged over 100, though his side made no sort of show in any of the competitions. He felt he had to do everything himself.

His 657 runs at an average of 93·85 in Australia in 1970-71 was the main prop of the England batting as they successfully sought to regain The Ashes.

Just 23 in his first full season, Boycott made 1,778 runs, and in 1964 he made 2,110. At first sight he was not obviously a batsman of the highest class, but his performances allowed no argument. On further analysis the observer would note his watchfulness, the way in which he moved into position, the fluency of his off-side strokes, especially against the ball just short of a length, and above all, his intense concentration. Although not possessing the natural gifts that many great batsmen have, he had worked out an effective method of playing, and he had the necessary application and temperament.

After his leap to fame, however, he had some difficult periods, and at the end of the 1969 season it seemed his later career was not quite fulfilling its immense early promise.

In some ways his concentration has not always been an unqualified asset to him. For at times when he has been below form, Boycott has fought on grimly, apparently oblivious to everything happening around him, playing a long, slow innings that may not have been in the best interests of the side and certainly was no pleasure to spectators. In 1967 he made 246 not out against India at Leeds but spent nearly six hours over the first 100. The selectors had previously called for a positive approach to batting, and this flagrant disregard for their requirements and the fact that it was not warranted by the state of the match caused Boycott to be dropped for the next Test as a disciplinary measure. In 1969 he played another painfully slow innings at Lord's against the West Indies, and there was talk that he might again be disciplined. No action was taken on this occasion, perhaps because that season he had to accustom himself to playing in contact lenses instead of spectacles.

These much publicized slow innings earned Boycott an undeserved reputation as a dull batsman. To anyone who had seen some of his batting in South Africa and in company with Bob Barber in Australia, where in the first hour of the England innings in the second Test at Melbourne they made over 80, this was ridiculous.

His best remembered innings in England is his 146 not out in the Gillette final of 1965. Overseas his most valuable innings have been one of 76 not out, which helped England to save the fourth Test at Johannesburg in 1964-65, and several in the West Indies in 1968.

**BOYCOTT Geoffrey**

Teams: Yorkshire and England

| Test series | | Tests | Runs | 100s | Avge |
|---|---|---|---|---|---|
| 1964 | v Australia | 4 | 291 | 1 | 48.50 |
| 1964-65 | in South Africa | 5 | 298 | 1 | 49.66 |
| 1965 | v New Zealand | 2 | 157 | — | 52.33 |
| 1965 | v South Africa | 2 | 75 | — | 18.75 |
| 1965-66 | in Australia | 5 | 300 | — | 42.85 |
| 1965-66 | in New Zealand | 2 | 13 | — | 4.33 |
| 1966 | v West Indies | 4 | 186 | — | 26.57 |
| 1967 | v India | 2 | 277 | 1 | 138.50 |
| *1967 | v Pakistan | 1 | 16 | — | 16.00 |
| 1967-68 | in West Indies | 5 | 463 | 1 | 66.14 |
| 1968 | v Australia | 3 | 162 | — | 32.40 |
| 1969 | v West Indies | 3 | 270 | 2 | 54.00 |
| 1969 | v New Zealand | 3 | 101 | — | 20.20 |
| 1970-71 | in Australia | 5 | 657 | 2 | 93.85 |
| 1971 | v Pakistan | 2 | 246 | 2 | 123.00 |
| 1971 | v India | 1 | 36 | – | 18.00 |
| 1972 | v Australia | 2 | 72 | — | 18.00 |
| 1973 | v New Zealand | 3 | 320 | 1 | 64.00 |
| Total | | 54 | 3,940 | 11 | 48.64 |

**Career runs:** 22,416 *Average:* 54.01
**Highest Test score:** 246* **v India, Leeds, 1967**
**Highest career score:** 260* **v Essex, Colchester, 1970**

* Not out
Career figures to the start of the 1973 season

# Bradman

## Sir Donald George (1908-    )

If a batsman had to be named as the greatest ever, the choice of many people would certainly be Australian cricketer Don Bradman. His record is unsurpassed, indeed unapproached, even though World War II and poor health took six years out of his career. Between 1927 and 1948 Bradman averaged 95.14 against the 56.10 of Walter Hammond, who had the next best record. In Test matches he averaged 99.94, over double the figure of the next most successful Australian batsmen, Bobby Simpson, Neil Harvey, and Bradman's two great contemporaries Bill Ponsford and Stan McCabe, all of whom averaged just over 48. In his 52 Test matches he made 29 centuries against the 22 of Hammond in 85 Tests.

These figures give an idea of Bradman's pre-eminence amongst batsmen of all times. Yet it was not only his consistency and freedom from error that made men marvel, but also the swiftness and facility with which he made his runs.

He undoubtedly saw the ball in flight as early as it can be seen by the human eye, but it was the speed of his reflexes that was at the heart of his genius. Quick-footed and perfectly balanced, he always seemed in position to play the stroke that the length of the ball required. And often the speed of his footwork would make the ball the length *he* wanted. He had all the strokes and a rare gift of improvisation. He was a wonderfully quick cutter and hooker, but if one stroke more than any other impressed itself on the memory of cricket fans, it was his hitting of the ball through mid-wicket, especially off the back foot. He seldom hit the ball in the air and always—it seemed—placed it wide of a fielder. His placing was a miracle of precision.

It has been said that on bad pitches he was but a shadow of the great batsman he was on hard, true pitches. But his record shows that he was a formidable figure even in adversity—in the 'body-line' series of 1932-33 he still averaged 56. It was also a significant tribute to his greatness that he was able to play again so successfully after the war. In 1948 he was nearly 40 and, to those who had watched him in his youth, was less spectacular and less imbued with the old quicksilver magic. But he still averaged 72 in the Test series and made 2,428 runs in first-class matches on the tour at an average of 89.92.

One of the first inklings the outside world had that a new cricket prodigy had arrived was a report early in 1927 that a certain Don Bradman of Bowral, New South Wales, had made 320 in a

*Sport and General*

*Topix*

**1 Don Bradman drives during a practice session at Lord's in 1948 when, on the last of his four tours to England, he was captain of a great Australian side. 2 Bradman hammers the Essex bowling to score 187 runs in 125 minutes.**

grade final. He had also exceeded 300 in the previous year's final.

Born in Cootamundra, New South Wales, on August 27, 1908, Bradman spent his boyhood in Bowral, some 80 miles from Sydney. He was only 19 when, in his first Sheffield Shield match, he made 118 for New South Wales against South Australia at Adelaide.

His first Test match, in the following season, was a grim experience for a young Australian for England won at Brisbane by 675 runs. Bradman was only twelfth man in the second Test. But he made 79 and 112 in the third and soon the idea of an Australian team without him became absurd. In the vital

Sheffield Shield match that season he made 340 not out against Victoria, the first of his big scores, and by the time he went to England in 1930 his reputation was enormous. Yet his achievements there were even greater. Beginning with 236, the first of three successive double centuries at Worcester, he made 2,960 runs, averaging 98.66. In Test matches he made four centuries and 974 runs, averaging 139.14.

At Lord's, Bradman's 254 was an innings that made watchers think, perhaps correctly, that they would never again see such dominating batting in this class of cricket. At Leeds he made 309 not out on the first day of the third Test, increasing it to 334 the next day. In a single day, Bradman had beaten a Test record that had stood since 1903 when R. E. Foster made 287 for England at Sydney. At the Oval he made 232. From his overwhelming mastery of English bowling and the subsequent series at home, when he made two centuries against the West Indies and four against South Africa, there developed 'body-line' with which England, under Douglas Jardine, countered Bradman and other successful batsman in 1932-33. But Bradman was back in England in 1934, no less devastating than four years before, and he returned as captain in 1938. Between these tours he had moved from New South Wales to South Australia.

It was a stroke of irony that his pre-war career of almost uninterrupted triumph should end with one of his few reverses. The last Test of 1938 was due to be played to a finish and England, batting first at the Oval, made 903 for 7 declared. Len Hutton's 364 in this innings took from Bradman one of the few records he surrendered in his playing career. In his younger days he had been a useful leg-break bowler and, as the England score mounted and his bowlers tired, he put himself on. But in bowling, he trod on a worn footmark and badly injured an ankle. He was carried from the field and took no further part in the match. England subsequently won the match by an innings and 579 runs, squaring the rubber.

When the war ended, it was not certain if Bradman's health would let him play again. But he made 76 and 106 in his first two matches against the MCC touring side of 1946-47, and 187 and 234 in the first and second Tests. He carried on at a level of brilliance only just below that of his pre-war days.

The physical attributes and the astonishing co-ordination that produced his peerless batting were supported by a temperament combining great application, an intense sense of purpose, and a streak of ruthlessness. These qualities served him well as a captain and he never lost a rubber. The unbeaten record of the great 1948 Australians was a suitable climax, though his own Test career finished at the Oval on a note of anti-climax. Coming in to play his last Test innings to a great ovation, he was bowled second ball by Eric Hollies. He had needed only four runs from that innings to average exactly 100 throughout his Test career.

It is now usual in Australia for great players to become active administrators, but Bradman, knighted in 1949, became almost as commanding a figure in Australian cricket off the field as he had been on it. He has been an immensely influential figure in the game in Australia, both as a selector and a member and chairman of the Board of Control. It was typical that when in the early 1960s he became convinced of the dangers to the game of illegal bowling and the growing number of 'throwers', the menace was stamped out more quickly and more thoroughly in Australia than anywhere else in the world.

**Don Bradman did not always hit the ball according to the text books, but his mixture of orthodox and unorthodox strokes brought him thousands of runs. 1 Bradman plays one of his favourite strokes and one many fans remember him playing—the pull through mid-wicket. 2 All eyes on the ball. Bradman's sweep may not have pleased the purists, but the power is obvious to the Leicestershire fieldsmen. His batting career was one of almost uninterrupted triumph**

| BRADMAN Sir Donald George | | | | |
|---|---|---|---|---|
| Teams: New South Wales, South Australia, and Australia | | | | |
| Test series | Tests | Runs | 100s | Avge |
| 1928-29 v England | 4 | 468 | 2 | 66.85 |
| 1930 in England | 5 | 974 | 4 | 139.14 |
| 1930-31 v West Indies | 5 | 447 | 2 | 74.50 |
| 1931-32 v South Africa | 5 | 806 | 4 | 201.50 |
| 1932-33 v England | 4 | 396 | 1 | 56.57 |
| 1934 in England | 5 | 758 | 2 | 94.75 |
| 1936-37 v England† | 5 | 810 | 3 | 90.00 |
| 1938 in England† | 4 | 434 | 3 | 108.50 |
| 1946-47 v England† | 5 | 680 | 2 | 97.14 |
| 1947-48 v India† | 5 | 715 | 4 | 178.75 |
| 1948 in England† | 5 | 508 | 2 | 72.57 |
| Total | 52 | 6,996 | 29 | 99.94 |

Career runs: 28,067 *Average:* 95.14
Highest Test score: 334 v England, Leeds, 1930
Highest career score: 452* New South Wales v Queensland, Sydney, 1929-30
*Not out    †Captain

Keystone

Topix

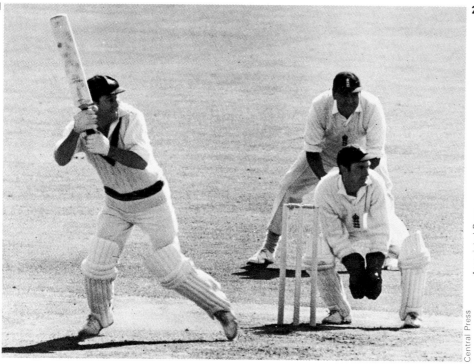

Associated Press

Central Press

# Chappell

Ian Michael (1943-    )

It must have been particularly galling for such a competitive cricketer as Ian Chappell that in his first match as captain of Australia, at Sydney in 1971, he had to concede The Ashes. Since then this aggressive stroke-maker, excellent slip and useful change spinner has shown that his captaincy is another talent.

A grandson of Vic Richardson who captained Australia in the 1930s, he played in his first Test against Pakistan at Melbourne in 1964-65. His next Test appearance was against England in the following year, on his home ground at Adelaide. The scorecard shows that he achieved little with bat or ball, but early in the match he held a magnificent slip catch from Geoff Boycott which helped set Australia on the road to victory and the retention of the Ashes.

In South Africa in 1966-67, he did not fulfil initial promise as a batsman, and his bowling was little used. But his batting made a

Ian Chappell—batting against England in 1968 (1), diving to dismiss Geoff Boycott in 1966 (2), and bowling in the 5th Test, again in 1968 (3).

considerable impact in England in 1968. He had played for Rams-bottom in the Lancashire League in 1963 and his technique proved more effective on English pitches than that of the other young Australian batsmen.

Back in Australia in 1968-69, he surpassed all his previous achievements by making 548 runs at an average of 68.50 in the Test series against West Indies. In the first Test he scored 117 and in the second 165. It was his dismissal for 96 in the last innings of the remarkable fourth Test at Adelaide that precipitated Australia's collapse when they were within sight of victory and gave them only a hard-earned draw. Outside Test matches in this golden season, Chappell played three more big innings against the tourists—188 not out for a Combined XI at Perth, 123 in the first match for South Australia, and 180 in the second.

Central Press

## CHAPPELL Ian Michael

Teams: South Australia and Australia

| Test series | Tests | Runs | 100s | Avge |
|---|---|---|---|---|
| 1964-65 v Pakistan | 1 | 11 | – | 11.00 |
| 1965-66 v England | 2 | 36 | – | 18.00 |
| 1966-67 in South Africa | 5 | 196 | – | 21.77 |
| 1967-68 v India | 4 | 212 | 1 | 30.28 |
| 1968    in England | 5 | 348 | – | 43.50 |
| 1968-69 v West Indies | 5 | 548 | 2 | 68.50 |
| 1969-70 in India | 5 | 324 | 1 | 46.28 |
| 1970    in South Africa | 4 | 92 | – | 11.50 |
| 1970-71 v England† | 6 | 452 | 2 | 37.66 |
| 1972    in England* | 5 | 334 | 1 | 33.40 |
| 1972-73 v Pakistan* | 3 | 341 | 1 | 68.20 |
| 1972-73 in West Indies* | 5 | 542 | 2 | 77.42 |
| Total | 50 | 3,436 | 10 | 40.90 |

Career runs: 13,748 Average: 48.75
Highest Test score: 196 v Pakistan, Adelaide, 1972-73
Highest career score: 209, Australians v Barbados, Bridgetown, 1972-73

*Not out    *Captain, †captain one test
Career figures to the end of the 1972-73 season

# Compton

Denis (1918-        )

Whether on the cricket pitch or the football field, Denis Compton was a popular and colourful sporting hero in the Britain of the 1940s. A natural at both games, he thrilled the crowds with his buccaneering spirit and his unorthodox, at times cheeky, play. Few sportsmen have captured, and held, the public imagination as Compton did. And if, perhaps, the statistics do not quite show him as the great all-rounder he undoubtedly was, the vivid memories he left with cricket and soccer fans of the immediate post-war years will long remain as tribute to the wonderful entertainment he provided in that age of austerity.

Compton's place among the greatest batsmen in the history of cricket cannot be disputed. If World War II had not taken six years out of his career at a time when he would have been at his peak, if he had not been handicapped by injury for over half his playing career, and if he had been more conscious of feats and figures, his record would have been even more outstanding than it was.

But it is for the gaiety and personality of his batting that he is remembered even more than for its quality. He had the gift of communicating to the spectator all his own feelings about the bowling, whether it be confidence or concern. This, with the fluency and apparent unorthodoxy of his stroke-play, made his batting fascinating to watch.

Technically he was thoroughly sound, and the strokes that he improvized with what many thought to be a flouting of the textbook in fact had a sound basis. He is associated in cricketer's minds with the sweep, which brought him many runs in safety but is often fraught with peril when imitated by others. But there were few other strokes that he did not play. His delayed drive square on the offside was a feature of his batting, as was the way in which he would step backward and hit the turning off-break to the off-side against the spin. And he was deadly in the placing of his masterfully executed on-drive.

In the field he became less mobile after sustaining a serious knee injury, though he was capable of spectacular catches. As a bowler he could bowl orthodox left-arm spin but he had more success with the chinaman and googly. He suffered from the usual inaccuracy that afflicts this type of bowling, but when he found a length he was capable of bothering the best batsmen.

Few English batsmen have risen to the top at an earlier age than Compton. When he was just 18 in 1936 he played his first match for Middlesex, against Sussex, batting No. 11 in the Whitsun match at Lord's. Within a month he had made the first of his 123 first-class hundreds, and by the end of the season there were many who thought that he should have gone to Australia with G. O. Allen's MCC side. He played in his first Test against New Zealand in the following year and in all the subsequent home Tests up to the outbreak of war, making 102 in his first innings against Australia, at Trent Bridge in 1938.

Towards the end of the war he played some first-class cricket in India and returned in excellent form for the 1946 season. In Australia that winter he made a hundred in each innings of the Adelaide Test, and back in England in 1947 he embarked on his golden year and his memorable record-breaking partnerships with Bill Edrich.

When he had made a hundred, he often considered that enough, unless the requirements of the side made it important for him to go on. In that season, with Middlesex

74

1 A sight Pakistan 'keeper Imtiaz must have become well accustomed to in the second of the 1954 Tests against England—Denis Compton sending the ball crashing to the leg-side boundary. Compton scored 278, his highest Test score. His second hundred was scored in just 80 minutes.

2 Compton grimaces in pain after being hit by a 'no-ball' bumper from Ray Lindwall. He was helped from the field and stitches were inserted. Then, with England at 119-5, he returned to play an admirable innings that yielded 145 runs before he ran out of partners.

3 Compton tumbles back onto his stumps after attempting to hook, and then ducking away from, a Keith Miller bumper. In an innings often hindered by bad light, and in which Miller was at his most hostile, he scored 184.

4 The famous Compton sweep. The stroke brought Compton hundreds of runs and was a delight to cricket fans.

5 The last stroke of the 1953 series against Australia. A moment after Compton had hit Arthur Morris for four, the crowd swarmed onto the Oval. England had won the Ashes.

6 Compton the footballer lashes one of the two goals he scored for Arsenal against Middlesbrough at Highbury in March 1948. Outside-left Compton played in the last third of Arsenal's successful 1947-48 league campaign, scored six goals, and won himself a championship medal.

7 February 1950, and Derby's Leuty is too late to stop Compton's flashing left foot. Despite his many knee operations, Compton went on in this, his last, season to gain a cup winners medal.

challenging successfully for the championship, he went on often. His record of 3,816 runs and 18 hundreds in the season is unlikely ever to be beaten, especially now that the amount of first-class cricket being played in England is decreasing.

However, in the last match of 1947 his knee let him down and he was seldom free of pain or discomfort afterwards. Yet in 1948 he played what many regard as his greatest innings—145 not out against Australia at Old Trafford, overcoming Lindwall at his most hostile and after being knocked out and retiring hurt early in his innings: He went to South Africa in 1948-49 and made his famous 300 in three hours at Benoni, easily the fastest 300 ever made. But though in the following season he reached the peak of his football career, he missed most of that cricket season through an operation which removed a fragment of bone from his knee. Characteristically he returned with a century

against Surrey in August, but the knee continued to trouble him. In 1954 he was still able to play an astonishing innings of 278 in 4 hours 50 minutes against Pakistan at Nottingham, but in November 1955 he had to have his kneecap removed. Again he returned with a hundred—against Somerset—and when fit enough to play in the last Test against Australia in 1956 he made a brilliant 94.

After the 1957 season he retired, making 143 and 48 in his last match for Middlesex. He became a regular commentator on Test matches for BBC television.

Compton's career as a footballer has been somewhat unjustly obscured by his prowess on the cricket field. He was a very good outside-left indeed, powerful, dangerous, quick, unorthodox, with a superb left foot, and also a useful header of the ball. He played eleven times for England during the war, and was thoroughly established in a brilliant forward-line with Stanley Matthews, Raich Carter, Tommy Lawton and Jimmy Hagan, before he was posted to India, with the Army, in 1944.

On his return, he had put on more weight than he was ever fully able to shed, though he won a 'Victory' international cap against Scotland at Hampden Park in 1946. Four years later, after missing a good deal of football through the demands of cricket tours, he played, with his brother Leslie, in Arsenal's cup winning team against Liverpool. It was from his corner that Leslie headed the equalizing goal against Chelsea at Tottenham in the semi-final, and he himself had scored with a tremendous left-footed drive against Burnley in an earlier round.

Compton joined Arsenal, like Leslie, from the Hampstead amateur club in 1935. By the time war broke out, he had already played 22 First Division matches for Arsenal, his league debut being in September 1936 against Derby County. In season 1942-43 he was a regular member of the powerful Arsenal team that won the League South and the League South Cup.

As a footballer, his confidence was limitless. He would casually bounce the ball on his head, before hooking it into the goalmouth, and he was an unflurried taker of penalty kicks, even in the most tense situations. There is little doubt that, had it not been for the war, he would have won numerous full caps for England.

| COMPTON Denis Charles Scott | | | | |
|---|---|---|---|---|
| **Teams:** Middlesex and England | | | | |
| Test series | Tests | Runs | 100s | Average |
| 1937 v New Zealand | 1 | 65 | — | 65.00 |
| 1938 v Australia | 4 | 214 | 1 | 42.80 |
| 1939 v West Indies | 3 | 189 | 1 | 63.00 |
| 1946 v India | 3 | 146 | — | 73.00 |
| 1946-47 in Australia | 5 | 459 | 2 | 51.00 |
| 1946-47 in New Zealand | 1 | 38 | — | 38.00 |
| 1947 v South Africa | 5 | 753 | 4 | 94.12 |
| 1948 v Australia | 5 | 562 | 2 | 62.44 |
| 1948-49 in South Africa | 5 | 406 | 1 | 50.75 |
| 1949 v New Zealand | 4 | 300 | 2 | 50.00 |
| 1950 v West Indies | 1 | 55 | — | 27.50 |
| 1950-51 in Australia | 4 | 53 | — | 7.57 |
| 1950-51 in New Zealand | 2 | 107 | — | 35.66 |
| 1951 v South Africa | 4 | 312 | 1 | 52.00 |
| 1952 v India | 2 | 59 | — | 29.50 |
| 1953 v Australia | 5 | 234 | — | 33.42 |
| 1953-54 in West Indies | 5 | 348 | 1 | 49.71 |
| 1954 v Pakistan | 4 | 453 | 1 | 90.60 |
| 1954-55 in Australia | 4 | 191 | — | 38.20 |
| 1955 v South Africa | 5 | 492 | 1 | 54.66 |
| 1956 v Australia | 1 | 129 | — | 129.00 |
| 1956-57 in South Africa | 5 | 242 | — | 24.20 |
| Total | 78 | 5,807 | 17 | 50.06 |

**Career runs:** 38,942 *Average:* 51.85
**Highest Test score:** 278 v Pakistan, Trent Bridge, 1954
**Highest career score:** 300, MCC v North-Eastern Transvaal, Benoni, 1948-49
**Career wickets:** 622 *Average:* 32.22
**Test Wickets:** 25 *Average:* 56.40
**Best Test bowling:** 5-70 v South Africa, Cape Town, 1948-49
**Best career bowling:** 7-36, MCC v Auckland, Auckland, 1946-47

Central Press

Keystone

| COMPTON Denis Charles Scott | | | |
|---|---|---|---|
| **Honours:** League Championship medal 1948; FA Cup winners medal 1950 | | | |
| Club | Season | League | |
| | | Mtchs | Gls |
| Arsenal | 1936-37 | 14 | 4 |
| | 1937-38 | 7 | 1 |
| | 1938-39 | 1 | |
| | 1946-47 | 1 | 1 |
| | 1947-48 | 14 | 6 |
| | 1948-49 | 6 | 2 |
| | 1949-50 | 11 | 1 |
| | Total | 54 | 15 |

# Cowdrey

## Michael Colin
## (1932-    )

No player in the world has spent longer at the top in post-war cricket than England's Colin Cowdrey, whose Test career began in Australia in 1954-55 when he was 21. His 109 Tests place him way at the head of the list of most-capped cricketers, and he would have undoubtedly played more had not a ruptured achilles tendon in May 1969 put him out of action. He scored more Test runs, 7,459, than any other Englishman, always in a manner of characteristic composure and elegance.

A gifted games player, Cowdrey reached the final of the Amateur Rackets Championship as an Oxford undergraduate and, while convalescing in 1969, proved himself a good enough golfer to win an important professional-amateur tournament at Turnberry with British Ryder Cup player Brian Huggett. Always heavily built, even as a prodigiously successful schoolboy cricketer, he has wonderfully quick reactions for someone of his size and he has long been one of the world's best slip catchers.

He first played for Kent in 1950, and was only 18 when he made an impressive 106 for the Gentlemen against a strong Players side at Scarborough. Two fifties for the Gentlemen against the Australians at Lords in 1953 confirmed his swift advance towards the England team. In 1954, when he was captain of Oxford, he was 12th man in the last Test against Pakistan at the Oval, and was a somewhat unexpected selection for the MCC tour of Australia and New Zealand.

The tour began tragically for him, for, on arrival in Perth, he learnt of the sudden death of his father, who had been a great inspiration to his cricket. However, it was Cowdrey's stand with Peter May, the first of many, that turned the second Test and the series in England's favour, and his remarkable innings of 102—out of a total of only 191—that in the third Test started England on the way to success. He returned to England as a Test player who had succeeded in the highest company and had an immense future.

Yet within a few weeks, a touch of controversy had entered his career, as he was rejected by the RAF because of a foot condition. And through the subsequent years, he tended to be underestimated in his own country, perhaps because it was felt that sometimes he did not make the most of his talent. Abroad he was a greatly respected figure among the cricket public. He toured Australia five times, and visited the other major cricket playing countries at least once. His comfortable, easy-going appearance led some at home to the conclusion that he was too gentle for

*Gerry Cranham/Transworld*

*Above*, **Colin Cowdrey, the Kent and England captain, sweeps a ball to the boundary. One of the most graceful and prolific batsmen in the history of cricket, he would almost certainly have passed Wally Hammond's record** Test aggregate of 7,249 runs in 1969 had an injury not put him out of action for the season. *Below*, Cowdrey thumps a majestic off-drive. His occasional reluctance to play strokes has sometimes led to criticism.

*Press Association*

captaincy, and his apparent reluctance at times to play strokes made him the target for criticism by people who felt that with his gifts he need not restrict himself.

The truth, perhaps, is that his method of batting, and his reliance on timing rather than on power, was better suited to the harder pitches and faster outfields abroad than to the many pitches in England on which the ball 'stops' and has to be assaulted with vigour if it is to reach the boundary.

English cricket history of the 1950s and 1960s is, however, packed with Cowdrey's achievements. At times he was converted into an opening batsman and at times he became captain. If he were unable to play, his batting and his slip-catching were sorely missed.

In his early days, England were strong in bowling but not in late-order batting, and the innings would often thrive or fall with May and Cowdrey. It was their historic stand of 411 at Edgbaston in 1957 that had a decisive effect on the series with West Indies, and Cowdrey, 150 at Edgbaston, followed with 152 in the next Test at Lords. As an opening batsman in West Indies in 1960, he met the West Indian fast bowlers with courage and success and, when Peter May was taken ill, assumed the captaincy that he had first taken over when May was ill in 1959.

In Australia in 1962-63, Cowdrey made his highest score—307

against South Australia in Adelaide. Later in 1963, in the Lords Test against West Indies, his arm was broken by a short ball from Wes Hall. At the end of a dramatic match he had to come in for the last two balls to earn England a draw—which he did, fortunately as the non-striker.

Cowdrey's next innings was eight months later when, having flown out as a reinforcement to the MCC team depleted by illness, he made a hundred in a Test match in Calcutta. Later that year he was dropped from the fourth Test against Australia but returned to make 93 not out in the last.

In 1966, Cowdrey became captain again in place of M. J. K. Smith. But after England had been beaten at Leeds he was replaced by Brian Close. He took over again when Close, having been recently censured for unfair play, was not acceptable to the MCC Committee for the tour of West Indies in 1968.

This proved to be one of Cowdrey's best tours, for his captaincy was happy and successful, and his 534 runs in the Test series played a big part in the final victory. As captain against Australia that summer he made a hundred in his 100th Test match, and in Pakistan in February 1969 he made his 91st first-class hundred and his 22nd Test hundred on a riot-interrupted day in Lahore. And though his Test days were over, he was still going strong for Kent in 1973, when he made his 100th century.

## COWDREY Michael Colin

**Teams:** Oxford University, Kent, and England

| Test series | | Tests | Runs | 100s | Average |
|---|---|---|---|---|---|
| 1954–55 | in Australia | 5 | 319 | 1 | 35.44 |
| 1954–55 | in New Zealand | 2 | 64 | — | 32.00 |
| 1955 | v South Africa | 1 | 51 | — | 25.50 |
| 1956 | v Australia | 5 | 244 | — | 30.50 |
| 1956–57 | in South Africa | 5 | 331 | 1 | 33.10 |
| 1957 | v West Indies | 5 | 435 | 2 | 72.50 |
| 1958 | v New Zealand | 4 | 241 | — | 60.25 |
| 1958–59 | in Australia | 5 | 391 | 1 | 43.44 |
| 1958–59 | in New Zealand | 2 | 20 | — | 10.00 |
| 1959 | v India | 5[1] | 344 | 1 | 57.33 |
| 1959–60 | in West Indies | 5[1] | 491 | 2 | 54.55 |
| 1960 | v South Africa | 5[*] | 312 | 1 | 34.66 |
| 1961 | v Australia | 4[1] | 168 | — | 21.00 |
| 1962 | v Pakistan | 4[2] | 409 | 2 | 81.80 |
| 1962–63 | in Australia | 5 | 394 | 1 | 43.77 |
| 1962–63 | in New Zealand | 3 | 292 | 1 | 146.00 |
| 1963 | v West Indies | 2 | 39 | — | 13.00 |
| 1963–64 | in India | 3 | 309 | 2 | 103.00 |
| 1964 | v Australia | 3 | 188 | — | 47.00 |
| 1965 | v New Zealand | 3 | 221 | 1 | 73.66 |
| 1965 | v South Africa | 3 | 327 | 1 | 65.40 |
| 1965–66 | in Australia | 4 | 267 | 1 | 53.40 |
| 1965–66 | in New Zealand | 3 | 196 | — | 49.00 |
| 1966 | v West Indies | 4[3] | 252 | — | 31.50 |
| 1967 | v Pakistan | 2 | 41 | — | 13.66 |
| 1967–68 | in West Indies | 5[*] | 534 | 2 | 66.75 |
| 1968 | v Australia | 4[*] | 215 | 1 | 35.83 |
| 1968–69 | in Pakistan | 3[*] | 133 | 1 | 33.25 |
| 1970–71 | in Australia | 3 | 82 | — | 20.50 |
| 1970–71 | in New Zealand | 1 | 99 | — | 49.50 |
| 1971 | v Pakistan | 1 | 50 | — | 25.50 |
| Total | | 109 | 7,459 | 22 | 45.48 |

**Career runs:** 39,306 *Average* 43.43
**Highest Test score:** 182 v Pakistan, Oval, 1962
**Highest career score:** 307, MCC v South Australia, Adelaide, 1962–63

*Captain in all Tests played, [1]Captain in 2 Tests, [2]Captain in 1 Test,
[3]Captain in 3 Tests. Career figures up to the start of the 1973 season

**1** Colin Cowdrey hooks on his first tour of Australia.
**2, 3** Cowdrey snaps up a half-chance to dismiss Rohan Kanhai against the West Indies in Trinidad.

# Davidson

## Alan Keith (1929-    )

Alan Davidson became Australia's leading bowler after the retirement of Lindwall, Miller, and Johnston, and he was one of the main reasons for the success of the far from powerful side captained by Richie Benaud between 1958-59 and 1962-63. Such a fine left-arm fast-medium bowler was he that the attempts to convert him into a slow left-arm spinner, when he first went to England in 1953, seem bizarre in retrospect.

'Davo', as he was known, also developed into a great all-rounder. Six feet tall with unusually broad shoulders, he was a powerful left-handed batsman and a brilliantly athletic fielder in any position. But it was his bowling that possessed the greatest quality. From a run of little over 15 yards, and from over the wicket, he moved the ball off the pitch in either direction and had a devasting late swing with the new ball. Tom Graveney is not the only famous batsman to have been bowled or lbw playing no stroke to a ball from Davidson which he had thought was slanting safely away outside his off-stump.

Davidson first played for New South Wales in 1949-50, when the leading Australian players were away in South Africa. He was such a highly promising fast-medium bowler that he went to New Zealand with a representative side at the end of that season.

The first of his three tours of England, in 1953, emphasized his promise, and he played in all five Tests, though with Lindwall, Miller, Johnston, and Archer in the side he was an auxiliary bowler rarely in the front line. He was used experimentally in a slower role after Johnston had been injured in a preliminary match at the start of the tour.

In 1956, on his second tour of England, he was dogged by injury and it was not until the visit to South Africa in 1957-58 that he began to reach his full stature as a Test player. Top of the tour bowling averages with 15.11 and third in the batting with 54.20, he took 25 wickets in the series. A year later in Melbourne he bowled a historic over at the start of the second Test against England—he had Richardson caught at the wicket, bowled Watson with a swinging full toss, and had Graveney lbw the next ball.

His highest Test score—80—was made in 1960-61 against the West Indies at Brisbane, in the famous tied Test—a match to which he made a massive contribution. Having scored 44 in the first innings and taken 11 wickets in the two West Indian innings, he was run out when Australia needed only another seven runs to win. He and Benaud added 134 for the seventh wicket.

His best-remembered innings in England is probably his 77 not out at Old Trafford later in 1961. He was Australia's main bowler on that tour and took 23 Test wickets, but it was his innings in the fourth Test that did more than anything to decide the series and keep the Ashes for Australia. Soon after the start on the last morning Australia were 157 runs ahead with only one second innings wicket left, after four days play in which England had always seemed to be just on top. But Davidson was still there. He hit David Allen, who had taken three wickets in 15 balls that morning, for 20 runs in one over. The last wicket stand of 98 with Graham McKenzie gave England too much to do—Australia won the match, the only one in the series that produced a result.

**1** Alan Davidson lofts a ball from England spinner David Allen during his fine innings of 77 not out in the fourth Test of the 1961 series. One of the great Australian all-rounders, 'Davo' was a vital member of Australia's Test teams of the Benaud era.
**2** Davidson's action may have lacked a classical grace but his swing and pace confused the world's best batsmen.

### DAVIDSON Alan Keith

Teams: New South Wales and Australia

| Test series | | Tests | Runs | Average | Wkts | Average |
|---|---|---|---|---|---|---|
| 1953 | in England | 5 | 182 | 22.75 | 8 | 26.50 |
| 1954-55 | v England | 3 | 71 | 14.20 | 3 | 73.33 |
| 1956 | in England | 2 | 8 | 8.00 | 2 | 28.00 |
| 1956-57 | in Pakistan | 1 | 40 | 20.00 | 2 | 7.50 |
| 1956-57 | in India | 1 | 16 | 16.00 | 1 | 42.00 |
| 1957-58 | in South Africa | 5 | 127 | 21.16 | 25 | 17.00 |
| 1958-59 | v England | 5 | 180 | 36.00 | 24 | 19.00 |
| 1959-60 | in Pakistan | 3 | 90 | 45.00 | 12 | 24.83 |
| 1959-60 | in India | 5 | 93 | 18.60 | 29 | 15.17 |
| 1960-61 | v West Indies | 4 | 212 | 30.28 | 33 | 18.54 |
| 1961 | in England | 5 | 151 | 30.20 | 23 | 24.86 |
| 1962-63 | v England | 5 | 158 | 22.57 | 24 | 20.00 |
| | Total | 44 | 1,328 | 24.59 | 186 | 20.58 |

**Career runs:** 6,804  *Average:* 32.86
**Highest Test score:** 80 v West Indies, Brisbane, 1960-61
**Highest career score:** 129, Australians v Western Province, Cape Town, 1957-58
**Career wickets:** 672  *Average:* 20.91
**Best Test bowling:** 7-93 v India, Kanpur, 1959-60
**Best career bowling:** 7-31, New South Wales v Western Australia, Perth, 1961-62

# Dexter

## Edward Ralph (1935- )

Capable of reaching great heights in almost anything he attempted, Ted Dexter, known throughout the cricketing world as 'Lord Ted', was one of the most dashing batsmen and most gifted all-round cricketers to play for England in modern times. His fielding could be brilliant either near or away from the wicket, and his belligerent aspect as he walked to the wicket, was a familiar sight. Yet a restless temperament and an apparent lack of concentration sometimes stopped him giving full vent to his talents, and he would exasperate the spectator by getting out needlessly through overconfidence and excessive contempt for the bowling.

From his early days at Radley College and Cambridge, he was also a fine golfer, a tremendous hitter of the ball for whom great things were forecast. These predictions were strengthened in 1969 when, after his retirement from first-class cricket, he was runner-up in the Oxford and Cambridge Golfing Society's President's Putter. As a batsman, too, Dexter was a tremendously hard driver, an especially strong and courageous player of fast bowling. Though he scored a number of centuries, he is best remembered by many people for his innings of 70 in 81 minutes in the Lord's Test of 1963 against the West Indian fast bowlers Wes Hall and Charlie Griffith, then in their menacing prime. And few Australians will ever forget his innings of 93 in the second Test of the 1962-63 series when he set England on the road to victory. In the first Test, he scored 70 and 99.

Dexter captained Cambridge in 1958 and two years later took over the captaincy of Sussex. He had matured early, and at 25 was already established in the front rank of English cricketers. While still at Cambridge, he had given an outstanding bowling performance in the 1957 Gentlemen v Players match. On a wet pitch, he took 5-8 in the Players' first innings and 3-47 in their second with his lively fast-medium bowling. As a bowler, he tended to fall between two stools because of the inability of his captains and himself to decide whether he should be used as a stock bowler or as a striking force. But he had moments of inspiration, and his ability to swing the ball a lot could make him devastating in typically English conditions. This was best illustrated in the Edgbaston Test of 1963 when he took five West Indies first innings wickets for 45. And if Freddy Trueman had not bowled out the West Indians in the second innings, Dexter might well have done so.

Having played in his first Test against the New Zealand tourists in 1958, Dexter was sent out to Australia during the 1958-59 MCC tour when Willie Watson and Ramon Subba Row were injured. He played in two Tests there, and on the New Zealand section of the tour made his maiden Test century, scoring 141 in the first Test, at Christchurch. A year later, after a modest home season, he was selected for the tour of the

**1** For once Ted Dexter's power driving lets him down as he holes out in the deep off Pakistan's leg spinner Intikhab Alam.
**2** The definitive Dexter drive. Dexter always believed in carrying the attack to the faster bowlers and loved to step onto the front foot to hit straight or through the covers.

Central Press

Central Press

West Indies. It was a much-criticized selection, but he proved one of the successes of the tour, playing the fast bowling with great zest, and topped the Test batting averages.

In a series in which bumpers were hurled at batsmen on both sides in liberal quantities, Dexter was at his most prolific. Batting at number six, he made a punishing 136 not out in the first innings of the series, and he never looked back.

His competitive temperament relished the confrontation with physical danger presented by the pace of the West Indies attack and he never flinched. He was batting at number three when he made his second century of the series at Georgetown. There, in company with Ramon Subba Row, he ensured that England could not lose the match. It was this series that above all established Dexter, whose class was never in doubt, as a batsman capable of big Test innings.

In the first Test of the 1961 series against Australia, he earned England a draw with a second innings of 180. And in the decisive Test of the series, at Old Trafford, he played a spectacular innings of 76 in 84 minutes which at one time put England in the position of needing only 106 runs from their last nine wickets. But with Dexter's dismissal, they collapsed.

Dexter became captain of England when he took the MCC side to India and Pakistan in 1961-62. In the home series against Pakistan the following summer, he was captain in the first two Tests, but Colin Cowdrey was preferred for the captaincy in the third. However, when Cowdrey was unfit, Dexter was appointed captain for the fourth Test and subsequently led England in Australia and New Zealand in 1962-63. He remained captain until he stood for Parliament in October 1964, and had to delay his acceptance of the invitation to tour South Africa. When he did eventually go, it was as vice-captain to Mike Smith. He did not captain England again and slipped out of regular first-class cricket, preferring to play on Sundays for the International Cavaliers.

When his county's batting was depleted by injury in 1968, Dexter returned to play for Sussex and made an immediate impact, scoring 203 against Kent at Hastings in his first innings. He was then selected for the last two Tests against the Australians.

He scored only 97 runs in his four innings, but the excitement his return caused further illustrated the great loss English cricket suffered when 'Lord Ted' retired from the first-class game. Cricket, especially in the 1960s, could ill-afford to lose one of its most dynamic characters.

He joined a Sunday newspaper as a working journalist, also commentating incisively on television. It was hardly surprising that someone with such natural talent should be successful in a new field. One always felt that whatever task Ted Dexter put his mind to he would perform it with flair.

## DEXTER Edward Ralph

Teams: Cambridge University, Sussex, and England

| Test series | | Tests | Runs | 100s | Average |
|---|---|---|---|---|---|
| 1958 | v New Zealand | 1 | 52 | — | 52.00 |
| 1958-59 | in Australia | 2 | 18 | — | 4.50 |
| 1958-59 | in New Zealand | 2 | 142 | 1 | 71.00 |
| 1959 | v India | 2 | 58 | — | 19.33 |
| 1959-60 | in West Indies | 5 | 526 | 2 | 65.75 |
| 1960 | v South Africa | 5 | 241 | — | 26.77 |
| 1961 | v Australia | 5 | 378 | 1 | 42.00 |
| 1961-62 | in Pakistan | 3* | 303 | 1 | 101.00 |
| 1961-62 | in India | 5* | 409 | 1 | 58.42 |
| 1962 | v Pakistan | 5† | 446 | 1 | 89.20 |
| 1962-63 | in Australia | 5* | 481 | — | 48.10 |
| 1962-63 | in New Zealand | 3* | 84 | — | 28.00 |
| 1963 | v West Indies | 5* | 340 | — | 34.00 |
| 1964 | v Australia | 5* | 384 | 1 | 48.00 |
| 1964-65 | in South Africa | 5 | 344 | 1 | 57.33 |
| 1965 | v New Zealand | 2 | 199 | — | 99.50 |
| 1968 | v Australia | 2 | 97 | — | 24.25 |
| Total | | 62 | 4,502 | 9 | 47.89 |

Career runs: 21,093 Average: 40.79
Highest Test and career score: 205 v Pakistan, Karachi, 1961-62
Career wickets: 419 Average: 29.90
Best career bowling: 7-24, Sussex v Middlesex, Hove, 1960

*Captain  †Captain in four Tests

1 Benaud bowled by Dexter for 2 in the fourth Test of the 1961 series. But the Australian captain gained revenge in the England second innings, bowling Dexter for 76 when he was in full flight and taking England to what seemed at the time an easy victory. Instead, with Dexter's dismissal, England collapsed and Australia won. Great rivals, Dexter and Benaud were two of cricket's outstanding personalities in the early 1960s. 2 Dexter drives Ken Mackay through cover in the first Test of the 1961 series. In a glorious display of batting, he scored 180 in England's second innings, hitting 31 boundaries, many of which came from his powerful driving.

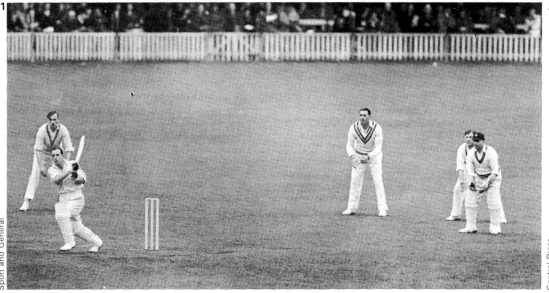

# Edrich

Bill (1916-    )

In 1934 a young cricketer made his debut for Norfolk in the Minor Counties championship. Thirty-five years later, in 1969, he was back playing for them. During that 35 years, though, Bill Edrich had gained fame as one half of the Compton-Edrich partnership that devasted bowling for Middlesex and England immediately after World War II.

Born at Lingwood in Norfolk, Edrich was also a good footballer, playing briefly for Tottenham Hotspur. But it was as a professional cricketer that he established himself at an early age. Qualifying for Middlesex in the 1937 season, he came on the county scene as his illustrious predecessor, Patsy Hendren, was in his last season and as another future giant, Denis Compton, was just starting out.

Though lacking the genius or the range of Compton, Edrich had other qualities—courage, fearlessness, resolution in adversity—that imprinted themselves on the imagination of the cricket public. And, unlike Compton, who had moments of vulnerability early in an innings, Edrich seemed merely to carry on where he had left off in the previous one. He was an especially fine player on bad pitches. Sturdily built, he was short of inches and yet when a fast bowler was imperilling the batsmen's existence, he seemed to relish it. A brave hooker and a quick cutter, he was particularly adept at the pulled drive. It was not a classic or attractive method, but allied to his pugnacious temperament it was good to watch and few would dispute its effectiveness.

In only his second full season for Middlesex, he joined the select group of batsmen who have made 1,000 runs before the end of May, and he played in four Tests against Bradman's 1938 Australians. But he met with little

success, and during both that series and the subsequent tour of South Africa, the selectors were often criticized for their persistence in picking him. However, in the last Test in South Africa—the notorious 'timeless' Test in Durban—he made 219 in the second innings. And then after the war the selectors' faith was handsomely justified.

Edrich returned to Middlesex after distinguished service in the RAF in which he won the DFC as a bomber pilot. He played only once against India in 1946, but was one of the successes of the 1946-47 tour of Australia, after which he turned amateur.

His partnerships with Compton in 1947, for Middlesex in their championship-winning year and for England against South Africa, are a legend. Among the most remarkable were an unbroken stand of 287 in $2\frac{3}{4}$ hours against Surrey at the Oval, another stand of 277 in 130 minutes at Leicester, and 370 in the Lord's Test. At Leicester they opened the second innings with 66 runs needed in 25 minutes and they made them with seven minutes to spare. In that season Edrich made 3,539 runs, an aggregate exceeded in cricket history only by Denis Compton (in that same year).

Edrich did not often approach the golden form in later seasons and was not chosen to go to Australia in 1950-51. But four years later, with England short of opening batsmen, he was picked as a tough, seasoned warrior who would not be overcome by the big occasion. As such, he did a useful job, although he never recaptured the fluency of former days.

In his heyday Edrich had been a fast bowler, who from a few yards run and with a slinging action worked up surprising pace and took some useful wickets. In later years, he acquired a happy touch as joint-captain of Middlesex, with Compton, for two seasons and as captain from 1953 to 1957.

**EDRICH William John**

Teams: Middlesex and England

| Test series | | Tests | Runs | 100s | Average | Wkts | Average |
|---|---|---|---|---|---|---|---|
| 1938 | v Australia | 4 | 67 | — | 11.16 | 4 | 34.75 |
| 1938-39 | in South Africa | 5 | 240 | 1 | 40.00 | 2 | 77.00 |
| 1946 | v India | 1 | — | — | — | 4 | 17.00 |
| 1946-47 | in Australia | 5 | 462 | 1 | 46.20 | 9 | 53.66 |
| 1946-47 | in New Zealand | 1 | 42 | — | 42.00 | 1 | 35.00 |
| 1947 | v South Africa | 4 | 552 | 2 | 110.40 | 16 | 23.12 |
| 1948 | v Australia | 5 | 319 | 1 | 31.90 | 3 | 79.33 |
| 1949 | v New Zealand | 4 | 324 | 1 | 54.00 | 2 | 48.50 |
| 1950 | v West Indies | 2 | 94 | — | 23.50 | 0 | — |
| 1953 | v Australia | 3 | 156 | — | 39.00 | — | — |
| 1954 | v Pakistan | 1 | 4 | — | 4.00 | — | — |
| 1954-55 | in Australia | 4 | 180 | — | 22.50 | 0 | — |
| Total | | 39 | 2,440 | 6 | 40.00 | 41 | 41.29 |

**Career runs:** 36,965 *Average:* 42.39
**Highest Test score:** 219 v South Africa, Durban, 1938-39
**Highest career score:** 267*, Middlesex v Northamptonshire, Northampton, 1947
**Career wickets:** 479 *Average:* 33.31
**Best Test bowling:** 4-68 v India, Oval, 1946
**Best career bowling:** 7-48, Middlesex v Worcestershire, Worcester, 1946

*not out

**1** Bill Edrich displays fine batting form in 1947—his finest season. **2** Edrich and Denis Compton—their partnerships for Middlesex and England are legend. **3** Edrich drives another four against South Africa in the 1947 series.

**1** The umpire takes evasive
action as John Edrich sends
a ball from Brian Yuile for
four. This match, the third
Test against New Zealand in
1965, was a personal triumph
for Edrich. Not selected for
the MCC side that toured
South Africa in 1964-65 and
ignored by the selectors for
the first two Tests, he made
an impressive comeback to the
Test arena by scoring 310
not out, so becoming only the
eighth batsman in the history
of Test cricket to score more
than 300. And as New Zealand
were forced to follow on, he
had the unusual distinction
of taking an active part in
the whole match. **2** Edrich
plays the ball square of the
wicket. One of his favourite
strokes, it has brought him
countless runs. **3** Edrich
goes up on his toes to play
a short-pitched ball from
Graham McKenzie in the final
Test of the 1968 series
against Australia. In seven
and three-quarter hours, he
scored 164 to set England on
the road to victory.
**4** Going down the wicket,
Edrich drives for four in his
innings of 115 against New
Zealand at Lord's in 1969.

# Edrich

## John Hugh (1937-    )

Tenacious, courageous and totally phlegmatic, John Edrich's left-handed batting served England loyally over ten years and 59 Tests. He had a particular liking for Australian bowling, making six centuries and scoring almost 2,000 runs in his 24 Tests against them.

A left-handed opening batsman who will bat number three with equal success, he tends to restrict himself to a few highly profitable strokes until he is thoroughly established. He misses little on or outside his legs, and off either back or front foot he scores many runs square of cover-point. Small and sturdily built, he is no classical stylist, but he has worked out a method of batting that is safer than it often looks and that, with his great resolution, serves him and his side well. And however vulnerable his small frame may make him look against fast bowling, he has met the best in the world successfully. In fact, any lack of success has usually been on slow pitches, such as those in Pakistan, where he has sometin.es got himself out trying to shake off the shackles that spinners can cast on the batsmen in those conditions.

A cousin of the former England and Middlesex batsman Bill Edrich, John left Norfolk for London some 20 years after his famed relation. But rather than go to Middlesex, he chose Surrey, where he had a better chance of standing on his own feet. After two years' national service, he played once in the championship in 1958, and then in 1959, his first full season, he made 1,799 runs, including a century in each innings of the second championship match of his career. This, moreover, was the first time he had opened an innings.

But then a broken finger slowed up his development, and it was 1963 before he played in his first Test, against West Indies. He went to India with M. J. K. Smith's MCC team that winter, but was one of many taken ill there, and it was not until his innings of 120 against Australia in the second Test at Lord's in 1964 that he established himself as a Test batsman. Yet despite this fine innings he was dropped for the final Test of the series and then left out of the MCC side that went to South Africa in 1964-65. But in 1965 he hit back with astonishing success.

From early June he played successive innings of 139 against the New Zealanders; 121 not out v Oxford University; 205 not out v Gloucestershire; 55 v Kent; 96 v Essex; 188 v Northamptonshire; 92 and 105 v Yorkshire—on a bad pitch at Bradford; and 310 not out in the Leeds Test against New Zealand. At this time he was using the pulled drive with great effect and was a prodigious hitter of sixes.

But then the run ended. In the first Test against South Africa, at Lord's, he was hit on the head by a ball bowled by Peter Pollock, and it was some time before he was fully fit. The valuable innings he played in Australia that winter, 109 in the second Test, 103 in the third, and 85 in the fifth—all at number three—were compiled in the more patient, controlled method with which he has been remarkably consistent since.

In 1969 when England lost, for various reasons, the bulk of her experienced batting—Ken Barrington, Colin Milburn, Colin Cowdrey, and Tom Graveney—there was still Edrich. He illustrated his pre-eminence by finishing the season far ahead of the field on top of the first-class averages, having made 2,238 runs at an average of 69.93. And among his eight centuries were two more in Tests—115 at Lord's and 155 at Trent Bridge and both against New Zealand.

He enjoyed a fine tour of Australia in 1970-71, but his consistent form then deserted him. In 1973, he was appointed captain of Surrey and his future playing career seemed to lie more in county rather than Test cricket.

5 Though he played in all five Tests against Australia in 1972. Edrich failed to make on fifty. This must have come as some relief to the Australians as he had shown an appetite for their bowling through the sixties.

# Grace

William Gilbert
(1848-1915)

No cricketer before or since has dominated the world of cricket as W. G. Grace did for nearly 40 years from the middle of the 1860s. In fact, he was said to be the most easily recognized figure in England along with the Prime Minister, William Ewart Gladstone. Tall, heavily built, and, from an early age, heavily bearded, W. G. (or 'The Doctor' as he was later called) was not only an all-round cricketer of great skill whose achievements in an unusually long career broke most of the records of the day but was also a man of formidable and striking personality who in his own time became a legend of dictatorial 'gamesmanship' blended with gruff kindliness.

A precocious boy in the 1860s, he played for the Gentlemen in the big match of the year when only just 17, and he linked the 'disorganized' cricket of those early years with the relatively modern times at the turn of the century of Fry, Ranji, Test matches, and the county championship. He retained his form so well that in 1895 he enjoyed one of his best seasons, becoming the first batsman ever to make 1,000 runs in May. And this was a few weeks short of his 47th birthday.

W. G.'s cricket background is well recorded. He was born the fourth of five sons to Dr Henry Grace and his wife Martha who lived near Bristol. His father was an enthusiastic cricketer but a hard-working doctor, and it was the redoubtable Mrs Grace who was the inspiration of the boys' cricket. Her enthusiasm and her considerable knowledge of the game were passed on in long hours in the family garden to the three youngest brothers of the five.

The third son of the five, Edward, was the first to win fame. Later he became generally known as 'The Coroner', because of his chosen occupation, and if there had been no W. G., he would have been the leading all-round cricketer of his time. He opened the innings with W. G. in the first Test match played in England in 1880. Their younger brother G. F., who died a fortnight later aged 30, was also in the side.

A tall, strong youth, W. G. made his first appearance in the top class in 1865 when he opened the innings for the Gentlemen at Lord's, making 34 in the second innings, and that same year he took seven wickets at the Oval for the Gentlemen. For some time previously, the Gentlemen and Players fixture had been so one-sided that on some occasions professionals were loaned to the Gentlemen to balance the match. But with the coming of W. G. it all changed. It was 20 years before

the Players won again at Lord's, and in the next 50 matches played between the sides on various grounds after W. G.'s arrival, they won only 7 while the Gentlemen won 31. W. G. was always at his best in this fixture, making 15 of his 126 centuries for the Gentlemen as well as taking 271 wickets for them with his rather round-arm, cleverly varied slow bowling. However, as W. G. did not qualify as a doctor until he was 31, there is little doubt that he received some money through his cricket and was not an amateur in the purest sense of the term.

As a batsman, he was entirely sound both in judgement of length and in execution of stroke. He was equally proficient off back foot and front, and was a masterly player of fast bowling, which on some of the rough pitches of the day could terrorize many able batsmen. And his record of 126 centuries stood until 1925 when Jack Hobbs passed it.

W. G.'s pre-eminence in the 1870s, soon after he and his family had played a big part in founding the Gloucestershire County Cricket Club, is evident from the fact that in 1871, one of his great years, he made 2,736 runs, an unheard of number, and averaged 78. The next highest average was the 34 of a very fine batsman, Richard Daft. In another season, 1876, he was almost as successful. Within eight days in August he made 344 against Kent, 177 against Nottinghamshire, and 318 not out against Yorkshire. A month later, he played what must have been one of his most remarkable innings—400 not out against '22 of Grimsby', a side composed on 22 players, all in the field on an outfield reported as being slow.

In 1872, Grace went on a tour to Canada and took a side to Australia in 1873-74. Yet surprisingly, perhaps, he was to go to Australia only once more, 18 years later. Meanwhile he captained Gloucestershire as he was to do for the first 29 years of their history, and played for England from the first home Test, in which he made 152. In 1886, he made 170 against Australia at the Oval, a score not exceeded in a Test match in England for 35 years. In 1888, he captained England for the first time and remained captain in England, and on the 1891-92 tour of Australia, until after the first Test of 1899, when he was replaced by A. C. MacLaren. By then, though, he was nearly 51 and finding his immobility in the field a tiresome handicap.

His record against Australia

**W. G. Grace, as portrayed by the cartoonist Spy. A skilful all-rounder, W.G., or 'The Doctor' as he was also known, was the outstanding personality in English cricket for nearly 40 years, becoming a legend in his own lifetime.**

Mary Evans

was good without ever being as exceptional as that in other cricket, but his best days were probably before Test cricket started. The glorious year of 1895, however, revealed him, to the general amazement, almost as all-conquering as ever. His 1,000 runs in May were in fact made in 22 days from the 9th to the 30th, and later that year he made his 100th century in an innings of 288 against Somerset. Against Kent at Gravesend, he was on the field throughout the three days, scoring 257 and 73 not out. It was little wonder that a shilling testimonial for W. G. that year produced £9,000.

In 1899 there was a sad episode —the Doctor's break with Gloucestershire. Enthusiasts in London started the London County Club to play near the Crystal Palace and W. G. accepted their invitation to become manager. He intended apparently to continue playing for Gloucestershire as well, but the Gloucestershire committee disapproved, and consequently he played solely for London County until 1904 when the venture died for financial reasons. He was still good enough to make 166 on the day after his 56th birthday and to score 150 runs and take 6 wickets against his native Gloucestershire. And it was while he was at the Crystal Palace with London County that W. G., an ardent bowls enthusiast as well, formed the London

County Bowling Club and played an important part in the formation of the English Bowling Association in 1903.

After 1904 his first-class cricket was played mainly for MCC and the Gentlemen, for whom he made 74 at the age of 58. He would doubtless have gone on making runs but for his cumbersomeness in the field. Yet in spite of this, his zest for cricket seems to have remained undulled and he made 69 not out for Eltham against Grove Park in July 1914—in his last match, 10 days before the outbreak of World War I. The next year he died, and was mourned far outside the world of cricket, for he had been a truly national figure.

### GRACE William Gilbert

**Teams:** Gloucestershire, London County, and England

| Test series | | Tests | Runs | 100s | Average | Wkts | Average |
|---|---|---|---|---|---|---|---|
| 1880 | v Australia | 1 | 161 | 1 | 161.00 | 3 | 22.66 |
| 1882 | v Australia | 1 | 36 | — | 18.00 | — | — |
| 1884 | v Australia | 3 | 72 | — | 18.00 | 3 | 12.66 |
| 1886 | v Australia | 3 | 200 | 1 | 50.00 | 1 | 22.00 |
| 1888 | v Australia | 3* | 73 | — | 18.25 | — | — |
| 1890 | v Australia | 2* | 91 | — | 30.33 | 2 | 6.00 |
| 1891-92 | in Australia | 3* | 164 | — | 32.80 | 0 | — |
| 1893 | v Australia | 2* | 153 | — | 51.00 | — | — |
| 1896 | v Australia | 3* | 119 | — | 19.83 | 0 | — |
| 1899 | v Australia | 1* | 29 | — | 14.50 | 0 | — |
| Total | | 22 | 1,098 | 2 | 32.29 | 9 | 26.22 |

**Career runs:** 54,904 *Average:* 39.52
**Highest Test score:** 170 v Australia, Oval, 1886
**Highest career score:** 344, MCC v Kent, Canterbury, 1876
**Career wickets:** 2,876 *Average:* 17.92
**Best Test bowling:** 2-12 v Australia, Lord's, 1890
**Best career bowling:** 10-49, MCC v Oxford University, Oxford, 1886

\* Captain (in two Tests in 1888)

**1** W. G.'s stature as a national figure is reflected in a *Punch* cartoon on the weather in 1898. The caption reads: 'Ninety in the shade—not out'; and umpire Punch is saying to W. G. Sol: 'By Jove, old man, you've "beaten the record" *this* time and no mistake!' **2** W. G. Grace with his younger brother G. F. and the Surrey bowler James Southerton in 1873. Another brother, E. M., was in the same England team, in 1880, as W. G. and G. F. But only W. G. went on to play in more Tests. **3** W. G. takes an interest in the Worcester Park beagles. **4** Grace scored just under 55,000 runs and took 2,876 wickets in his career.

# Grout

## Arthur Theodore Wallace (1927-1968)

Between 1957 and 1965 Wally Grout kept wicket for Australia in 51 Test matches, the last of them less than three years before his much lamented death through heart failure. Short and sturdily built, he was very much a player for the big occasion and very few chances escaped him in a Test match. His bag of 187 victims, 163 caught and 24 stumped, is an astonishing one for 51 Tests, and is exceeded only by Godfrey Evans' 219 from 91 Tests.

Though he first played for Queensland in 1946-47, he was second string to Don Tallon and did not win a regular place in the State side until Tallon's retirement following the 1953 tour of England. Gil Langley succeeded Tallon as the Australian wicket-keeper though, and it was not until the tour of South Africa in 1957-58 that Grout, then 30, played in his first Test. Once in the side, he was not to be dislodged, even though throughout his Test career Australia had an outstanding second wicket-keeper in Barry Jarman, who was a better batsman. Grout's own batting, however, was far from negligible and he could be difficult to dislodge in a crisis. He made 74 against England at Melbourne in 1958-59 but his most important innings was probably his 37 at Leeds in 1964. His ninth wicket stand of 89 with Peter Burge gave Australia a first innings lead that enabled them to win the only finished Test of the series.

In his first Test he held six catches in an innings, four of them off Alan Davidson, who provided him with many chances in the early years of his Test career. This number has been equalled but never exceeded in Test cricket. However, his feat of taking eight catches in an innings for Queensland against Western Australia in 1959-60 was still without parallel 10 years later.

Grout is especially remembered in England for a characteristically quick and fair act during the first Test of 1964 at Trent Bridge. One of the England opening batsmen, Titmus, had collided with the bowler, Hawke, and had been knocked over. The ball was thrown to Grout, who could have broken the wicket and run Titmus out at leisure, but having seen what had happened, he allowed the batsman to reach the crease.

**1 As ever Australia's Wally Grout takes the ball cleanly. He missed few chances in his 51 Test Matches.**

*Melbourne Herald*

*Press Association*

**2 For once Grout is just beaten in his attempt to run out the West Indian fast bowler Wesley Hall. The Australian wicket-keeper did not play his first Test until he was 30, on the tour of South Africa in 1957-58. But once he won his place, he hung on to it with the same determination that he clung on to his spectacular diving catches. His total of 187 Test victims is second only to the Test record of 219 held by England's Godfrey Evans, who took 91 Tests to reach that total.**

## GROUT Arthur Theodore Wallace

**Teams:** Queensland and Australia

| Test series | Tests | Runs | Average | Catches | Stumpings |
|---|---|---|---|---|---|
| 1957-58 in South Africa | 5 | 93 | 18.60 | 16 | 3 |
| 1958-59 v England | 5 | 119 | 19.83 | 17 | 3 |
| 1959-60 in Pakistan | 3 | 98 | 49.00 | 8 | 4 |
| 1959-60 in India | 4 | 147 | 36.75 | 14 | 2 |
| 1960-61 v West Indies | 5 | 72 | 8.00 | 20 | 3 |
| 1961 in England | 5 | 47 | 7.83 | 20 | 1 |
| 1962-63 v England | 2 | 17 | — | 7 | 2 |
| 1963-64 v South Africa | 5 | 84 | 10.50 | 13 | 1 |
| 1964 in England | 5 | 84 | 16.80 | 10 | 0 |
| 1964-65 in India | 1 | 12 | 6.00 | 4 | 0 |
| 1964-65 in Pakistan | 1 | 0 | 0.00 | 5 | 0 |
| 1964-65 in West Indies | 5 | 83 | 13.83 | 14 | 4 |
| 1965-66 v England | 5 | 34 | 6.80 | 15 | 1 |
| Total | 51 | 890 | 15.09 | 163 | 24 |

**Career runs:** 5,167 *Average:* 22.56
**Highest Test score:** 74 v England, Melbourne, 1958-59
**Highest career score:** 119, Queensland v South Australia, Brisbane, 1960-61
**Career dismissals:** 586, *Catches,* 472 *Stumpings:* 114
**Best Test wicketkeeping:** 8 dismissals (6 ct 2 st) in match, v Pakistan, Lahore, 1959-60
8 dismissals (all ct) in match, v England, Lord's 1961
**Best career wicketkeeping:** 8 dismissals (all ct) in innings, Queensland v Western Australia, Brisbane, 1959-60

Central Press

Popperfoto

# Hall

## Wesley Winfield
## (1937-    )

When tall, gangling Wes Hall first went to England with John Goddard's West Indies team in 1957, he was not particularly successful, taking only 27 wickets and not playing in a Test match. But he was then only 19, and had a superb action for a fast bowler. Within two years he had profited from the experience gained in England and was quickly becoming the best fast bowler in the world, a position which he maintained for much of the early 1960s. His run, like that of other fast bowlers, could be criticized as over-long and contributing to a slow over-rate, but his fluent, lissom action, his accelerating run-up to the wicket, his strength, stamina, and speed made him exciting to watch.

Born in Bridgetown, Barbados —much later he moved to Trinidad as a coach—Wes Hall first played as a batsman-wicket-keeper. But by the time he went to England his potential as a fast bowler was widely acknowledged and his batting consisted mostly of a few whirlwind minutes later in the innings.

In 1958-59 he established himself by taking 46 Test wickets during the tour of India and Pakistan, including a hat-trick at Lahore. He followed with

22 wickets against Peter May's England team in the West Indies and 21 against Australia in the famous series of 1960-61. For a while he played for Queensland in the Sheffield Shield as well as in the Lancashire League for Accrington, and he reached the peak of his fame in England in 1963 with the controversial Charlie Griffith as his partner.

While Hall's action was a joy to watch, Griffith's at times seemed to many people to be outside the law and it is a strange thought that Hall, undoubtedly the finer bowler of the two, does not appear in *Wisden* as a Cricketer of the Year. Griffith was honoured in 1963 when he took 32 wickets, twice as many as Hall, though clearly he could scarcely have achieved so much without his great partner. And it may be significant that when Hall and Griffith returned to England in 1966 on another successful tour and Griffith's action was closely watched, Hall took more wickets. By then, however, he was beginning to show signs of decline. These became more evident during MCC's tour of the West Indies in 1968, and he played in only two Tests on the tour of Australia a year later.

One of Hall's most remarkable bowling performances was at Lord's in 1963 on the last day of a memorable second Test. He bowled throughout the 3 hours 20 minutes play possible, taking

The classic action of West Indies fast bowler Wes Hall caught (1) just before delivery and (2) just after. He was one of the fastest and most ferocious bowlers in the world in the 1960s, and with Charlie Griffith produced a Test spearhead that no other country could rival at that time.

4-93, and when play finished, England, with their last batsmen in, still needed six runs for victory. In this match, as at other times, he bowled short, and there were moments when his onslaught with Griffith on lively pitches was not pleasant to watch and considerably less fun to face.

But he was an immensely likeable personality with something of the clown about him.

This was especially so in his batting, though some of his performances were of widely contrasting styles. In 1963 he made a spectacular 102 not out against Cambridge University in 65 minutes. But in 1968 in Trinidad, he batted throughout the last two hours with Gary Sobers to save the first Test against England and he revealed for once a stalwart defence.

| HALL Wesley Winfield | | | |
|---|---|---|---|
| **Teams:** Barbados, Queensland, and West Indies | | | |
| Test series | Tests | Wkts | Average |
| 1958-59 in India | 5 | 30 | 17.66 |
| 1958-59 in Pakistan | 3 | 16 | 17.93 |
| 1959-60 v England | 5 | 22 | 30.86 |
| 1960-61 in Australia | 5 | 21 | 29.33 |
| 1961-62 v India | 5 | 27 | 15.74 |
| 1963    in England | 5 | 16 | 33.37 |
| 1964-65 v Australia | 5 | 16 | 28.37 |
| 1966    in England | 5 | 18 | 30.83 |
| 1966-67 in India | 3 | 8 | 33.25 |
| 1967-68 v England | 4 | 9 | 39.22 |
| 1968-69 in Australia | 2 | 8 | 40.62 |
| 1968-69 in New Zealand | 1 | 1 | 42.00 |
| Total | 48 | 192 | 26.38 |

**Career wickets:** 546 *Average:* 26.13
**Best Test bowling:** 7-69 v England, Kingston, 1959-60
**Best career bowling:** 7-51, West Indies v Glamorgan, Swansea, 1963
**Highest Test score:** 50* v India, Port of Spain, 1961-62
                        50 v Australia, Brisbane, 1969-61
**Highest career score:** 102*, West Indies v Cambridge University, Cambridge, 1963

*Not out. Career records to the end of the 1972-73 season

# Hammond

## Walter Reginald
## (1903-1965)

Walter Hammond ranks as one of the greatest cricketers in the history of the game. Mostly thought of as a batsman, he was, however, also a lively and intelligent fast-medium bowler, who took 83 Test wickets, and one of the greatest slip-fielders of his time.

Hammond's first-class career for Gloucestershire and England fell almost entirely between the two world wars. It followed an unusual course, for his first reputation was as a hitter, albeit a polished one. But it was soon clear he was more than that, and he went on an MCC tour to the West Indies early in 1926. There, however, he caught a bug which prevented him from playing during the 1926 season, and it was not until the next year that his talent was fulfilled.

Few players have returned to the game after illness so sensationally. He made 1,000 runs in May and 2,969 in the season, averaging nearly 70. In one famous innings at Old Trafford, he scored 187 in three hours off bowling that included the great Australian speed merchant McDonald and which was to win Lancashire the championship that year. This was in the second innings; in the first he had made 99. In 1927-28 he toured South Africa where he played in the first of his 85 Test matches.

Hammond was now a batsman of impressive command, a superbly balanced athlete, quick and powerful at the crease, with a classical off-drive. The adventure of his youth had been curbed and he had a more considered approach to batting that was in contrast to that of a few years before. He seldom hooked now.

In 1928-29, when he was still only 25, he turned on the Australians, who had been spared a first meeting with him in 1926 by his illness. In the series he made 905 runs, an aggregate exceeded only by Don Bradman's 974 in 1930. Twice he passed 200, and in the fourth Test at Adelaide, which England won by 12 runs, he made 119 not out and 177.

His feats in the next 10 years were sometimes overshadowed by those of his great contemporary, Bradman, but they nevertheless included many superb innings. Of his 22 Test hundreds, 9 were against Australia, 6 against South Africa, and 4 against New Zealand. One of the latter—his 336 not out at Auckland in only $5\frac{1}{4}$ hours—remained the highest innings in Test cricket until Len Hutton's 364 at the Oval in 1938.

He went through a relatively unsuccessful period in Test cricket in the early 1930s, but he was back at his best in 1936, scoring 167 and 217 against India. And with G. O. Allen's team in Australia in 1936-37 he made 231 not out at Sydney. In 1938 he turned amateur and was appointed captain

**Although Walter Hammond will always be remembered as one of cricket's great batsmen, he was also a first-class all-rounder, a fine fast-medium bowler with 83 Test victims, and a great slip fielder.**

| HAMMOND Walter Reginald | | | | | | |
|---|---|---|---|---|---|---|
| **Teams:** Gloucestershire and England | | | | | | |
| **Test series** | **Tests** | **Runs** | **100s** | **Average** | **Wkts** | **Average** |
| 1927-28 in South Africa | 5 | 321 | — | 40.12 | 15 | 26.60 |
| 1928 v West Indies | 3 | 111 | — | 37.00 | 3 | 34.33 |
| 1928-29 in Australia | 5 | 905 | 4 | 113.12 | 5 | 57.40 |
| 1929 v South Africa | 4 | 352 | 2 | 58.66 | 1 | 95.00 |
| 1930 v Australia | 5 | 306 | 1 | 34.00 | 5 | 60.40 |
| 1930-31 in South Africa | 5 | 517 | 1 | 64.62 | 9 | 26.66 |
| 1931 v New Zealand | 3 | 169 | 1 | 56.33 | 2 | 34.00 |
| 1932 v India | 1 | 47 | — | 23.50 | 3 | 8.00 |
| 1932-33 in Australia | 5 | 440 | 2 | 55.00 | 9 | 32.33 |
| 1932-33 in New Zealand | 2 | 563 | 2 | 563.00 | 0 | — |
| 1933 v West Indies | 3 | 74 | — | 24.66 | 0 | — |
| 1934 v Australia | 5 | 162 | 1 | 20.25 | 5 | 72.80 |
| 1934-35 in West Indies | 4 | 175 | 1 | 25.00 | 0 | — |
| 1935 v South Africa | 5 | 389 | — | 64.83 | 6 | 24.33 |
| 1936 v India | 2 | 389 | 2 | 194.50 | 1 | 94.00 |
| 1936-37 in Australia | 5 | 468 | 1 | 58.50 | 12 | 25.08 |
| 1937 v New Zealand | 3 | 204 | 1 | 51.00 | 4 | 25.25 |
| 1938 v Australia | 4† | 403 | 1 | 67.16 | 0 | — |
| 1938-39 in South Africa | 5† | 609 | 3 | 87.00 | 3 | 53.66 |
| 1939 v West Indies | 3† | 279 | 1 | 55.80 | – | — |
| 1946 v India | 3† | 119 | — | 39.66 | 0 | — |
| 1946-47 in Australia | 4† | 168 | — | 21.00 | – | — |
| 1946-47 in New Zealand | 1† | 79 | — | 79.00 | – | — |
| Total | 85 | 7,249 | 22 | 58.45 | 83 | 37.83 |

**Career runs:** 50,551    *Average:* 56.10
**Highest Test and career score:** 336* v New Zealand, Auckland, 1932-33
**Career wickets:** 732    *Average:* 30.58
**Best Test bowling:** 5-36 v South Africa, Johannesburg, 1927-28
**Best career bowling:** 9-23, Gloucestershire v Worcestershire, Cheltenham, 1928

*Not out    †Captain

Sport and General

Central Press

of England in that summer's series against Australia. He made 240 in the Lord's Test and led England to the victory that squared the series at the Oval, though he himself scored only 59 of England's mammoth 903-7. He led MCC in South Africa in 1938-39 and made three centuries, including 140 in the last innings of the famous timeless Test at Durban when England made 654-5 and the match was left unfinished after 10 days.

After service in the RAF, much of it in South Africa, Hammond returned to Gloucestershire for the 1946 season, and at the age of 43 headed the first-class averages with 84.90. He was the obvious choice for the captaincy in Australia that winter, but his talents at last failed him. Nor, as a rather aloof and silent, unbending figure, was he a successful captain of a side of much younger men, and apart from the odd match for Gloucestershire he did not play

again. He went to live in South Africa, and remained cut off from English cricket until, a few months before his death, he became a frequent and welcome visitor to the headquarters of M. J. K. Smith's MCC team when they were playing in Durban in 1964-65.

Some of the many records Walter Hammond set up were still standing at the start of the 1970s: his tally of 78 catches in the 1928 season and his 10 in a match—two more than any other fielder. His record of 7,249 runs remained for almost 25 year suntil finally beaten by Colin Cowdrey, a player of equal grace and power in the making of strokes. Among English batsmen, only Hobbs has made more runs against Australia, and only Hobbs and Hendren have made more first-class hundreds. But it was the manner in which most of them were made, even more than the runs themselves, for which Hammond is remembered.

*Below,* **Neil Harvey, one of the world's greatest left-handed batsmen after World War II, makes a typical forcing stroke. He came into the Australian side as an 18-year old on the 1947-48 tour of India and he held his place until his retirement in 1963. His 6,149 Test runs make him the second most prolific Australian to Don Bradman.**

*Above* **Wally Hammond hits a boundary off Clarke in the Test against West Indies at Manchester in the last pre-war series in 1939. During the war, Hammond served in the R.A.F. and spent much of that time in South Africa. He developed a great affection for the country and after a few years in post-war cricket he retired to live there. His total of 7,249 runs in Test Matches was for over twenty years the largest in the history of the international game until first beaten by Colin Cowdrey and then by Garfield Sobers. Only Jack Hobbs, Frank Woolley, Patsy Hendren, Philip Mead and W. G. Grace scored more runs in first-class cricket and all five of them played more innings and averaged less per innings.**
**Hammond's total of 167 centuries in the first-class game is the third highest in history—behind the 197 of Jack Hobbs and the 170 of Patsy Hendren. Had it not been for the Second World War, he must have threatened Hobbs' record. On seven separate occasions he struck two hundreds in a match, the only batsman to do so, and he averaged a century just under once every five visits to the crease.**
**As a superbly gifted stroke-maker, his talents lay particularly on the off-side of the wicket. A driver in the classic mould, he was equally forceful off the back foot in front of and behind the wicket. He was more limited on the on-side, though he had a liking for the sweep which he played precisely and with very little risk.**

# Harvey
## Robert Neil (1928-    )

Until his retirement in 1963, Neil Harvey was the outstanding batsman produced by Australia since World War II. A quick-footed left-hander, he was superbly equipped with strokes and possessed an ever-present urge to attack. He was also a fielder of the highest class, whether in the slips or moving like lightning in the covers—a not unexpected accomplishment of one who was also a successful baseball player.

One of the qualities that lifted him above the other leading Australian batsmen of his time was his skill on bad pitches. This

was especially apparent in England in the 1950s, and he was the most formidable adversary of the strong England bowling of those years. Harvey's playing career covered 17 years from 1946 to 1963, a long span for an Australian. However, he started unusually young. He was just 18 when he first played for Victoria—he was to move to New South Wales 12 years later in 1958—and he was only 19 when he went to England with Sir Donald Bradman's great 1948 side. Though he had played in the last two Test matches against India in the previous home season and had made 153 in the last, at Melbourne, in just over four hours with scarcely a mistake, he was inevitably looked on by many people in England as a hope for the future who would probably not find a place in this strong team of established players.

He did not play in the first three Tests, but he did in the fourth, and he joined the select band of Australians who have made a hundred in their first Test against England. It was, moreover, a brilliantly fluent innings of 112 made in just over three hours. This was the historic Test in which Australia scored 404-3 to win on the last day, and the young Harvey was at the crease with Bradman when the winning run was scored.

For the next 15 years Harvey was the mainstay of Australian batting, scoring more runs in Test matches than any other Australian except Bradman. In South Africa in 1949-50 he made 660 runs, (average 132) in Test matches, including four centuries, and broke all records for an Australian batsman in South Africa. It was here that his fine technique on bad pitches became evident, for in the third Test at Durban he played a remarkable innings of 151 not out on a crumbling pitch and won the match for Australia after they had been bowled out for 75 in the first innings and had been 59 for three in the second.

Three seasons later he scored 834 runs in the home series against South Africa, averaging 92.66. When he went to England in 1953 on the second of his four tours, he made 10 hundreds and scored over 2,000 runs. Only Bradman and McCabe had scored more than 2,000 runs in an English season previously.

In the next two series against England, in 1954-55 and 1956, his reputation continued to grow. He made 162 at Brisbane when Australia won their only victory against Len Hutton's team, and he played a masterly innings of 92 not out, exactly half the total, when Australia were going down to defeat before Tyson and Statham in the second Test. On the wet and often unpredictable pitches in England in 1956, his average of 19 may seem disastrous compared with the 90 of Peter May for England, but Australia had the worst of the pitches and were up against better bowling, and Harvey played two or three highly skilled innings in testing conditions.

He was less successful in South Africa in 1957-58 than on his first visit. But in 1958-59 he played a vital innings of 167 in a total of 308 which helped Australia to beat England in the second Test. And on his last visit to England, in 1961, he began with a hundred at Edgbaston in the first Test. In the second Test, at Lord's, he captained Australia for the only time, Richie Benaud being unable to play, and won a fine victory by five wickets. At Leeds, where Australia lost on a bad pitch, he was top scorer in each innings with 73 and 53.

Against Ted Dexter's England team in 1962-63, he was not at his best, and his 154 in the fourth Test, the last of his 21 Test hundreds, owed something to early dropped catches. However, he was still a force in Sheffield Shield cricket and made a characteristically vigorous 231 not out, the highest score of his career, in 5 hours for New South Wales against South Australia. At the end of the season, though, he announced his retirement, and in 1964 was awarded the MBE.

One of the most important parts of Harvey's make-up throughout his long career was the temperament that left him unruffled in the most unnerving situations. There is no stronger evidence of his flair for rising to the occasion than his record in his early days when, though lacking experience of the top class of cricket, he had a better record in it than he did in domestic cricket in Australia. Of his first 31 first-class hundreds, no less than 11 were in Test matches and only four were in the Sheffield Shield.

*Below right* **A characteristically wristy shot by Neil Harvey.**
*Below* **A rare moment of trouble for Harvey who scored 21 hundreds for Australia.**

Radio Times Hulton Picture Library

Sport & General

### HARVEY Robert Neil

**Teams:** Victoria, New South Wales, and Australia

| Test series | Tests | Runs | 100s | Average |
|---|---|---|---|---|
| 1947-48 v India | 2 | 166 | 1 | 83.00 |
| 1948 in England | 2 | 133 | 1 | 66.50 |
| 1949-50 in South Africa | 5 | 660 | 4 | 132.00 |
| 1950-51 v England | 5 | 362 | — | 40.22 |
| 1951-52 v West Indies | 5 | 261 | — | 26.10 |
| 1952-53 v South Africa | 5 | 834 | 4 | 92.66 |
| 1953 in England | 5 | 346 | 1 | 34.60 |
| 1954-55 v England | 5 | 354 | 1 | 44.25 |
| 1954-55 in West Indies | 5 | 650 | 3 | 108.33 |
| 1956 in England | 5 | 197 | — | 19.70 |
| 1956-57 in Pakistan | 1 | 6 | — | 3.00 |
| 1956-57 in India | 3 | 253 | 1 | 63.25 |
| 1957-58 in South Africa | 4 | 131 | — | 21.83 |
| 1958-59 v England | 5 | 291 | 1 | 48.50 |
| 1959-60 in Pakistan | 3 | 273 | — | 54.60 |
| 1959-60 in India | 5 | 356 | 2 | 50.85 |
| 1960-61 v West Indies | 4 | 143 | — | 17.87 |
| 1961 in England | 5† | 338 | 1 | 42.25 |
| 1962-63 v England | 5 | 395 | 1 | 39.50 |
| **Total** | **79** | **6,149** | **21** | **48.41** |

**Career runs:** 21,699 *Average:* 50.92
**Highest Test score:** 205 v South Africa, Melbourne, 1952-53
**Highest career score:** 231*, New South Wales v South Australia, Sydney, 1962-63

*Not out †Captain in one Test

# Hobbs

Sir John Berry
(1882-1963)

A complete batsman, classical in method, calm in temperament, and supremely efficient in execution, Jack Hobbs was the greatest batsman of his generation. He was known to his friends until his death as 'the Master', and roughly from the retirement of W. G. Grace to the hey-day of Don Bradman he was without doubt the world's most accomplished batsman. He made more hundreds —197—in first-class cricket than any other batsman, and it is a tribute to his skill that he made 98 of them after he reached 40, when most batsmen, certainly today, would have been considered past their best.

Hobbs went to Surrey and the Oval from Cambridge, and so followed in the path of Tom Hayward who, from 1905 until World War I, was to be his opening partner for Surrey and a strong influence upon him. He had to qualify by residence, but made an immediate impact when he began to play for the county in 1905. He was already 22, by which age both Grace and Bradman in their respective eras were breaking records.

'W. G.' did in fact captain the Gentlemen of England in the first match Hobbs played for Surrey and in which he made 88. Only two weeks later, in his first championship match, against Essex, he scored 155 and was given his county cap.

Hobbs' career for Surrey was to last for 30 historic years until 1934, and it was only four years before his retirement that he ceased to play for England. And even after his death in 1963, many of his records stood. As well as the 197 centuries, his aggregate of 61,237 runs was still the highest ever made, and his 316 not out against Middlesex in 1926 was the highest innings ever played at Lord's. His 266 not out at Scarborough in 1925 was the highest in the long history of the Gentlemen and Players match, and no one equalled his 16 centuries in the fixture.

During his career, he had four opening partners with whom he was especially successful— Hayward and Andy Sandham for Surrey, and Wilfred Rhodes and Herbert Sutcliffe for England. His 352 with Hayward against Warwickshire at the Oval in 1909 was their highest partnership together, and in 1907 they had shared in no less than four opening stands of over 100 within a week against Cambridge University and Middlesex, a feat without parallel.

The best remembered stand between Hobbs and Rhodes was their 323 at Melbourne against Australia in 1911-12, which, at the beginning of the 1970s, was

Press Association

still the highest ever made for the first wicket for England against Australia.

After World War I, Sandham succeeded Hayward, and with him Hobbs made 428 against Oxford University at the Oval in 1926. Altogether they shared in 63 stands of over 100. But it is probably Hobbs' opening partnerships with the Yorkshireman Herbert Sutcliffe that are best remembered. In 1924-25 they had three consecutive opening stands in Test matches of 157, 110, and 283. Seven times they exceeded 200 together, and on 26 occasions, (15 in Test matches), they passed 100.

The partnership of Hobbs and Sutcliffe was remarkable for their understanding of each other's running and their joint mastery of difficult pitches, such as that at the Oval in 1926 when England won back the Ashes last held before the war. At the start of the second innings they had to bat on a drying pitch, but they made 172 together, Hobbs, 100, coming through the worst of the difficulties and steering England to ultimate victory. In Melbourne three years later, another superb stand of 105 turned a possible defeat into victory in equally difficult conditions.

Hobbs' method had no outstanding idiosyncrasy. It was simple, graceful, and correct, based on a fine eye, a supreme judgement of length, the gift of timing, and an ability always to be in the right position. Like all the great players he was very effective off the back foot, and without appearing to bludgeon the bowler, he would dictate to

him and maintain a steady flow of scoring strokes. Slim and of medium height, he was also a brilliant fielder in the covers and in his early days a useful swing bowler. In South Africa in 1909-1910 he opened the bowling in three Tests.

Those who saw Hobbs on either side of World War I have said that maturity, while increasing his command, had taken away a little of the dashing side of his batting. But in the 1920s he stood supreme on all pitches and against all types of bowling, and when he was taken ill with appendicitis during the 1921 series against Australia, it was akin to a national disaster. He was amazingly consistent, never appearing to be out of form. In 1923 he passed 100 hundreds and advanced on W. G.'s record 126

*Above,* **Jack Hobbs scores the 100th run of his 126th century, at Taunton in 1925, to equal the record set by W. G. Grace.**

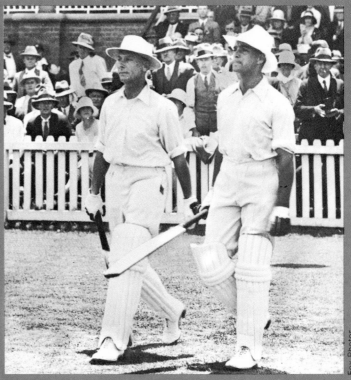

*Above,* **Hobbs (left) and Herbert Sutcliffe—a superb opening partnership that often set England on the road to victory.**

*Above,* **'The Master'. Hobbs' batting was simple, graceful, and correct, based on a fine eye, supreme judgement of length, and an ability always to be in the right position.**

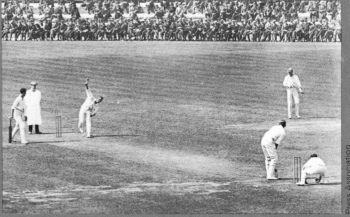

*Above,* **The first picture ever taken of Jack Hobbs bowling, in 1920 for Surrey against Oxford University. Ten years earlier, he had opened the bowling in three Tests against South Africa.**

amid a fervour of excitement. Each time he failed to make a hundred, he was said to have 'failed again'. He reached 125 with 12 hundreds in the early part of 1925, and was in tremendous form even for him, but the tension built up, and from July 25th to August 15th he and the cricket public waited. Eventually at Taunton against Somerset the 126th 100 was made, and in the second innings the 127th. He went on to make 16 in the season, a record that stood until Denis Compton beat it in 1947.

He went to Australia on five MCC tours and to South Africa twice, before World War I. Just as he had overlapped the Grace era in his youth, so he overlapped the Bradman era in 1930 when he played in his last series, at the age of 47. He started well with 78 and

74 in the first Test, which England won by 93 runs, but did not pass 50 again. The last of his 61 tests was the one at the Oval in which England made 405 in the first innings, Hobbs 47, and were beaten eventually by an innings.

In his last season, 1934, he played in only a few matches. He was in his 52nd year and entitled to treat gently what had been a sound but never a robust physique. The fluency of the strokes might have faded a little but the technique was still superb, and when asked by George Duckworth to play in his benefit match at Old Trafford, he went out and scored 116 and 51 not out. With Sandham once again, he put on 184. Lancashire were champions that year, and Hobbs' century was the only one scored against them in the championship.

## HOBBS John Berry

**Teams:** Surrey and England

| Test series | | Tests | Runs | 100s | Average |
|---|---|---|---|---|---|
| 1907-08 | in Australia | 4 | 302 | — | 43.14 |
| 1909 | v Australia | 3 | 132 | — | 26.40 |
| 1909-10 | in South Africa | 5 | 539 | 1 | 67.37 |
| 1911-12 | in Australia | 5 | 662 | 3 | 82.75 |
| 1912 | v Australia | 3 | 224 | 1 | 56.00 |
| 1912 | v South Africa | 3 | 163 | — | 40.75 |
| 1913-14 | in South Africa | 5 | 443 | — | 63.28 |
| 1920-21 | in Australia | 5 | 505 | 2 | 50.50 |
| 1921 | v Australia | 1 | — | — | — |
| 1924 | v South Africa | 4 | 355 | 1 | 71.00 |
| 1924-25 | in Australia | 5 | 573 | 3 | 63.66 |
| 1926 | v Australia | 5 | 486 | 2 | 81.00 |
| 1928 | v West Indies | 2 | 212 | 1 | 106.00 |
| 1928-29 | in Australia | 5 | 451 | 1 | 50.11 |
| 1929 | v South Africa | 1 | 62 | — | 31.00 |
| 1930 | v Australia | 5 | 301 | — | 33.44 |
| **Total** | | **61** | **5,410** | **15** | **56.94** |

**Career runs:** 61,237 *Average:* 50.65
**Highest Test score:** 211 v South Africa, Lord's, 1924
**Highest career score:** 316*, Surrey v Middlesex, Lord's, 1926
*Not out

# Hutton
## Sir Leonard (1916-    )

Len Hutton won recognition as one of the greatest batsmen in cricket history through many prodigious feats, one of the earliest being his 364 in the Oval Test of 1938. Made when he was only 22, it was the longest as well as the highest Test innings at that time and it remains the highest innings played in the long England *v* Australia series. Yet probably his most remarkable feat was in resuming his career for Yorkshire and England with no loss of skill after World War II when, as a result of an accident in an Army gymnasium, his left arm was shorter and less strong than his right.

Hutton is also remembered as the first professional in modern times to captain England, which he did with much success for three years from 1952. He was captain when England regained the Ashes in 1953 and when they retained them on the triumphant tour of 1954-55 by beating Australia 3-1. A profound thinker

*Left,* **Len Hutton (in cap) is congratulated after passing Bradman's record test score of 334 at the Oval in 1938. The 22-year-old Hutton scored 364. Such was Hutton's skill and tactical cunning that he became the first modern professional to captain an England side.** *Below,* **Hutton, record-bound, skies a ball to leg. His innings was the longest in test cricket.**

on the game, he liked to be captain and to be able to put his theories into practice. But the off-the-field commitments of an England captain took more out of this quiet, reserved man and dedicated professional than was fully realized at the time. And at the height of his success as a Test captain—he had never been appointed captain of Yorkshire—he dropped out of first-class cricket in 1955, partly because he was not at his fittest but mostly because he had had enough. He was still only 38 and though on his recent tour of Australia he had not made as many runs as usual, there was no reason to think that his powers were in decline.

However, an interrupted season for Yorkshire in 1955 was his last, and the next year he was knighted for his services to cricket. Since then, he has lived away from his native Yorkshire, near London, absorbed in business interests, though his elder son, Richard, has followed him into the Yorkshire side, as an all-rounder.

Len Hutton's influence on the English cricket of his time was often described as dour and defensive. But though he was a tough, practical captain against Australia, the patience he showed in his batting often tended to obscure its great quality. When he really unloosed his superb strokes, it was a sight not to be forgotten, and his 37 in 24 minutes one morning in a Sydney Test is regarded as a great innings in cameo form.

But it was as a technician that he was pre-eminent. No sensible critic would have tried to compare him with his great contemporary Denis Compton, for they were entirely different in approach and execution. But he was a marvellously correct batsman, stylish if not spectacular, and always in the right position, even though he seldom used his feet to move out to the pitch of the ball. Colin Cowdrey, whose first Test matches were played under Hutton's leadership, once said that he was the most complete batsman he had ever seen.

Hutton's early years with the Yorkshire second XI left little doubt that another England batsman had been found, though few perhaps guessed that in a country where batsmen mature late his impact would be so swift. Born in Pudsey, the home of Herbert Sutcliffe, he came, at an early age, under the eye of another great Yorkshireman, George Hirst, the county coach. He was also a useful leg-break bowler then, and throughout his career he was a competent fielder, mostly near the bat.

He played in his first first-class match for Yorkshire at Cambridge in 1934 and failed to score, as he was to do in his first Test only three years later. Of medium height, he was not strongly built, and in his first two seasons

Yorkshire used him sparingly, but awarded him his county cap in the third when he made 1,000 runs for the first time. In later years, he made more than 2,000 runs in a season 10 times and in 1949 scored 3,429 runs, a seasonal aggregate bettered only by Denis Compton, Bill Edrich, and Tom Hayward.

By 1937 Hutton was scoring 10 centuries in the season, but in his first Test against New Zealand that year he made 0 and 1. In his second though he made the first of 19 Test hundreds.

He began the 1938 series against Australia with another 100 and an opening stand of 219 with Charles Barnett. He finished it with his record-breaking 364 made in 13 hours 20 minutes. In the last season before the war, he made 196 against West Indies at Lord's and, in the last pre-war Test, 73 and 165 not out at the Oval. He was the young master with a magnificent future to come.

The injury to his arm occurred early in the war, and subsequently he had three seasons of local and services cricket in which to overcome his disability before first-class cricket began again in 1946. In 1945 he opened in services matches with Cyril Washbrook, with whom he was to share a famous Test partnership, and with Compton and Bill Edrich in their prime there was apparently no shortage of English batting in the post-war years. But Compton was soon affected by his knee injury and Australia had formidable bowling sides in those years. Therefore many of Hutton's most important innings before the advent of May and Cowdrey were played sustaining an uncertain England batting side. Once, at Lord's in 1948, he batted so unimpressively that he was dropped for the next Test; a strange decision in retrospect, for he played Lindwall and Miller at their fastest supremely well. This was especially so in 1950-51 when he averaged 88.83, 50 more than the next batsman.

In South Africa in 1948-49 he batted with Washbrook all through a day's play in Johannesburg and they scored 359 for the first wicket. In 1951 he made his 100th hundred, at the Oval against Surrey, and the next year he captained England against India.

At Lord's in 1953, he made 145 against Australia and that winter became the first professional to take an MCC side overseas. In the West Indies, England lost the first two Tests but won the third and fifth in which the captain made 169 and 205 respectively. He missed part of the first series against Pakistan in 1954, returning to lead England in the Test they lost at the Oval. But his mind was on the tour of Australia, and though he averaged only 24 in the 1954-55 series, he led England

shrewdly and effectively to one of their most decisive victories against Australia.

For Hutton it was the fulfillment of burning ambition to redress the lack of success on his two previous tours. As a batsman his only real innings of the series came appropriately enough in the Fourth Test, which England won to retain The Ashes.

In reply to Australia's score in first innings of 323, Hutton carefully showed the way with a painstaking 80. It took four and and half hours and it was his only fifty of the series. But it guided England to a first innings lead after which came Tyson and Statham at their best and eventual victory.

His form in the tour matches was as impeccable as ever— he made over a thousand runs in Australia—but after the two Tests against New Zealand on the way back to England, he left international cricket, and he announced his retirement from the game after injuries had restricted his appearances for Yorkshire in 1955. England did not lose a Test series under his command—a record which pays tribute to his leadership.

After retiring he continued to be involved in the game from the Press box. His deep and thinking appreciation of the game finding a new and most successful outlet.

**1 Hutton hits out at the Oval against South Africa in 1947.**
**2 On the Oval balcony, Hutton and Lindsay Hassett shake hands after England had regained the Ashes in 1953, after a 20-year gap.**
**3 Though for England he often had to bat patiently in the team cause, Hutton played all the attacking shots with textbook correctness, and was quite capable of accumulating runs quickly when the situation dictated.**

### HUTTON Sir Leonard

Teams: Yorkshire and England

| Test series | | Tests | Runs | 100s | Average |
|---|---|---|---|---|---|
| 1937 | v New Zealand | 3 | 127 | 1 | 25.40 |
| 1938 | v Australia | 3 | 473 | 2 | 118.25 |
| 1938-39 | in South Africa | 4 | 265 | – | 44.16 |
| 1939 | v West Indies | 3 | 480 | 2 | 96.00 |
| 1946 | v India | 3 | 123 | – | 30.75 |
| 1946-47 | in Australia | 5 | 417 | 1 | 52.12 |
| 1947 | v South Africa | 5 | 344 | 1 | 43.00 |
| 1947-48 | in West Indies | 2 | 171 | – | 42.75 |
| 1948 | v Australia | 4 | 342 | – | 42.75 |
| 1948-49 | in South Africa | 5 | 577 | 2 | 64.11 |
| 1949 | v New Zealand | 4 | 469 | 2 | 78.16 |
| 1950 | v West Indies | 3 | 333 | 1 | 66.60 |
| 1950-51 | in Australia | 5 | 533 | 1 | 88.83 |
| 1950-51 | in New Zealand | 2 | 114 | – | 38.00 |
| 1951 | v South Africa | 5 | 378 | 1 | 54.00 |
| 1952 | v India | 4* | 399 | 2 | 79.80 |
| 1953 | v Australia | 5* | 443 | 1 | 55.37 |
| 1953-54 | in West Indies | 5* | 677 | 2 | 96.71 |
| 1954 | v Pakistan | 2* | 19 | – | 6.33 |
| 1954-55 | in Australia | 5* | 220 | – | 24.44 |
| 1954-55 | in New Zealand | 2* | 67 | – | 22.33 |
| Total | | 79 | 6,971 | 19 | 56.67 |

Career runs: 40,140    Average: 55.51
Highest Test and career score: 364, England v Australia, Oval, 1938
*Captain

Central Press

## 3

Sport & General

# Laker
## James Charles (1922-    )

Jim Laker will always be remembered for one of the most extraordinary feats in cricket history—his 19 wickets for 90 runs for England against Australia at Old Trafford in 1956. No one else in the history of the first-class game had ever taken more than 17 wickets in a match. Yet Laker, with his offspin, took 19 in a Test match against Australia and, inexplicably, while another highly skilled spin bowler, Tony Lock, perhaps the most prolific wicket-taker of the time, was taking only one at the other end. Just three weeks before, Lock himself had taken 16 wickets for Surrey against Kent at Blackheath, including all 10 in the second innings. Laker's feat was spread over four days in a rain-interrupted match. The pitch took spin from an early stage, but it was not as lethal as many to be met at that period.

Tall and strong, Laker had a lively, high action, great powers of spin, and immaculate control of the variations of length, pace, and flight with which he plagued batsmen. In England he mostly pushed the ball through at a pace that kept the batsmen from moving out to him but still allowed the ball to turn. On the harder pitches in Australia, South Africa, and the West Indies, where he had a good but less spectacular record, he would flight it more, yet with equal control. Laker began to bowl off-breaks at 17

**Jim Laker, Surrey master of spin. Australia felt the bite of his off-breaks when he took 19 for 90 in one Test.**

Central Press

Central Press

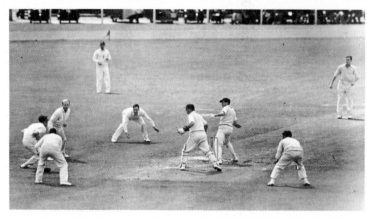

*Left,* **Though he won renown as an off-spinner, Jim Laker was a useful batsman and once scored 113 for Surrey against Gloucestershire at the Oval.** *Above,* **One of all 10 Australian wickets captured by Laker in their second innings of the 4th Test at Old Trafford in 1956, when he took his match tally to a record 19: Keith Miller walks to the pavilion, bowled Laker.** *Right,* **Ken Mackay is caught by Oakman off Laker for 0—for Mackay a repeat of his first innings dismissal.**

Central Press

just before World War II, having been a batsman and fast bowler at school. Before Yorkshire could become interested in him, the war broke out, but while serving in the RAOC in the Middle East he showed high promise in the good-class cricket played in Cairo. Stationed in London on his return home, he was soon introduced to Surrey who, after a time, convinced him that his future lay in cricket rather than in the banking career on which he had started. Whether Yorkshire would have given permission for Surrey to engage him had they seen more of him will never be known, but in 1946 the memories of his schooldays were over seven years old and they let him go. Within two years of his first-class debut, he was playing for England.

In his first full season of 1947, he finished seventh in the first-class averages with 79 wickets, and that winter went to the West Indies with G.O. Allen's MCC team, playing in his first Test in Barbados and taking 7-103 in the first innings. Back in England, he played in three Tests against Australia, making 63 in a total of 165 in the first. As a batsman, he was a hearty swinger of the bat at around No. 9 with an effective slash that earned him many runs on the off-side.

The Australians of 1948 played him with a confidence their successors seldom emulated, and after they had made their 404-3 in the last innings at Leeds,

Laker, who had had several chances dropped off him but was still really learning the offspinner's trade, was one of those dropped. For a while his career marked time, but he burst into the record books in the Test trial at Bradford in 1950, when on a drying pitch he took eight 'Rest' wickets for two runs, completely ruining the match as a trial. However, the selectors were still not convinced that he was a valuable bowler on good pitches as well, and he was not a regular choice for England, though his 10-119 against South Africa at the Oval in 1951 had much to do with England's victory there.

In 1952 Surrey's seven-year run of championship successes began, with Laker playing an important part, and in 1953 he and Lock bowled out Australia at the Oval when the Ashes where recovered after 19 years. But there still remained a tendency to identify him too closely with the helpful pitches in vogue at the time, especially at the Oval, and another great bowler, Bob Appleyard, was preferred on Len Hutton's successful tour of Australia in 1954-55.

Laker's greatest triumphs, however, were to come in 1956 when he took 46 wickets in the series against Australia at an average of 9.60 and at Old Trafford accomplished a feat that will almost certainly never be equalled, especially not in a Test match. In addition to his overall bag of 19 wickets, he

became the first player to take 10 wickets in a Test innings, and only the fourth player to take 10 wickets in an innings more than once—he had accomplished the feat earlier in the season with 10-88 for Surrey, also against the Australians.

Sadly, his later years with Surrey were marred by disagreements, and after his retirement in 1959—when he was only 37 and still a great bowler—he wrote a controversial book which caused MCC to withdraw his honorary membership and Surrey his pavilion privileges. Happily, these were restored within a few years

and the incident has been long forgotten.

Laker returned to first-class cricket for a time in the early 1960s, playing in a number of matches, mostly at home, for Essex, The pitches by now possessed more grass and had changed in character but though he rarely had figures, to compare with those of earlier years he was still a model bowler for young cricketers to watch and he was seldom played with comfort. When he finally left the first-class scene, he maintained his association with cricket, becoming a successful television commentator.

## LAKER James Charles

Teams: Surrey, Essex, and England

| Test series | | Tests | Wkts | Average |
|---|---|---|---|---|
| 1947-48 | in West Indies | 4 | 18 | 30.33 |
| 1948 | v Australia | 3 | 9 | 52.44 |
| 1949 | v New Zealand | 1 | 4 | 22.25 |
| 1950 | v West Indies | 1 | 1 | 86.00 |
| 1951 | v South Africa | 2 | 14 | 14.85 |
| 1952 | v India | 4 | 8 | 23.62 |
| 1953 | v Australia | 3 | 9 | 23.55 |
| 1953-54 | in West Indies | 4 | 14 | 33.50 |
| 1954 | v Pakistan | 1 | 2 | 19.50 |
| 1955 | v South Africa | 1 | 7 | 12.00 |
| 1956 | v Australia | 5 | 46 | 9.60 |
| 1956-57 | in South Africa | 5 | 11 | 29.45 |
| 1957 | v West Indies | 4 | 18 | 24.88 |
| 1958 | v New Zealand | 4 | 17 | 10.17 |
| 1958-59 | in Australia | 4 | 15 | 21.20 |
| **Total** | | **46** | **193** | **21.23** |

**Career wickets:** 1,944 *Average:* 18.40
**Best Test and career bowling:** 10-53 v Australia, Old Trafford, 1956
**Highest Test score:** 63 v Australia, Trent Bridge, 1948
**Highest career score:** 113, Surrey v Gloucestershire, Oval, 1954

# Larwood

Harold (1904-    )

Many people well placed to judge believe that Harold Larwood was the fastest and best fast bowler in cricket history. It was, therefore, all the sadder that his career should have declined among the bitterness of the bodyline controversy in which he was one of the two central figures and which left unpleasant memories of what, in most ways, was a glorious record.

Fair haired and of only medium height, he did not at first sight possess all the fast bowler's requirements, certainly not in 1925 when he first appeared for Nottinghamshire as a slim 20-year-old from one of the mining villages with which that county abounds. But his run-up, relatively short, yet beautifully balanced and accelerating gradually, at once attracted attention, and his marvellously supple, easy, textbook action left no doubt of his quality. In the following year, he was playing for England against Australia.

Although his pace was exceptional, it was the accuracy derived from his perfect action that made him so deadly and, in time, the ideal instrument of Jardine's bodyline policy in Australia in 1932-33.

Larwood's Test career before that series had not been outstanding. On A. P. F. Chapman's tour of 1928-29, he was never fully fit and at home in 1930 he was thwarted by a combination of Don Bradman and mild pitches. His most successful Test to date had

been the first Test of 1928-29 at Brisbane when he took 6-32 and 2-30 and scored 70 and 37. As a batsman at around No. 9 for England, he hit the ball hard and had a sound basic technique.

Before the 1932-33 tour, he had taken only 45 Test wickets. But under the captaincy of A. W. Carr, he had been a great force for Notts, playing a big part in their championship win of 1929. Eight times in all he took 100 wickets in a season, with a best performance of 9-41 against Kent at Trent Bridge in 1931.

In Australia on that unhappy tour, he bowled superbly to his orders. Though it was the short ball, fast and accurate, that undermined the batsmen, he could put in a devastating yorker at will. In addition, he was helped

*Popperfoto*

---

| LARWOOD Harold | | | |
|---|---|---|---|
| **Teams:** Nottinghamshire and England | | | |
| **Test series** | | Tests | Wkts | Avge |
| 1926 | v Australia | 2 | 9 | 28.00 |
| 1928 | v West Indies | 2 | 6 | 19.00 |
| 1928-29 in Australia | | 5 | 18 | 40.44 |
| 1929 | v South Africa | 3 | 8 | 23.25 |
| 1930 | v Australia | 3 | 4 | 73.00 |
| 1931 | v New Zealand | 1 | — | — |
| 1932-33 in Australia | | 5 | 33 | 19.51 |
| Total | | 21 | 78 | 28.41 |

**Career wickets:** 1,427 *Average:* 17.51
**Best Test bowling:** 6-32 v Australia, Brisbane, 1928-29
**Best career bowling:** 9-41, Nottinghamshire v Kent, Trent Bridge, 1931
**Highest Test score:** 98 v Australia, Sydney, 1932-33
**Highest career score:** 102*, Nottinghamshire v Sussex, Trent Bridge, 1931

*Not out

---

*Right,* The bowling action of Harold Larwood. He was feared by batsmen in England for his accuracy and speed, and in Australia for his devastating 'bodyline' technique. Larwood (below) and Voce were a Notts-England pair without equal.

*Popperfoto*

by the fact that there were other fine fast bowlers in the side— G. O. Allen, who did not bowl bodyline, and Bill Voce, Larwood's partner from Notts. In the first Test, Larwood took five wickets in each innings and thereafter he was the spearhead of England's attack, taking 33 wickets in all. And in the last Test, at Sydney, which was to be the last of his career, he went in as nightwatchman and made 98 in two and a quarter hours.

His departure from Test cricket was not entirely due to the aftermath of bodyline and the reluctance of selectors to open old

wounds, but to an injury to his left foot. It had been under great pressure, not only through the ordinary demands of fast bowling but through those extra times he thumped the ball in short of a length. He played on for Notts until 1938, but latterly was merely a fast-medium bowler operating off a short run. His name at that time inevitably had unpleasant associations in Australia, but after World War II he, his wife, and five daughters emigrated there. His part in the 1932-33 series had been forgiven and forgotten, and he became a much respected Australian citizen.

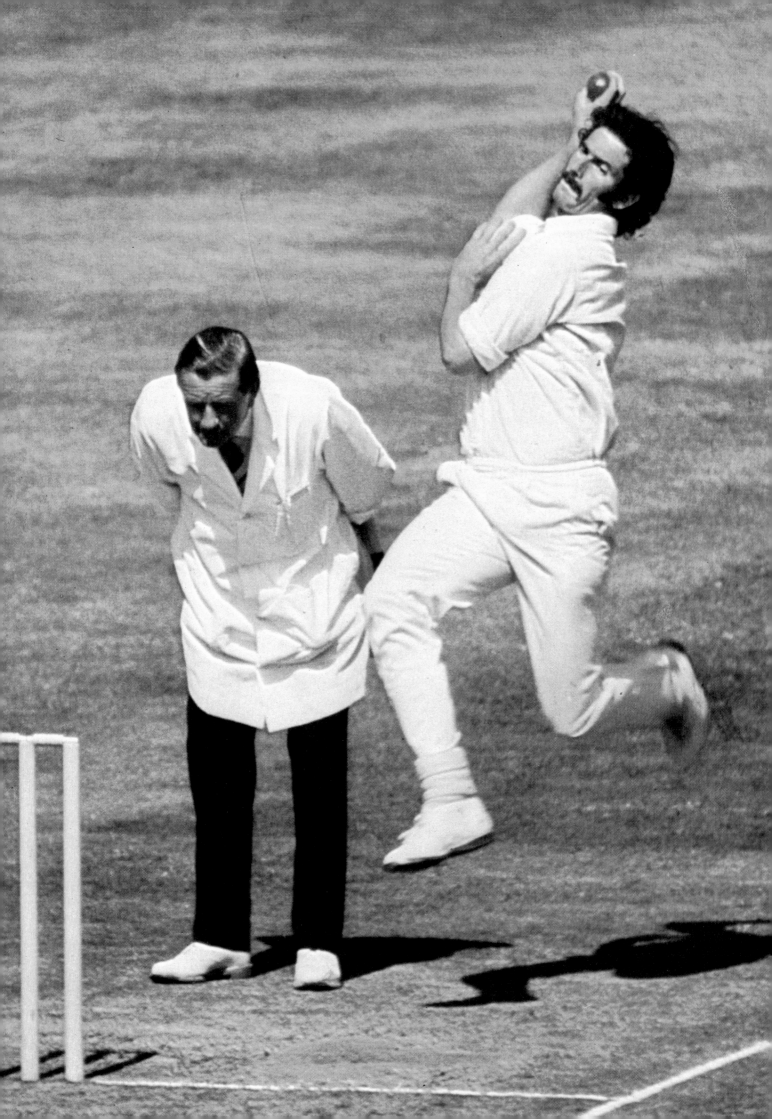

# Lillee

## Dennis Keith
## (1949-    )

As England reeled under the pace and aggression of Dennis Lillee's bowling in the 1972 Test series, they might have recalled the old proverb about biting the hand that fed you.

Lillee himself points to a season spent in the Lancashire League as one of the significant developments in a career which progressed from sheer pace to the ability to move the ball without any appreciable loss of speed. The result was shown in a magnificent series for Lillee in which he took 31 wickets, the most by any Australian in England.

Sadly, it seems, the effort has taken its toll. After playing against the Pakistanis the following winter, he broke down on the tour of West Indies in the early part of 1973, an already suspect back weakening under the strain of genuine fast bowling. An attempted change of action seemed the only solution to the problem.

Lillee's own competitive instincts and loyalty to his side had been largely to blame for the breakdown in Jamaica. The previous month in the Third and final Test against Pakistan, he was feeling the injury. But with Pakistan only needing 159 to win in the last innings, he willingly lent his frame to the cause. He bowled throughout that innings—a spell of eleven overs one evening and twelve the following day—and played a vital part in a famous Australian victory. He bowled at a reduced speed and wore a sleeveless sweater throughout his stint, but he removed three front-line batsmen, Nasim, Zaheer and Mushtaq.

Lillee first appeared for his state, Western Australia, at the age of 19, finding the life in his home strip at Perth very

*Left* **The power of Dennis Lillee in full cry in England in 1972. After taking 51 wickets in 11 Tests his career was threatened by a severe back injury.**

suitable for the pace of his bowling. His speed attracted the selectors who were looking for support for Graham McKenzie. Lillee was chosen for the 'B' tour to New Zealand at the end of the 1969-70 season, and responded with 18 first-class wickets which cost him only 18 runs each.

The following year, as Australia sought to counter in a series against England which John Snow was winning with pace, he was called into the full national side for the Fifth Test. Though England batted well, he took 5 for 84 in the first innings, doing the statutory job of a good quick bowler by briskly polishing off the tail.

He kept his place and though the 1971 tour by the South Africans was cancelled, Lillee opened the Australian attack against a World XI and in the second representative game he really came of age. The World XI were shot out for 59 and in 57 balls Lillee captured 8 for 29, including Garry Sobers for a duck. He followed with four more victims in the second innings and Australia won convincingly by an innings.

Despite problems with his back early on the tour, he carried the same form into the Tests in England the following summer. He bowled a lengthy 59 overs in the First Test at Old Trafford for match figures of 8 for 106, including an impressive 6 for 66 in the second innings.

His hostility proved a potent weapon for Ian Chappell, and throughout the series he was rarely mastered. The three principle batsmen in the 1970-71 series, Boycott, Edrich and Luckhurst, averaged 93.85, 72.00 and 56.87 respectively. In 1972 their returns were 18.00, 21.80 and 24.00. Much of the credit for such a turnabout belonged to Lillee.

Wickets were a little harder to come by against Pakistan, but he must have anticipated a rewarding series on the hard West Indian pitches until his back finally complained once too often to undermine the prospects of a thrilling career.

# Lindwall

## Raymond Russell
## (1921-    )

Ray Lindwall burst upon the cricket world after World War II as a great fast bowler and the more lethal, and more orthodox, in the redoubtable partnership of Lindwall and Miller that made Sir Donald Bradman's unbeaten Australians of 1948 such a devastating attacking force. Of medium height but strongly built, he recalled to many the great English fast bowler Harold Larwood, who also had an easy, perfectly balanced, accelerating run-up and a model action.

Lindwall possessed all the great fast bowler's arts—accuracy, genuine pace achieved without undue effort, subtle variations of pace, and the ability to swing the ball. At first the movement was mainly away from the bat, but while playing in the Lancashire League he developed the inswinger because slip catches off outswingers bowled

by someone of his pace were not readily taken. So considerable was his ability to move the ball in the air that he remained an effective bowler long after the sharp edge had gone off his pace, and his Test career continued until he was 38. When experiments were being made in England in 1953 with a smaller ball, he swung it about so absurdly in the nets at Lord's that the project was dropped. He was probably at his best in the heavier atmosphere of England, though the first of his three tours there was easily his most successful.

A promising rugby league player before the war, he used his speed and sure-handling to good effect in the field, often making catches of seemingly impossible chances. Such a catch was the one he took to dismiss Peter May at Headingley in 1956. Fielding at square leg, he took the ball only inches from the ground. As a vigorous batsman, he made two Test centuries, one against England at Melbourne, in

**Although purists found Ray Lindwall a joy to watch, batsmen facing him rarely found time to appreciate his balanced, accelerating run-up and model action.**

| LILLEE Dennis Keith | | | |
| --- | --- | --- | --- |
| **Teams:** Western Australia and Australia | | | |
| **Test series** | **Tests** | **Wickets** | **Average** |
| 1970-71 v England | 2 | 8 | 24.87 |
| 1972    in England | 5 | 31 | 17.67 |
| 1972-73 v Pakistan | 3 | 12 | 29.41 |
| 1973    in West Indies | 1 | — | — |
| | 11 | 51 | 24.15 |

**Career wickets:** 243 *Average:* 23.02
**Best Test bowling:** 6-66 v England, Old Trafford, 1972
**Best career bowling:** 8-29, Australia v Rest of the World, Perth, 1971-72
**Highest Test score:** 14 v Pakistan, Adelaide, 1972-73
**Highest career score:** 36, Australians v Windward Islands, Grenada, 1973

Career figures to the end of the 1972-73 season

1946-47, the other in Barbados against West Indies six years later.

The lack of first-class cricket in the war years meant that when Lindwall played in his first Test against England, at Brisbane in 1946, he was merely a name to most people outside Australia. He had had little of the build-up that would have attended a fast bowler of his class in ordinary times. Yet at 25 he was already a mature cricketer and the best fast bowler in the world, waiting only for the opportunity to prove it by performance in the highest class.

He had come under the eye of Bill O'Reilly, then captain of the St George club in Sydney, at an early age, and played for New South Wales in 1941. For some years thereafter he was on war service in New Guinea and the Solomon Islands, and it was not until 1945-46 that he returned to inter-state cricket, with immediate success.

Towards the end of the season he toured New Zealand, and the following season began his long confrontation with English batsmen, quietly at first, for he developed chicken-pox during the first Test and did not play in the second. But in the third, batting at No. 9, he shared in a stand of 154 in 87 minutes with Don Tallon in the second innings, making 100 himself in under two hours. In the fourth Test he took six wickets and in the fifth nine, including 7-63

*Right*, **Ray Lindwall was not always prepared to let the ball go past. An aggressive batsman, he scored just over 1,500 runs in Test cricket, including two centuries.** *Below*, **Lindwall bowling in 1956 on his last English tour.**

Popperfoto

| LINDWALL Raymond Russell | | | |
|---|---|---|---|
| **Teams:** New South Wales, Queensland, and Australia | | | |
| **Test series** | **Tests** | **Wkts** | **Average** |
| 1945-46 in New Zealand | 1 | 2 | 14.50 |
| 1946-47 v England | 4 | 18 | 20.38 |
| 1947-48 v India | 5 | 18 | 16.88 |
| 1948 in England | 5 | 27 | 19.62 |
| 1949-50 in South Africa | 4 | 12 | 20.66 |
| 1950-51 v England | 5 | 15 | 22.93 |
| 1951-52 v West Indies | 5 | 21 | 23.04 |
| 1952-53 v South Africa | 4 | 19 | 20.15 |
| 1953 in England | 5 | 26 | 18.84 |
| 1954-55 v England | 4 | 14 | 27.21 |
| 1954-55 in West Indies | 5 | 20 | 32.15 |
| 1956 in England | 4 | 7 | 34.00 |
| 1956-57 in Pakistan | 1 | 1 | 64.00 |
| 1956-57 in India | 3† | 12 | 16.58 |
| 1958-59 v England | 2 | 7 | 29.85 |
| 1959-60 in Pakistan | 2 | 3 | 40.66 |
| 1959-60 in India | 2 | 6 | 37.00 |
| Total | 61 | 228 | 23.05 |

**Career wickets:** 794 *Average:* 21.36
**Best Test bowling:** 7-38 v India, Adelaide, 1947-48
**Best career bowling:** 7-20, Australians v Minor Counties, Stoke-on-Trent, 1953
**Highest Test score:** 118 v West Indies, Bridgetown, 1954-55
**Highest career score:** 134*, New South Wales v Queensland, Sydney, 1945-46

*Not out †Captain in one Test

in the first innings.

In 1948 Lindwall was helped by the fact that a new ball was available after only 55 overs, in contrast to 85 today, and he swept aside almost all opposition, taking 86 wickets on the tour and 27 in the Test series.

His accuracy is reflected by the fact that half of his 86 victims were bowled. With Keith Miller and Bill Johnston also at the peak of their powers, the England batsmen had an unhappy summer that reached its gloomiest point for them when they were bowled out for 52 and 188 at the Oval, Lindwall taking 6-20 and 3-50.

In a weaker Australian side that lost the Ashes in 1953, he was little less successful himself, taking 26 Test wickets at 18 apiece. Miller came next with 10 wickets.

The first signs that England batsmen were beginning to find him less of a problem came in

Australia in 1954-55, when Len Hutton's team held the Ashes and Lindwall took only 14 wickets at 27 apiece. But his 3-27 and 2-50 had helped to win the first Test. In 1956 in England, he took only seven Test wickets, and it seemed, as Australia went home in disarray after that tour, that Lindwall, then 35, must be one of those who had played his last Test. But he was recalled for the fourth Test of the 1958-59 series, taking three wickets in that match and four in the fifth Test.

His return was the more popular for allowing Test crowds another look at a perfect action at a time when some doubtful ones were in vogue. A year later, crowds in Pakistan and India had the same opportunity, for Lindwall was a member of Richie Benaud's side there, and he took the last 9 of his 228 Test wickets. He retired on returning home, and in 1965 he was awarded the MBE.

# McKenzie

### Graham Douglas
### (1941-    )

Though fast bowlers are wont to leap from obscurity into world fame more quickly than other cricketers, few have been more completely unknown than Graham McKenzie when he went on his first tour to England in 1961. He had played two matches for Western Australia at the end of the 1959-60 season, but he took 4-41 in the state match against the West Indians at the start of the next season and did so well in the Sheffield Shield that he was picked for the tour. Yet up to the time of departure, the Australian captain, Richie Benaud, had not even seen him.

In England he proved to have been an inspired selection. He became Alan Davidson's partner in the opening attack, took 5-37 in the second innings of the Lord's Test, and played a big part with the bat in the two Tests that Australia won. At Lord's, he shared in stands that added 102 vital runs for the last two wickets and at Old Trafford he made 32 in a famous last wicket stand of 98 with Davidson. In later years, his batting has not developed as seemed likely then, and his record as a bowler in Test matches has nearly always been better than that in minor matches.

McKenzie's great ability has lain in the fact that he bowled so well on good pitches. A powerfully built 6-footer, he has a short, relaxed run-up and a beautiful action. From this action is derived the ability to thump the ball into an unhelpful pitch, so producing an extra high bounce. He is not especially accurate, but he can produce the ball that will undo the best of batsmen in good conditions.

Gentle, quietly spoken, almost dreamy, McKenzie has none of the fast bowler's traditional belligerence, but from his first tour at the age of 19 it has seemed certain that he would break all Australian records for the number of wickets taken in Tests. His career, however, has not quite been one of uninterrupted success. In 1965-66 the selectors dropped him from the team chosen to play in the fourth Test in Adelaide, but his replacement broke down before the match and he was recalled. His 6-48 in the first innings gave England a disastrous start from which they never quite recovered.

On joining Leicestershire in 1969 he had no immediate success. And though he did unexpectedly well for a fast bowler in India later that year, taking 26 wickets, he took only one in three Tests in South Africa. Blessed with exceptional soundness of limb and muscle through the years, he may not have been at his fittest in South Africa, and a minor technical flaw had crept into his action.

He played in only three Tests against Ray Illingworth's tour team, though he continued to be a force under Illingworth's leadership in county cricket for Leicestershire.

*Below left,* **Graham McKenzie at Lord's in 1961. Just 20, the Australian fast bowler took 5-37 in England's second innings.**
*Below,* **Nine years later, McKenzie was again at Lord's, opening the bowling for the Rest of the World against England.**

### McKENZIE Graham Douglas

**Teams:** Western Australia, Leicestershire, and Australia

| Test series | | Tests | Wkts | Avge |
|---|---|---|---|---|
| 1961 | in England | 3 | 11 | 29.36 |
| 1962-63 | v England | 5 | 20 | 30.95 |
| 1963-64 | v South Africa | 5 | 16 | 43.06 |
| 1964 | in England | 5 | 29 | 22.55 |
| 1964-65 | in India | 3 | 13 | 16.46 |
| 1964-65 | in Pakistan | 1 | 8 | 16.27 |
| 1964-65 | v Pakistan | 1 | 7 | 20.00 |
| 1964-65 | in West Indies | 5 | 17 | 39.82 |
| 1965-66 | v England | 4 | 16 | 29.18 |
| 1966-67 | in South Africa | 5 | 24 | 26.00 |
| 1967-68 | v India | 2 | 13 | 24.00 |
| 1968 | in England | 5 | 13 | 45.76 |
| 1968-69 | v West Indies | 5 | 30 | 25.26 |
| 1969-70 | in India | 5 | 21 | 21.00 |
| 1969-70 | in South Africa | 3 | 1 | 333.00 |
| 1970-71 | v England | 3 | 7 | 50.14 |
| Total | | 60 | 246 | 29.78 |

**Career wickets:** 1016 *Average* 27.68
**Best Test and career bowling:**
8-71 v West Indies, Melbourne, 1968-69
**Highest Test and career score:**
76 v South Africa, Sydney, 1963-64

Career figures up to the start of the 1973 season

Sport & General

Full of elegance and power, Surrey and England captain Peter May was perhaps the finest batsman of the 1950s. *Left* The elegant May mounts up his score in the first Test against West Indies at Edgbaston in 1957. He amassed a career best of 285 not out and, with Colin Cowdrey, put on 411—a Test record for the 4th wicket and the highest stand ever made for England. The partnership ensured England's domination of the series.

# May

## Peter Barker Howard
(1929-    )

For a period in the 1950s, Peter May was regarded as the best batsman in the world. And to many he has, more than a decade after his retirement, no superiors in England among post-war batsmen. His Test career spanned less than 10 years, yet in that time, as well as his feats as a batsman, he captained England a record 41 times.

Fine though his record is, however, it conceals two all-important facts. One is that during his career for Surrey, whom he captained for four years—twice to the championship—he was batting on pitches at the Oval that were far from ideal. In fact, the great Surrey bowlers of the day—Bedser, Loader, Laker, and Lock—reaped hundreds of wickets there. The second is that in Test matches, as well as batting on frequently imperfect wickets, he was continually under pressure, sustaining England batting that had no established opening partnership and had the obdurate but relatively unproductive Trevor Bailey at No. 6 with little afterwards. For years he can seldom have gone to the crease without feeling that a crisis was on, and that if he failed the side failed. Such pressure, along with that of work, a period of ill-health, and the burden of captaincy, was probably a contributory factor to his early retirement in 1961 when only 31.

Tall, elegant, and powerful,

Peter May had an almost orthodox method, played very straight, and had all the strokes except perhaps the hook, which he did not often seem to need to play. He combined, as few others have, the grace, strength, and classic mould of the old-fashioned amateur with the professional competitiveness now needed in the highest class.

He was already a batsman of limitless potential when he came under the eye of former England and Leicestershire player George Geary, then coach at Charterhouse. At both Charterhouse and Cambridge, May's talents developed on good pitches, and he played his first match for Surrey in 1950. A year later he was playing for England against South Africa at Leeds and it was a sign of the concentration and phlegmatic temperament he was to show so often later that he made 138 in that first Test.

After playing against India in 1952, he became the first target of the Australian bowlers in 1953. Ray Lindwall bowled superbly to him at the Oval in the Surrey match, and when he was out cheaply in the first Test the England selectors dropped him until the vital fifth Test. He returned then to play two important innings and was soon acknowledged as the batsman who would take over the mantles of Hutton and Compton.

He was vice-captain to Len Hutton on the triumphant tour of Australia in 1954-55, and it was his 104 at Sydney in the second Test that turned the series towards England after they had lost the first Test and been 74 runs behind

in the first innings of the second. On returning to England May found himself appointed captain, Hutton being ill, and he led England 35 times in succession, beginning with the magnificent series of 1955 against South Africa. He himself scored a brilliant hundred at Lord's and another at Old Trafford, averaging 72 in the series.

The next year he had an even more remarkable record in a low-scoring series against Australia, averaging 90 and sharing a memorable fourth wicket partnership of 187 with the veteran Cyril Washbrook at Leeds after England had lost three wickets for 17.

May was then at his peak of brilliance, and his failure in the Test series in South Africa in 1956-

57 has never been satisfactorily explained. He played as well as ever in other matches but fell to brilliant catches and the like in the Tests. But at home in 1957 he soon showed this was merely a fleeting failure, for when England began their second innings in the first Test at Edgbaston 288 behind West Indies, May batted for nearly 10 hours, making 285 not out and sharing in a record fourth-wicket stand of 411 with Colin Cowdrey. The baffling Sonny Ramadhin was never the same again, and England went on to win the series easily.

Early in 1958, May played two of his best innings for Surrey—174 against Lancashire at Old Trafford and 165 against the New Zealanders at the Oval when the next highest score in the match was 25. But that winter in Australia he led an ageing side, and though he still batted well himself he were well beaten by Richie Benaud's more aggressive Australians.

In 1959, May suffered a painful illness midway through the season. He was struck down again during the tour of West Indies that winter, and missed the 1960 season, but returned to play against Australia in 1961 before retiring. Throughout his career he had played as an amateur, and his services to cricket did not stop with his wonderful record on the field. Since retiring, he has served as a Test selector and on innumerable committees for Surrey and MCC.

| MAY Peter Barker Howard | | | | |
|---|---|---|---|---|
| **Teams:** Cambridge University, Surrey, and England | | | | |
| **Test series** | Tests | Runs | 100s | Average |
| 1951    v    South Africa | 2 | 171 | 1 | 57.00 |
| 1952    v    India | 4 | 206 | — | 34.33 |
| 1953    v    Australia | 2 | 85 | — | 28.33 |
| 1953-54 in West Indies | 5 | 414 | 1 | 46.00 |
| 1954    v    Pakistan | 4 | 120 | — | 24.00 |
| 1954-55 in Australia | 5 | 351 | 1 | 39.00 |
| 1954-55 in New Zealand | 2 | 71 | — | 23.66 |
| 1955    v    South Africa | 5† | 582 | 2 | 72.75 |
| 1956    v    Australia | 5† | 453 | 1 | 90.60 |
| 1956-57 in South Africa | 5† | 153 | — | 15.30 |
| 1957    v    West Indies | 5† | 489 | 2 | 97.80 |
| 1958    v    New Zealand | 5† | 337 | 2 | 67.40 |
| 1958-59 in Australia | 5† | 405 | 1 | 40.50 |
| 1958-59 in New Zealand | 2† | 195 | 1 | 195.00 |
| 1959    v    India | 3† | 150 | 1 | 50.00 |
| 1959-60 in West Indies | 3† | 83 | — | 16.60 |
| 1961    v    Australia | 4‡ | 272 | — | 38.85 |
| **Total** | 66 | 4,537 | 13 | 46.77 |

**Career runs:** 27,592 *Average:* 51.00
**Highest Test and career score:** 285* v West Indies, Edgbaston, 1957

*Not out  †Captain  ‡Captain in 3 Tests

Press Association

# Miller
## Keith Ross (1919-  )

Perhaps the most exciting personality on the cricket scene in the years following World War II, Keith Miller moved into the press box when his playing days ended and continued his lively association with the game.

As a player, he was unpredictable in everything he did, and the public loved him for it. At times, he looked the greatest fast bowler the game has seen, yet it is well known that bowling was often irksome to him. He was much happier hitting the ball to all corners of the ground. But if the runs were too easy to obtain, he would not be averse to throwing his wicket away. His off-the-field life was equally unexpected. Full of fun and often a practical joker, he had moments of extreme seriousness. And his love of classical music contrasted sharply with his fondness for gambling.

Standing 6 ft. 1 in. tall, lithe, handsome, and debonair, Miller gave the appearance of the perfect athlete, and he became a hero to young and old, male and female. Born in Melbourne while Keith Smith and Ross Smith were making the first flight from England to Australia, he was given the Christian names of the two airmen, and though it is difficult to know whether or not he gained inspiration from the names, he developed the same adventurous spirit.

Early ideas of becoming a jockey had to go by the board when Miller grew more than a foot soon after his 16th birthday.

Even when small, he had shown promise as a cricketer, but with increased build came more power, and he developed quickly, especially as a free-hitting batsman. He first played for Victoria in 1937-38, soon making his mark. But the war intervened, and he went to England where he served as a night fighter pilot. It was then that he suffered the back injury that at times handicapped him as a player. Not that he ever let that be an excuse for a poor performance: indeed he would never admit he was in difficulty.

It was in England that Miller blossomed as an all-rounder, and his bowling in the 'victory' Tests for Australia against England was a foretaste of what was to come. Also that season, 1945, he hit himself into the headlines with an innings of 185 in 165 minutes for a Dominions' XI against England at Lord's. It included seven sixes, one of them among the biggest hits ever seen on the ground.

His reputation established, Miller returned to Australia and transferred from Victoria to New South Wales, becoming an automatic Test choice and developing with his great friend Ray Lindwall, a fearsome fast bowling combination that kept Australia on top of the cricket world for seven years. Rarely did he fail with both bat and ball, and his all-round skill brought him 2,958 runs and 170 wickets in 55 Tests. Not that he concerned himself with figures. They were incidental in the course of thoroughly enjoying himself and communicating that enjoyment to others.

Fast bowling brought him the majority of his wickets, and there were times when his fierce pace, vicious bumper, and ability to make the ball kick from a length made him almost unplayable. Not that he was an out-and-out pace man. Few who saw his bowling at Lord's in 1956 will ever forget it. Approaching the end of his career, the 36-year-old Miller, bowling medium-pace and moving the ball either way, took 5-72 and 5-80. On other occasions, he turned to off-breaks, and in fact his best Test bowling performance, 7-60, came with spin on a sticky pitch in the first Test against England at Brisbane in 1946-47. Yet even when apparently bowling at his fastest and best, Miller would show the refusal to conform that was so characteristic of him by suddenly slipping in a leg-break, googly, off-break, or a round-arm slinging ball. Or he would unexpectedly turn round when walking back to his mark and send down a delivery of rare pace off only a yard-or-so run.

The highlights of Miller's Test batting were three centuries against England and four against West Indies—three of them in the 1954-55 season. When the mood took him, he could annihilate the finest bowling attack with an

**Few cricketers have generated excitement on the cricket field as much as Keith Miller. As a bowler, he was unpredictable, likely to send down a fast bumper or a leg-break; as a batsman he provided enormous entertainment with his powerful hitting.**

Popperfoto

Fox Photos

Power and grace go into a Keith Miller sweep. In full cry, he could devastate the most powerful bowling attacks in the world.

## Mitchell

### Bruce (1909- )

Opening batsman and anchor of many South African innings for a period of 20 years, Bruce Mitchell first played for his country in England in 1929. He went there at the age of 20, and though he had almost no experience of turf pitches he astonished everyone by his skill on them. Later, he became renowned for his patience and imperturbable temperament. He was often regarded as a dull batsman, but his method was immensely sound and he had an agreeable style.

It is often said, with justice, that predominantly defensive batsmen may save matches but never win them. Mitchell, however, played an all-important part in the victory at Lord's in 1935 that gave South Africa their first win over England in a rubber in England. He batted 5½ hours in the second innings to make 164 not out before South Africa declared at 278-7. His first Test hundred had come against England in Cape Town in 1930-31, when he and I. J. Siedle scored 260 together, 40 years later still the South African record opening stand.

Mitchell was 38 when he returned to England with Alan Melville's South African side in 1947. His form for the Transvaal had suggested that he had lost little of his old reliability in the war years, and after a slow start he soon made four hundreds in six innings and batted stolidly through the tour to a remarkable climax. At the Oval in the fifth Test, he made 120 in the first innings and then, when South Africa went in needing 451 to win, batted to the end of the match when his side was only 28 short of the target and he himself had made 189 not out. He was off the field for less than 15 minutes in the four days. In all, he made eight hundreds on the tour and averaged 61.

His last series was against England in 1948-49, when he made the last of his eight Test hundreds and missed a ninth by just 1 run in his final Test.

### MITCHELL Bruce

**Teams:** Transvaal and South Africa

| Test series | | Tests | Runs | 100s | Average |
|---|---|---|---|---|---|
| 1929 | in England | 5 | 251 | — | 31.37 |
| 1930-31 | v England | 5 | 455 | 1 | 50.55 |
| 1931-32 | in Australia | 5 | 322 | — | 32.20 |
| 1931-32 | in New Zealand | 2 | 166 | 1 | 55.33 |
| 1935 | in England | 5 | 488 | 2 | 69.71 |
| 1935-36 | v Australia | 5 | 251 | — | 31.37 |
| 1938-39 | v England | 5 | 466 | 1 | 58.25 |
| 1947 | in England | 5 | 597 | 2 | 66.33 |
| 1948-49 | v England | 5 | 475 | 1 | 52.77 |
| Total | | 42 | 3,471 | 8 | 48.88 |

**Career runs:** 11,395 *Average:* 45.39
**Highest Test score:** 189* v England, Oval, 1947
**Highest career score:** 195, South Africans v Surrey, Oval, 1935

*Not out

Bruce Mitchell scored two centuries in the 1947 Oval Test, being eighth out in the first innings and not out in the second. He had a liking for the Surrey ground because on the South African tour twelve years earlier, he made his best career score, 195, against the county side.

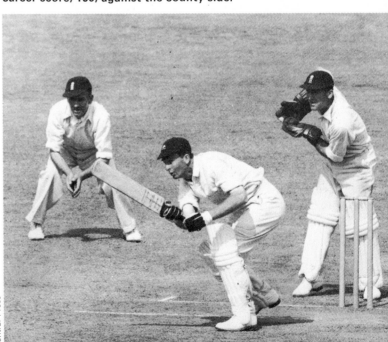

Central Press

impressive repetoire of strokes that included powerful drives and the most delicate cutting. He is one of the few cricketers to have scored a century and taken 6 wickets in the same innings of a Test. In the fifth Test against West Indies at Kingston in 1954-55, he scored 109 in Australia's first innings after taking 6 West Indies wickets for 107. Add to this an ability to pick up brilliant catches, especially in the slips, and Miller has claims to rank among the finest all-round cricketers of all time.

### MILLER Keith Ross

**Teams:** Victoria, New South Wales, and Australia

| Test series | | Tests | Runs | 100s | Average | Wkts | Average |
|---|---|---|---|---|---|---|---|
| 1945-46 | in New Zealand | 1 | 30 | — | 30.00 | 2 | 3.00 |
| 1946-47 | v England | 5 | 384 | 1 | 76.80 | 16 | 20.87 |
| 1947-48 | v India | 5 | 185 | — | 37.00 | 9 | 24.77 |
| 1948 | in England | 5 | 184 | — | 28.26 | 13 | 23.15 |
| 1949-50 | in South Africa | 5 | 246 | — | 41.00 | 17 | 22.94 |
| 1950-51 | v England | 5 | 350 | 1 | 43.75 | 17 | 17.70 |
| 1951-52 | v West Indies | 5 | 362 | 1 | 40.22 | 20 | 19.90 |
| 1952-53 | v South Africa | 4 | 153 | — | 25.50 | 13 | 18.53 |
| 1953 | in England | 5 | 223 | 1 | 24.77 | 10 | 30.30 |
| 1954-55 | v England | 4 | 167 | — | 23.85 | 10 | 24.30 |
| 1954-55 | in West Indies | 5 | 439 | 3 | 73.16 | 20 | 32.00 |
| 1956 | in England | 5 | 203 | — | 22.55 | 21 | 22.23 |
| 1956-57 | in Pakistan | 1 | 32 | — | 16.00 | 2 | 29.00 |
| Total | | 55 | 2,958 | 7 | 36.97 | 170 | 22.97 |

**Career runs:** 14,183 *Average:* 48.90
**Highest Test score:** 147 v West Indies, Kingston, 1954-55
**Highest career score:** 281*, Australians v Leicestershire, Leicester, 1956
**Career wickets:** 497 *Average:* 22.29
**Best Test bowling:** 7-60 v England, Brisbane, 1946-47
**Best career bowling:** 7-12, New South Wales v South Australia, Sydney, 1955-56

* Not out

# Morris

## Arthur Robert (1922-    )

Arthur Morris could be called 'The Quiet Australian'. A pleasant, modest, and kind man, he was liked wherever he went as well as being regarded as perhaps the best left-handed opening batsman the game has known. In keeping with his manner, Morris was more of a gentle persuader of runs rather than an aggressive acquirer. So successful were his methods that in 24 matches against England he scored 2,080 runs, including eight centuries, and averaged just over 50. A player of complete calm with a sound defence and neat style, he excelled in placing his strokes wide of fieldsmen, and often he would upset bowlers by walking down the pitch and putting them off their length.

His consistency meant that England, in the early days of Morris at least, rarely managed the good start that usually gives a side encouragement. Not that Morris began his Test career auspiciously. He scored just 2 and 5 in his first two games, but the selectors persisted with him, and in the third Test, at Melbourne, England had a sample of his skill when he scored 155 in the second innings. This was followed by 122 and 124 not out at Adelaide, the first time an Australian had hit a century in each innings of a Test in his own country. In the same game, Denis Compton also scored a hundred in each innings. Morris finished the series with an average of 71.85.

He did even better on his first tour of England in 1948 and headed the Test averages, above Bradman and Barnes, with 87.00. He hit 196 at the Oval, 182 at Headingley, and 105 at Lord's. At Headingley, he and Bradman put on 301 for that second wicket and helped Australia to a remarkable victory by seven wickets when set to get 404 in 345 minutes on the last day.

Morris was unable to maintain such a high level in his next three series against England, although he did score 206, the highest of his career, in the fourth Test at Adelaide in 1950-51. In that series and the next, 1953, Morris so often fell victim of Alec Bedser that he became known as 'Bedser's Bunny'. Against all countries, Morris played in 46 Tests and averaged 46.48. His career average in first-class games was over 55 and included 46 hundreds.

Morris began his cricketing days at school as a slow left-arm bowler and a No. 11 batsman. He was still regarded only as a bowler in his high school days, but gradually his batting improved, and when 16 he hit a century against Sydney University. That led to his being tried as an opening batsman, and he stayed in that position.

While still a schoolboy, Morris was asked to play for New South Wales Second XI against the Victorian Second XI, and was only 19 when he shook the cricket world by scoring a century in each innings of his first Sheffield Shield match, 148 and 111 against Queensland at Sydney in December 1940. During the war years Morris played little cricket, being stationed for most of the time in New Guinea, and it was not until the 1946-47 MCC visit that he returned to cricket full-time. He gave up the game seriously at the all too early age of 33.

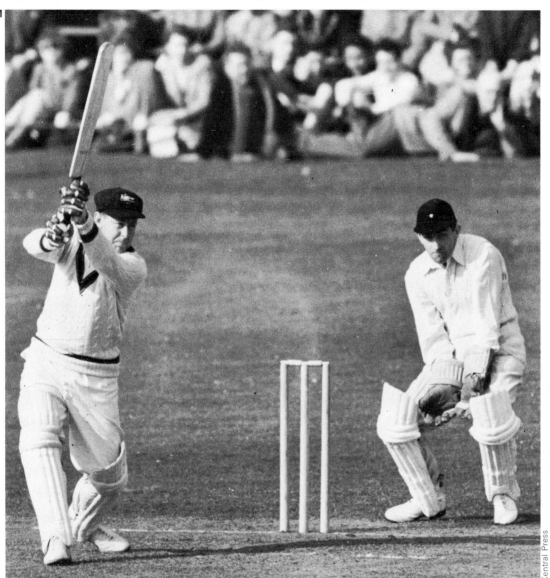

**1** A text-book cover drive by Australian opener Arthur Morris. A persuader of runs, he excelled in placing the ball wide of fieldsmen.
**2** A more aggressive stroke sends fielders ducking and the ball to the boundary.

*Central Press*

*Sport & General*

| MORRIS Arthur Robert | | | | |
|---|---|---|---|---|
| **Teams:** New South Wales and Australia | | | | |
| **Test series** | **Tests** | **Runs** | **100s** | **Average** |
| 1946-47 v England | 5 | 503 | 3 | 71.85 |
| 1947-48 v India | 4 | 209 | 1 | 52.25 |
| 1948    in England | 5 | 696 | 3 | 87.00 |
| 1949-50 in South Africa | 5 | 422 | 2 | 52.75 |
| 1950-51 v England | 5 | 321 | 1 | 35.66 |
| 1951-52 v West Indies | 4* | 186 | — | 23.25 |
| 1952-53 v South Africa | 5 | 370 | — | 41.11 |
| 1953    in England | 5 | 337 | — | 33.70 |
| 1954-55 v England | 4* | 223 | 1 | 31.85 |
| 1954-55 in West Indies | 4 | 266 | 1 | 44.33 |
| Total | 46 | 3,533 | 12 | 46.48 |

**Career runs:** 12,489  *Average:* 55.01
**Highest Test score:** 206 v England, Adelaide, 1950-51
**Highest career score:** 290, Australians v Gloucestershire, Bristol, 1948

*Captain in 1 Test

# Pollock

## Peter Maclean
## (1941-    )

Far from being overshadowed by the brilliance of his younger brother Graeme, Peter Pollock established himself as a vital member of the South African team as a deadly fast bowler.

*Left,* **Peter Pollock sends one down against Hampshire in 1965. Though less famous than his younger brother Graeme, he had by 1970 taken more Test wickets for South Africa than any bowler except Hugh Tayfield.** *Below,* **Pollock in action for the Rest of the World against an England XI.**

Patrick Eager

Standing just over 6 ft. 2 in. tall and well built, he made good use of his physique for both speed and stamina. At one time he relied on sheer pace with plenty of bouncers to unsettle batsmen, but with experience came variation. His extremely long run-up usually meant he took a long time to deliver an over, but he found that he lost effectiveness when he tried to take fewer paces.

At school Peter Pollock used to open both batting and bowling, but his coach George Cox advised him to concentrate on bowling. He was only 17 when he made his first-class debut, and in 1961 he toured England with the Fezelas, a team that included most of South Africa's best young talent. Making excellent progress with Eastern Province, he began his Test career against New Zealand at Durban in 1961-62 with outstanding success. In the first innings he took 3-61 and followed with 6-38 in the second. The 1963-64 tour of Australia showed him to be a top-class bowler. He began with 6-95 in the first Test at Brisbane, claimed 5-83 at Sydney, and altogether took 25 wickets in the series, heading the South African bowling averages. He followed with 15 wickets in New Zealand at the end of the tour of Australia, including 6-47 at Wellington, so that in eight successive Tests he captured 40 wickets.

He did not have a good series against Mike Smith's Englishmen in 1964-65, but he came back well during the short tour of England in 1965, taking 20 wickets in three Tests for 366 runs. He fell away again against Australia in 1966-67, but on the next Australian visit in 1970 he was well to the fore, his 15 wickets for 258 runs including 5-39 at Johannesburg and 4-20 at Cape Town. And during the 1970 England v Rest of the World series, he was reporting the matches when he was unexpectedly called upon to replace Graham McKenzie in the third match at Edgbaston.

Sport & General

### POLLOCK Peter MacLean

Teams: Eastern Province and South Africa

| Test Series | Tests | Wkts | Avge |
|---|---|---|---|
| 1961-62 v New Zealand | 3 | 17 | 17.58 |
| 1963-64 in Australia | 5 | 25 | 28.40 |
| 1963-64 in New Zealand | 3 | 15 | 17.20 |
| 1964-65 v England | 5 | 12 | 37.08 |
| 1965 in England | 3 | 20 | 18.30 |
| 1966-67 v Australia | 5 | 12 | 39.16 |
| 1969-70 v Australia | 4 | 15 | 17.20 |
| Total | 28 | 116 | 24.18 |

**Career wickets:** 485 *Average:* 21.89
**Best Test bowling:** 6-38 v New Zealand, Durban, 1961-62
**Best career bowling:** 7-19, Eastern Province v Western Province, Port Elizabeth, 1962-63
**Highest Test score:** 75* v Australia, Cape Town, 1966-67
**Highest career score:** 79, Eastern Province v Transvaal, Johannesburg, 1962-63

*Not out. Career figures up to the end of the 1972-73 season

Always aggressive, Graeme Pollock hammered the Hampshire attack to the tune of 94 in 66 minutes in this 1965 innings. (see page 108)

# Pollock

## Robert Graeme
## (1944-    )

The opportunity came in the summer of 1970 to compare the merits of Graeme Pollock and Gary Sobers, two of the best left-handed batsmen cricket has known. They played in the same Rest of the World side against England, but unfortunately for those who claimed that Pollock was every bit as good as the great West Indian, he failed to show his best form.

Despite that, however, Pollock is acknowledged to be a master of his art, and those who see him play a big innings are enthralled. He makes batting look so easy that most of his partners and opponents suffer badly when in contact with him. At times he hardly seems to put any power behind a stroke, yet the ball races over the turf and defies all efforts to cut it off before the boundary. His off-side shots in particular are played in a lazy, almost contemptuous manner, and his placing in the arc from third man to long off has rarely been bettered. When he decides to put the full strength of his 6 ft. $2\frac{1}{2}$ in. frame behind a drive, a six is almost inevitable. With Pollock, timing is everything and he is a real joy to the eye. A noticeable point about him is that he appears to have no nerves and all his play shows a lack of tension.

Pollock was born in Durban, and his father, a Scot, was a keen cricketer who kept wicket for Orange Free State. An exceptional schoolboy player, he hit a century and took 10 wickets in one match when only nine, and like his father, he did everything with his right hand except bat. Until the age of 12 he bowled fast like his brother Peter, but he was then persuaded to try leg-breaks instead. After spending four years in the Grey High School XI, starting at 13 and finishing as captain, he moved to Eastern Province and, at the age of 16 years 335 days, became the youngest player to hit a century in the Currie Cup competition.

He owed a lot to the coaching of George Cox, the Sussex batsman, and when visiting England with his parents in 1961 he played six innings for the county's Second XI. Continuing his remarkable progress in South Africa, he became the youngest South African to hit a double century when he scored 209 not out against Richie Benaud's Cavaliers side at Port Elizabeth. He was then 19 years 20 days old, and he was just 20 when he was appointed captain of Eastern Province.

Graeme Pollock made his Test debut in Australia in 1963-64 and quickly made himself a personality with a brilliant 127 not out in the second important match of the tour, against a Combined XI at Perth, his century taking no more

than 85 minutes. His first two Tests were far from distinguished, but a change came in the third at Sydney where he made 122, the second 50 of his century coming in 17 scoring strokes. The next Test brought a real triumph, for with Eddie Barlow he added 341 for the third wicket, the highest stand in South African Test

**1 A subdued Pollock playing for the Rest of the World in England in 1970. His form disappointed and his only major innings came at the Oval where he made 114. 2 In full flow against Australia in the 1969-70 series in which he made 517 runs, including his best ever score of 274.**

history. Barlow made 201 and Pollock 175, a great innings for a 19-year-old.

When England visited South Africa in 1964-65 Pollock was again slow to get started, but in his last seven innings he scored over 50 five times, with the highlight his 137 and 77 not out in the fifth Test on his own ground at Port Elizabeth. The following English summer, 1965, Pollock toured England and scored 291 runs in the three Tests, including 125 at Trent Bridge. When he had scored 28 in that innings he became, at little more than 21, the youngest batsman to reach 1,000 runs in Test cricket. Between the first and second Tests, Pollock made 203 not out at Canterbury,

an innings that contained 5 sixes and reminded Kent followers of their own great left-hander, Frank Woolley.

Pollock has taken a real toll of Australian bowling, especially in his own country. In 1966-67 he hit 90 in the first Test and helped South Africa gain their first home victory over their opponents in 64 years. That was followed by a tremendous 209 at Cape Town, although it still failed to save South Africa from defeat. He maintained his form with 67 not out in the Third Test at Durban and 105 in the final match at Port Elizabeth, so playing a vital part in South Africa's winning the series 3-1.

When Australia next visited South Africa in 1970, Pollock scored 517 runs in seven innings, with his magnificent 274 at Durban the highest score ever made for South Africa in a Test match. Later that year he visited England again, to represent the Rest of the World, but his only worthwhile innings was 114 in the final game at the Oval.

| **POLLOCK Robert Graeme** | | | |
|---|---|---|---|
| **Teams:** Eastern Province and South Africa | | | |
| **Test series** | **Tests** | **Runs** | **100s** | **Avge** |
| 1963-64 in Australia | 5 | 399 | 2 | 57.00 |
| 1963-64 in New Zealand | 1 | 53 | – | 26.50 |
| 1964-65 v England | 5 | 459 | 1 | 57.37 |
| 1965 in England | 3 | 291 | 1 | 48.50 |
| 1966-67 v Australia | 5 | 537 | 2 | 76.71 |
| 1969-70 v Australia | 4 | 517 | 1 | 73.85 |
| Total | 23 | 2,256 | 7 | 60.97 |

**Career runs:** 10,590 *Average:* 52.16
**Highest Test and career score:**
274 v Australia, Durban, 1969-70

Career figures up to the end of the 1972-73 season

score 1,000 runs and take 50 wickets in a South African season, and in 1961-62 his tour aggregate of 1,915 runs eclipsed Denis Compton's 13-year-old record. Also on that second tour he headed both the Test and tour batting and the tour bowling averages, as well as being the leading fielder with 22 catches. His seven centuries included 203 against Western Province and 142 in the fourth Test, and his 4-44 off 45 overs following a hard-hit 69 played a vital part in New Zealand's fifth-Test victory that squared the series.

Outstanding at both cricket and rugby as a Wellington schoolboy, Reid made his first-class debut in 1947, and in 1949, at 20, went to England with Walter Hadlee's side, soon establishing himself as its leading all-rounder. His batting was solid and included Test innings of 50 and 93, his bowling at times was as fast as that of anyone in English cricket, and he proved a capable wicket-keeper in the fourth Test at the Oval. He returned to England in 1952 for three seasons with Heywood in the Central Lancashire League, and it was while playing there that he changed to bowling off-cutters. His immaculate length and control proved their worth in South Africa in 1953-54, and two years later in India and Pakistan he headed the Test bowling averages in both series as well as scoring 1,032 runs on the tour.

It was on his first South African tour that Reid discovered the value of playing off the back foot rather than the front, and subsequently adapted his technique so that he rarely went forward except to drive. The change, however, did not restrict his natural desire to attack, and many bowlers suffered from his powerful driving and savage hooking. One attack to wilt before a Reid on-slaught was that of Northern Districts in a 1962-63 Plunket Shield match with Wellington. His 296 included a record number of sixes for an innings—15. Not so productive but equally attacking had been his innings of 84 that started New Zealand on the way to victory over West Indies at Auckland in 1956.

He was an automatic choice as New Zealand's captain from that success until his retirement following the 1965 tour of India, Pakistan, and England. There were times when he alone seemed to hold the New Zealand side together, and he often went in to bat knowing that so much depended on him. Consequently his performances at times suffered. Had he been a member of an established side, though, his record may well have been even greater.

**Considered by many to be New Zealand's best-ever cricketer, John Reid was also the country's most successful captain. When he retired, he had scored more runs and taken more wickets than any other New Zealander, and it was under his leadership that the Kiwis won their first Test victory, in 1956 against West Indies. In 1962-63, his powerful batting produced a world record 15 sixes in an innings of 296.**

Sport & General

# Reid

## John Richard (1928-    )

New Zealand's outstanding cricketer in the 1950s and early 1960s, John Reid was worthy of a place among the leading all-rounders of his time. His 58 consecutive Test appearances were a record, and, in what was perhaps the highlight of his career, he had the distinction of leading his country to her first ever Test victory, against West Indies in 1956. It was just his third Test as captain.

More than any place else, Reid demonstrated his all-round ability most consistently in South Africa. On his first tour there, in 1953-54, he became the first cricketer to

### REID John Richard

**Teams:** Wellington, Otago, and New Zealand

| Test series | | Tests | Runs | 100s | Avge | Wkts | Avge |
|---|---|---|---|---|---|---|---|
| 1949 | in England | 2 | 173 | – | 43.25 | 0 | – |
| 1950-51 | v England | 2 | 72 | – | 24.00 | 0 | – |
| 1951-52 | v West Indies | 2 | 9 | – | 3.00 | 0 | – |
| 1952-53 | v South Africa | 2 | 17 | – | 5.66 | 2 | 56.00 |
| 1953-54 | in South Africa | 5 | 263 | 1 | 29.22 | 12 | 32.00 |
| 1954-55 | v England | 2 | 106 | – | 26.50 | 4 | 19.00 |
| 1955-56 | in Pakistan | 3 | 136 | – | 22.66 | 7 | 31.57 |
| 1955-56 | in India | 5 | 493 | 2 | 70.42 | 6 | 45.16 |
| 1955-56 | v West Indies | 4† | 203 | – | 25.37 | 7 | 36.85 |
| 1958 | in England | 5* | 147 | – | 16.33 | 6 | 31.16 |
| 1958-59 | v England | 2* | 44 | – | 14.66 | 3 | 17.66 |
| 1961-62 | in South Africa | 5* | 546 | 1 | 60.66 | 11 | 19.72 |
| 1962-63 | v England | 3* | 263 | 1 | 52.60 | 2 | 85.50 |
| 1963-64 | v South Africa | 3* | 88 | – | 14.66 | 12 | 23.16 |
| 1964-65 | v Pakistan | 3* | 229 | – | 38.16 | 4 | 35.50 |
| 1964-65 | in India | 4* | 198 | – | 28.28 | 3 | 59.33 |
| 1964-65 | in Pakistan | 3* | 296 | 1 | 59.20 | 5 | 27.00 |
| 1965 | in England | 3* | 148 | – | 24.66 | 1 | 54.00 |
| Total | | 58 | 3,431 | 6 | 33.31 | 85 | 33.41 |

**Career runs:** 16,067  *Average:* 41.62
**Highest Test score:** 142 v South Africa, Johannesburg, 1961-62
**Highest career score:** 296, Wellington v Northern Districts, Wellington, 1962-63
**Career wickets:** 458  *Average:* 22.51
**Best Test bowling:** 6-60 v South Africa, Dunedin, 1963-64
**Best career bowling:** 7-20, Otago v Central Districts, Dunedin, 1956-57

*Captain    †Captain in 3 Tests

Central Press

# Richards

### Barry Anderson
### (1945-    )

Barry Richards is something of a throwback in cricket. The modern theory that batsmen, especially those going in first, cannot score quickly against present-day bowling and scientific field-placing has no place in his make-up. He believes that the aim of a batsman is to dominate an attack from first to last, and because of this outlook is one of the most attractive and successful batsmen in the game.

After making an early impact in his home town of Durban, Richards captained the South African schools side that visited England in 1963 and made his first-class debut for Natal in 1964-65. Along with Mike Procter, also from Natal, he played for Gloucestershire's Second XI in 1965—they could not appear in the County Championship because of the qualification rules. They did appear together, though, for the first eleven against the South Africans, and both did so well that Gloucestershire hoped they would remain in England and so qualify by residence. Instead they went home to South Africa, although Procter later returned on special registration for Gloucestershire and Richards went to Hampshire.

In his first season for Hampshire, Richards hit 2,039 runs in the Championship, and finished second to Geoff Boycott in the overall averages, with 2,395 runs

at an average of 47.90, his five centuries including 206 against Nottinghamshire at Portsmouth. The following season, despite injuries, he averaged 57.60 for 1,440 runs, and in 1970 scored 1,667 runs (averaging 53.77). In 1970-71 he went to Australia where, playing for South Australia, he scored 224 against MCC followed a little later by 356 in the Sheffield Shield match against Western Australia and 146 in the second game with MCC. He also broke Don Bradman's South Australian record of 1,448 in a season.

Richards had a brilliant first Test series, scoring 508 runs in seven innings against Australia in South Africa in early 1970, hitting 140 in his second Test at Durban and 126 in the fourth at Port Elizabeth. He also played in all five matches for the Rest of the World against England in 1970, but was not at his best and his highest score was only 64. Ideally suited to the one-day quick-fire cricket, Richards has many excellent performances in the Gillette Cup and John Player League.

Cricket can only be the loser as the political situation in South Africa has prevented Richards in his prime from gracing the Test arena in no more than that initial series against Australia. But any personal disappointment has not affected his performances either for Hampshire or for Natal, for whom he assumed the extra responsibility of captaincy with considerable success.

*Above left* **Barry Richards' belief in attacking cricket make him one of the game's most exhilarating batsmen.** *Above* **He compiles his runs in text-book fashion, a complete master of every shot, particularly the drive. His appeal to the spectator lies in the fact that he is so rarely inhibited from displaying his repertoire in any form of cricket.**

---

**RICHARDS Barry Anderson**

**Teams:** Natal, Hampshire, and South Africa

| Test series | Tests | Runs | 100s | Average |
|---|---|---|---|---|
| 1969-70 v | | | | |
| Australia | 4 | 508 | 2 | 72.57 |

**Career runs:** 16,751 *Average:* 56.78
**Highest Test score:** 140 v Australia, Durban, 1969-70
**Highest career score:** 356, South Australia v Western Australia, Perth, 1970-71

Career figures to the start of the 1973 season

# Snow

## John Augustine (1941- )

By the end of the 1970-71 MCC tour of Australia, John Snow was generally regarded as the best and most hostile fast bowler of the period, and his 31 wickets in the series had gone a long way towards England's regaining the Ashes after a gap of 12 years.

Like many of the leading fast bowlers the game has known, Snow is a controversial character, either loved or hated depending on what part of the world he is playing in. He sends down a liberal supply of bouncers that some batsmen find intimidating, but he is at his most dangerous when getting the ball to lift from a length—something he can do more than most. He is also a man of moods, and there have been times when he has looked far from the bowler he can be. Without question he needs the stimulus of a big occasion or a challenge in order to prove himself, and the contrast in his character is shown by the fact that a man who can be so aggressive on the field is also someone who writes poetry.

His father, a vicar in Sussex and keenly interested in cricket, gave Snow his first lessons on the vicarage lawn, and at Christ's Hospital school, where he stayed nine years, he began as a batsman. In later years, however, he developed as a fast bowler. He began at Sussex in 1961, but not until 1964 did he gain a regular place in the side, being awarded his county cap that summer. The next year, when he took over 100 wickets, his form was good enough to attract the attention of the Test selectors, and he began his Test career with one match against New Zealand and one against South Africa.

In 1966 he captured 126 wickets and began to establish himself as an England bowler. His best bowling and best batting figures up to 1971 came in that year, and he was chosen for three games against West Indies, taking 12 wickets. His most memorable feat, though, was with the bat, for at the Oval he scored 59 not out and with Ken Higgs took part in a last-wicket stand of 128. At this stage of his career, he had not yet developed his real menace, but it burst forth in the West Indies in 1967-68, when he took 7-49 at Kingston, 5-86 at Bridgetown, and 6-60 at Georgetown, altogether capturing 27 wickets for 504 runs in the series.

In the home series with Australia in 1968 he took 17 wickets, and England, appreciating the Australians' discomfort against true fast bowling, looked to him as their main shock bowler in the 1970-71 series. If that edge was slightly blunted in the 1972 series, he still finished with 24 wickets and though the arm was slightly lower he remained England's quickest bowler in 1973.

### SNOW John Augustine

**Teams:** Sussex and England

| Test series | | | Tests | Wkts | Average |
|---|---|---|---|---|---|
| 1965 | v | New Zealand | 1 | 4 | 20.00 |
| 1965 | v | South Africa | 1 | 4 | 36.50 |
| 1966 | v | West Indies | 3 | 12 | 37.58 |
| 1967 | v | India | 3 | 10 | 26.40 |
| 1967 | v | Pakistan | 1 | 3 | 42.00 |
| 1967-68 | in | West Indies | 4 | 27 | 18.66 |
| 1968 | v | Australia | 5 | 17 | 29.88 |
| 1968-69 | in | Pakistan | 2 | 4 | 21.25 |
| 1969 | v | West Indies | 3 | 15 | 27.06 |
| 1969 | v | New Zealand | 2 | 3 | 51.33 |
| 1970-71 | in | Australia | 6† | 31 | 22.83 |
| 1971 | v | India | 2 | 6 | 28.16 |
| 1972 | v | Australia | 5 | 24 | 23.12 |
| 1973 | v | New Zealand | 3 | 13 | 24.61 |
| Total | | | 41 | 173 | 25.87 |

**Career wickets:** 853 *Average:* 22.39
**Best Test bowling:** 7-40 v Australia, Sydney, 1970-71
**Best career bowling:** 7-29, Sussex v West Indians, Hove, 1966
**Highest Test and career score:** 73 v India, Lords, 1971

*Not out.   †Excludes abandoned Melbourne Test.
Career figures up to the start of the 1973 season

1 The return of the Ashes to England in 1970-71 was in no small part due to John Snow, who established himself as perhaps the best and most hostile bowler of his time. 2 Snow, the batsman, on the receiving end: the bowler, Australia's 'Froggy' Thomson.

Patrick Eager

Central Press

# Sobers

## Garfield St Aubrun (1936- )

A number of cricketers could claim the title of 'the best all-rounder the game has known', but few could have such a strong claim as the West Indian left-hander Gary Sobers. He could hold his place in any side on either his batting or bowling alone. But to these must be added amazing reflexes in the field that enable him to bring off brilliant catches close to the wicket. Nor is he merely a fine player. He is an astute captain and his approach to the game makes him one of its true characters.

Nobody seeing Sobers going out to bat could fail to be thrilled with expectation—the familiar walk with shoulders slightly stooping, quick strides peculiarly his own; the air of a man eager to get on with the slaughter of bowlers. Rarely is the spectator disappointed. There have been others more elegant in style, but hardly anyone has hit the ball with such power and certainly while obviously enjoying every moment of his stay at the crease. Glamorgan's Malcolm Nash knows to what extent a bowler can suffer at Sobers' hands. At Swansea in August 1968 playing against Nottinghamshire, he had the mortifying experience of being struck for six off every delivery of a 6-ball over. Never before had a bowler been subjected to such treatment. That particular innings —76 not out in 35 minutes—contained seven sixes and six fours, and it showed the extent to which Sobers can pulverize an attack.

Another world record to his credit is his 365 not out against Pakistan in the third Test at Kingston in 1957-58. As he amassed the highest score in Test history, Sobers shared a second-wicket stand of 446 with Conrad Hunte, the highest partnership ever for West Indies.

When Sobers sets himself for a big hit, he puts everything behind it. His lithe body winds up and then uncoils like a compressed spring released; the ball comes off the bat with terrific velocity, and many a fieldsman has had bruised hands trying to stop it. His driving on either side of the wicket is equally skilful, his hooks and pulls are thunderous, and his cutting can be at times vicious, at other times delicate. He is, in effect, the complete batsman, for although he believes and proves that aggression pays, he can also defend as well as most.

As a left-arm bowler, Sobers is three men in one. Opening the attack off a medium-length lolloping run-up he can be fast. His action is well nigh perfect, with a beautiful, classical side-on delivery, and his ability to make the ball swing in late or run away to the slips after pitching makes him a real menace, especially while the shine is on the ball. Later in an innings he often switches to slow bowling. If the pitch is helpful, he bowls orthodox spinners; on other occasions he tries off-breaks and googlies from the back of the hand. As a result of his many talents, he is always in the game, and it is not very often that he fails to make an impression in one form or other.

From the moment he entered the first-class arena as a 16-year-old in June 1953, Gary Sobers made his mark. His figures of 22-5-50-4 and 67-35-92-3 for Barbados against that year's Indians were highly commendable, and a year later he was in the Test side against England at Kingston. He claimed 4-75 with his slow spinners in the England innings of 414. His batting was developing all the time, too, and early in 1955 he opened the innings against Australia in the fourth Test at Bridgetown. Ray Lindwall and Keith Miller were hit for 43 in 15 minutes.

Touring England in 1957 he scored 1,664 runs in first-class matches, including 219 not out against his future county Nottinghamshire, but his Test record was

**For spectators there are few more exciting sights than Gary Sobers in full flow: a bowler may think otherwise.**

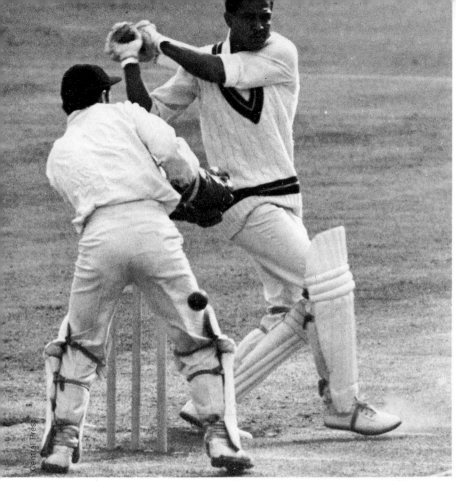

only modest. It was against Pakistan back home that winter that he came into his own with a vengeance, his maiden Test century being the treble hundred at Kingston that beat Len Hutton's 20-year-old Test record by one run. In the next game, at Georgetown, he scored 125 and 109 not out, and there was little doubt that Sobers the international batsman had arrived. Realizing his attraction as a crowd-pleaser, Radcliffe, the Central Lancashire League club, signed him as a professional, and it was with them that he developed the arts of fast bowling.

But when he went with the West Indian side to India and Pakistan in 1958-59 he found the pitches unsympathetic to speed and so changed his style once more— this time trying off-breaks and 'chinamen'. Meanwhile his batting thrived in the conditions, and in successive innings in the first three Tests he made 25, 142 not out, 4, 198, and 106 not out. This meant he had scored six centuries in six successive Test matches.

Against the England touring side of 1959-60 he hit 154 for Barbados, and a few days later scored 226 in the first Test, sharing a stand of 399 with Frank Worrell (197 not out). It began at 4.50 p.m. on the Friday and ended at 11.40 a.m. on the Tuesday—a total of 9½ hours—and was the best fourth-wicket stand for the West Indies. In that series he also made 147 at Kingston and 145 at Georgetown, scoring 709 runs and averaging 101.28. In Australia in 1960-61 he played a notable part in the tie at Brisbane, scoring 132, and later,

Few players can have as much claim to the title of the 'best all-rounder in cricket' as Gary Sobers. Whether he is batting, bowling, or fielding, he is capable of taking a game by the scruff of the neck and changing its whole course. In 1966, England felt the full effect of his talents when he scored 722 runs, including 3 centuries, and took 20 wickets for West Indies in the series.

at Sydney, made 168. South Australia were so impressed that they persuaded him to sign for them, and he stayed there for three seasons, the state finishing third, second, and first respectively while he was there. In 1962-63, he created an Australian record by becoming the first player to score 1,000 runs and take 50 wickets in a season.

Many other notable performances with bat and ball followed, and he gained fresh fame when he took over the leadership of West Indies in 1965. He had another spell in English league cricket, with Norton in the North Staffordshire League, and in late 1967 joined Nottinghamshire. Taking over the captaincy in 1968 he helped them jump from 15th to 4th place that season, and in 1970 his genius was further rewarded when he was appointed captain of the Rest of the World team that played England. Injury interrupted his run of success and he missed the 1973 series against Australia. But later that year he returned against England, with more Test runs to his name than any other player.

### SOBERS Garfield St Aubrun

Teams: Barbados, South Australia, Nottinghamshire, and West Indies

| Test series | | Tests | Runs | 100s | Average | Wkts | Average |
|---|---|---|---|---|---|---|---|
| 1953-54 | v England | 1 | 40 | – | 40.00 | 4 | 20.25 |
| 1954-55 | v Australia | 4 | 231 | – | 38.50 | 6 | 35.50 |
| 1955-56 | in New Zealand | 4 | 81 | – | 16.20 | 2 | 24.50 |
| 1957 | in England | 5 | 320 | – | 32.00 | 5 | 71.00 |
| 1957-58 | v Pakistan | 5 | 824 | 3 | 137.33 | 4 | 94.25 |
| 1958-59 | in India | 5 | 557 | 3 | 92.83 | 10 | 29.20 |
| 1958-59 | in Pakistan | 3 | 160 | – | 32.00 | 0 | — |
| 1959-60 | v England | 5 | 709 | 3 | 101.28 | 9 | 39.55 |
| 1960-61 | in Australia | 5 | 430 | 2 | 43.00 | 15 | 39.20 |
| 1961-62 | v India | 5 | 424 | 2 | 70.66 | 23 | 20.56 |
| 1963 | in England | 5 | 322 | 1 | 40.25 | 20 | 28.55 |
| 1964-65 | v Australia | 5† | 352 | – | 39.11 | 12 | 41.00 |
| 1966 | in England | 5† | 722 | 3 | 103.14 | 20 | 27.25 |
| 1966-67 | in India | 3† | 342 | 0 | 114.00 | 14 | 25.00 |
| 1967-68 | v England | 5† | 545 | 2 | 90.83 | 13 | 39.07 |
| 1968-69 | in Australia | 5† | 497 | 2 | 49.70 | 18 | 40.72 |
| 1968-69 | in New Zealand | 3† | 70 | – | 14.00 | 7 | 43.00 |
| 1969 | in England | 3† | 150 | – | 30.00 | 11 | 28.90 |
| 1971 | v India† | 5 | 597 | 3 | 74.62 | 12 | 33.50 |
| 1971-72 | v New Zealand† | 5 | 253 | 1 | 36.14 | 10 | 33.20 |
| Total | | 86 | 7,626 | 25 | 58.66 | 215 | 34.46 |

Career runs: 25,795 Average: 55.83
Highest Test and career score: 365* v Pakistan, Kingston, 1957-58
Career wickets: 967 Average: 27.67
Best Test bowling: 6-73 v Australia, Brisbane, 1968-69
Best career bowling: 9-49, West Indians v Kent, Canterbury, 1966

*Not out.     †Captain.     Career figures up to the start of the 1973 season

# Statham

## John Brian (1930-     )

Known by his cricketing friends as 'George', England and Lancashire opening bowler Brian Statham could be considered the ideal professional. During a career lasting 19 years, he was a highly popular player both on and off the field, everyone admiring the level-headed manner in which he took adversity as well as adulation. Most fast bowlers possess a volatile nature that sometimes gets them into trouble, but there was never the slightest suggestion of Statham giving offence. In this way, he contrasted markedly with his England partner Fred Trueman. The Yorkshireman was all fire and brimstone, the Lancastrian gentlemanly and phlegmatic.

Not that batsmen could ever regard him with anything but the greatest respect, for he was a formidable opponent. At times, the critics would say he was too accurate, meaning that batsmen, even if they found him difficult to score off, knew what to expect. Against that, however, it was claimed that his very accuracy meant that batsmen took more risks than they normally would have done at the other end. Time and time again he would see the ball beat the bat without reward. Other men would have found this galling, but Statham took it all in his stride and continued to try to the limit.

He possessed the philosophical approach to the vagaries of fortune experienced by all bowlers. But it never weakened his resolve to keep plugging away, always aiming at the stumps. Few bowlers have attained such accuracy at such a biting pace, but Statham had his own dictum and his own motivation—"If they miss, I hit," he would explain with a wry smile, and the number of defeated batsmen who went back to the pavilion "b Statham" accounted for a high proportion of his victims.

After doing his National Service in the RAF, Statham joined Stockport in the Central Lancashire League. He did nothing exceptional there, but his potential was recognized and MCC suggested Statham contact his county club, who offered him a trial. Taken on in May 1950, he came under the guidance of Harry Makepeace, the Lancashire coach, and made such rapid progress that within two months he was making his Championship debut against Kent at Old Trafford—on June 17, his 20th birthday. A few weeks later he gained a regular place in the county side. Though he was somewhat raw and his action looked ungainly, there was no denying the speed he possessed, and he had several successes, notably at Bath where in one spell he took 5

Somerset wickets for 5 runs. His remarkably quick advance was far from over, and before the summer ended he had been awarded his county cap. Then that winter, together with his team-mate Roy Tattersall, he was called upon to reinforce the injury-hit MCC team in Australia. He did not play in any Tests there, but made his England debut against New Zealand at Christchurch.

Lancashire were naturally delighted with his progress, and in his second season he made his mark with 97 wickets at 15.11 apiece. Slim and wiry, Statham was known for a time as 'The Whippet', but gradually he filled out and developed powerful shoulders, which gave him added pace. As a left-handed batsman, he often provided amusing entertainment for the crowd—but not always for his opponents, who found he sometimes stayed at the crease longer than expected. He was also a fine outfield with a sure pair of hands that rarely missed a catch, and a long accurate throw from the deep.

From the time he made his Test debut, Brian Statham was usually an automatic choice for England, featuring in the strong sides that won and retained the Ashes in the 1950s. His partnerships with Frank Tyson and Trueman often found him playing a supporting role, but neither would deny the large part he played in their own successes. With just a little bit of luck, however, he himself could easily have been the more successful partner. After 1963, it seemed that Statham's Test career was over, but he came back for one match against South Africa at the Oval in 1965 and with 5-40 and 2-105 completed 250 Test wickets. Among those were his 7-39 against South Africa at Lord's in 1955 and his 7-57 against Australia at Melbourne in 1958-59.

Outside Test cricket, he topped 100 wickets in 13 seasons, 10 in succession from 1957 to 1966, and his triumphs included three hat-tricks—against Sussex at Old

 *(caption marker "2")*

## STATHAM John Brian

**Teams:** Lancashire and England

| Test series | | Tests | Wkts | Average |
|---|---|---|---|---|
| 1950-51 | in New Zealand | 1 | 1 | 47.00 |
| 1951 | v South Africa | 2 | 4 | 19.50 |
| 1951-52 | in India | 5 | 8 | 36.62 |
| 1953 | v Australia | 1 | 2 | 44.00 |
| 1953-54 | in West Indies | 4 | 16 | 28.75 |
| 1954 | v Pakistan | 4 | 11 | 19.36 |
| 1954-55 | in Australia | 5 | 18 | 27.72 |
| 1954-55 | in New Zealand | 2 | 12 | 7.58 |
| 1955 | v South Africa | 4 | 17 | 21.35 |
| 1956 | v Australia | 3 | 7 | 26.28 |
| 1956-57 | in South Africa | 4 | 14 | 24.92 |
| 1957 | v West Indies | 3 | 13 | 33.30 |
| 1958 | v New Zealand | 2 | 7 | 18.57 |
| 1958-59 | in Australia | 4 | 12 | 23.83 |
| 1959 | v India | 3 | 17 | 13.11 |
| 1959-60 | in West Indies | 3 | 10 | 28.60 |
| 1960 | v South Africa | 5 | 27 | 18.18 |
| 1961 | v Australia | 4 | 17 | 29.47 |
| 1962 | v Pakistan | 3 | 16 | 17.37 |
| 1962-63 | in Australia | 5 | 13 | 44.61 |
| 1963 | v West Indies | 2 | 3 | 81.00 |
| 1965 | v South Africa | 1 | 7 | 20.71 |
| **Total** | | **70** | **252** | **24.84** |

**Career wickets:** 2.260   *Average:* 16.36
**Best Test bowling:** 7-39 v South Africa, Lord's, 1955
**Best career bowling:** 8-34, Lancashire v Warwickshire, Coventry, 1957
**Highest Test score:** 38 v India, Lord's, 1959
**Highest career score:** 62, Lancashire v Leicestershire, Old Trafford, 1955

Trafford in 1956, for MCC against Transvaal at Johannesburg in 1956-57, and against Leicestershire at Old Trafford in 1958. At Coventry in 1957 he took 15 wickets (8-34 and 7-55) in the match with Warwickshire, and another 15 (7-71 and 8-37) came against Leicestershire in 1964.

Statham's benefit in 1961 showed the esteem in which the public held him, for it brought him over £13,000. In 1965, he took over the captaincy of Lancashire and in the New Year's Honours List of 1966 was awarded the CBE. The next season, however, he relinquished the county leadership, and in 1968 his career came to an end.

**1** A confident appeal by Brian Statham, 'keeper Jim Parks, and slips Colin Cowdrey and Ken Barrington is rewarded with Colin Bland's dismissal. Statham, aged 35 and out of Test cricket since 1963, was recalled to the England side for the last Test against the 1965 South Africans and celebrated his return with 5-40 in the Springboks' first innings, the fifth giving him his 250th wicket in Tests.
**2** As a batsman, Statham enjoyed a tail-ender's slog.
**3** Statham in action in his last Roses match in 1968 and **4** in Adelaide on his last tour of Australia in 1962-63.

 *(caption marker "1")*

 *(caption marker "4")*

Central Press

Ray Green

Central Press

Sport & General

# Trueman

## Frederick Sewards (1931- )

Characters in cricket, and no doubt in other walks of life, are often not appreciated until they have retired or at least reached a seniority that gives their peculiar individuality a loveable quality. In the young it would be merely bumptiousness. Thus it was some time before Fred Trueman, 'Fiery Fred' to many, was fully appreciated in all quarters. For most of a first-class career that lasted from 1949 to 1968, however, he was seen by the public as a rugged personality epitomizing the down-to-earth Yorkshireman. For almost as long, his sayings, most of them impromptu and born of a quick wit and unfettered tongue, were a legend in the cricket world. One of the most polite and most well known is that when he was asked if he thought any other bowler would ever take 300 wickets in Test cricket. 'Aye', he said, 'but whoever does will be bloody tired.'

When he first played for Yorkshire, Trueman already had the makings of a fine, almost classical fast bowler's method. The gently curving run-up was on the long side, but the acceleration was right and all that was needed was greater control. He had a natural movement away from the bat, which at the pace he could obviously work up would make him a menace to the best batsmen. But there was a wildness about him, perhaps stemming partly from his not looking at the batsman in the delivery stride, and this temporarily delayed his development. Soon, however, when not much over 20, he was routing the Indians of 1952 and being recognized as one of the world's most formidable fast bowlers.

He was especially welcome in England, where there had been no bowlers of genuine pace since the war until he and Brian Statham appeared, shortly to be followed by Frank Tyson. Nevertheless, throughout Fred Trueman's career there was plenty of competition, and his progress was not unopposed. In a less prosperous period in English cricket, he might have played many more than 67 Test matches. He was not picked to go to Australia in 1954, when Tyson, Statham, and Peter Loader were preferred, but the quality of his bowling became more and more appreciated, especially his ability to move the ball in the air and off the pitch at a high speed. Though he himself was often quoted as claiming to be 'the fastest bloody bowler in the world' and as issuing bloodcurdling threats to unwary batsmen, he soon realized that pace alone was not everything. Thus he remained a very good bowler until well into his late 30s.

Nor was bowling his whole cricket life. He was renowned as a mighty hitter, showing no respect whatsoever for the textbook dictum that the right hand should play an unobtrusive part in most strokes. But he could also turn successfully to defence if the situation demanded. He was a brilliant close fielder and, unusually, could throw almost equally well with either arm.

The son of a miner, Trueman worked briefly as one before, at 18, making his first appearances for Yorkshire. His immense promise was obvious, but he was brought along gradually during the next few years, two of which were spent doing national service in the RAF. He was in some ways lucky to play his first Tests in 1952 against Indian batsmen unused to fast bowlers on lively pitches, and in four Tests he took 29 wickets at 13.31 apiece, including 8-31 at Old Trafford. The next year, however, he played only once against Australia. That winter he went to the West Indies with Len Hutton's team, but in the turbulent atmosphere of cricket there, his brash, forthright manner frequently had him in trouble, and though he took 134 wickets at home in 1954 the

selectors did not call on him for Australia. The Ashes were won without him. He was not fit in 1956, and he was again left out of a touring side, this time to South Africa.

At this stage he had had several successful but, at the highest level, disappointing seasons. He had now, however, gained experience, and from about 1957 to 1963 was at his peak. In 1960 he had his best home season, taking 175 wickets, and it was not until 1967 that he took fewer than 100 again. In all he took 100 wickets in a season 12 times, and among bowlers of comparable pace only Brian Statham, 13 times, has done it more often. In his later years, a touch of prudence made his batting more productive overall, and his three first-class hundreds were made between 1963 and 1965.

Valuable though he was to Yorkshire, it was in Test matches that the real class of his bowling was shown by his ability to surprise the world's best players. Between 1958 and 1964 he missed only odd matches for England. In 1960 in the West Indies he took 21 Test wickets and kept clear of the controversy that had surrounded him on the previous tour. At home that year he took 25 wickets against South Africa and in 1961 20 more against Australia, including 5-58 and 6-30 at Leeds, where he made the most of a poor pitch and enabled England to win by eight wickets.

At Lord's in 1962 he took 6-31 when Pakistan were bowled out for 100 on the first day and in the series added 22 Test wickets to the growing list. Against Frank Worrell's triumphant West Indians of 1963 he took 11 wickets in the famous Lord's Test, followed by 12 at Edgbaston. His 7-44 in the last innings there brought England their only win and was a model of how conditions allowing the ball to move in the air and off the

seam should be exploited. In that series his tally of wickets was 34—against the next most successful English bowler's bag of 15.

In the previous Australian season of 1962-63, with Ted Dexter's MCC side, he had refuted the theory that fast bowlers over 30 are past their best in Australia and had taken 20 wickets. But that was his last official tour. In the 1964 series against Australia he was still the major wicket-taker with 17, but he was dropped for the fourth Test and there were suggestions that his Test career might be over. At this point he was easily the biggest wicket-taker in Test history, and there was widespread hope that he would have a chance to reach 300. He was then on 297. Recalled for the final Test at the Oval, he was for a long time far from dangerous, but eventually, coming on for another spell, he dismissed Redpath and McKenzie with successive balls and soon afterwards made Neil Hawke the 300th victim amid universal jubilation.

The end of his Test career was not delayed for long. He played in only the first two of the six Tests against New Zealand and South Africa in 1965, and after three more seasons liberally sprinkled with bursts of characteristic brilliance, he retired from Yorkshire cricket too. He might almost have stage-managed his farewell season. Yorkshire won their third successive championship and, with Trueman at the helm, inflicted the first defeat on the 1968 Australians. It was Yorkshire's first defeat of an Australian side since 1902, and Trueman took 6 wickets in the match for 83 runs. Trueman was Yorkshire to the core which made incongruous a brief return for Derbyshire.

Patrick Eager

1 All eyes on Colin Cowdrey as he takes the catch from Neil Hawke that gave Fred Trueman (left) his 300th wicket in Test cricket.
2 The England team surround Trueman to congratulate him on his feat. After his last Test, and his 307th Test wicket, Trueman had taken 55 more Test wickets than any other bowler from any country.
3 In the last few years of his career, Trueman developed into a sound batsman, as well as preserving the smooth bowling action (4) which accounted for 2,304 batsmen in a first-class career lasting from 1949 to 1968.

Patrick Eager

## TRUEMAN Frederick Sewards

Teams: Yorkshire and England

| Test series | | Tests | Wkts | Average |
|---|---|---|---|---|
| 1952 | v India | 4 | 29 | 13.31 |
| 1953 | v Australia | 1 | 4 | 22.50 |
| 1953-54 | in West Indies | 3 | 9 | 46.66 |
| 1955 | v South Africa | 1 | 2 | 56.00 |
| 1956 | v Australia | 2 | 9 | 20.44 |
| 1957 | v West Indies | 5 | 22 | 20.68 |
| 1958 | v New Zealand | 5 | 15 | 17.06 |
| 1958-59 | in Australia | 3 | 9 | 30.66 |
| 1958-59 | in New Zealand | 2 | 5 | 21.00 |
| 1959 | v India | 5 | 24 | 16.70 |
| 1959-60 | in West Indies | 5 | 21 | 26.14 |
| 1960 | v South Africa | 5 | 25 | 20.32 |
| 1961 | v Australia | 4 | 20 | 26.45 |
| 1962 | v Pakistan | 4 | 22 | 19.95 |
| 1962-63 | in Australia | 5 | 20 | 26.05 |
| 1962-63 | in New Zealand | 2 | 14 | 11.71 |
| 1963 | v West Indies | 5 | 34 | 17.47 |
| 1964 | v Australia | 4 | 17 | 23.47 |
| 1965 | v New Zealand | 2 | 6 | 39.50 |
| Total | | 67 | 307 | 21.57 |

Career wickets: 2,304  Average: 18.29
Best Test bowling: 8-31 v India, Old Trafford, 1952
Best career bowling: 8-28, Yorkshire v Kent, Dover, 1954
Highest Test score: 39* v New Zealand, Oval, 1958
Highest career score: 104, Yorkshire v Northamptonshire, Northampton, 1963

*Not out

# Underwood

## Derek Leslie (1945- )

Quiet and undemonstrative, with a shuffling, unathletic gait, Derek Underwood does not, at first sight, look the type of cricketer to break records and upset traditions. But he has enjoyed a career probably unique among English bowlers. Most bowlers, particularly those relying on length and accuracy, need many years to learn their job. Underwood appeared unheralded in first-class cricket in 1963 aged 17, and that season took 101 wickets. By 1971 he had already taken more than 1,000 first-class wickets and over 100 in Test matches.

Underwood's method is unusual too. His slow-medium pace is faster than that of the normal left-arm spinner. And he does not attempt to spin the ball prodigiously, relying instead on numerous subtle variations that can surprise batsmen on the best of pitches. On bad pitches he can be next to unplayable, so quickly can he make the ball turn or lift.

After his remarkable first season, when he became the youngest bowler ever to take 100 wickets, he took 9-28 the next year against Sussex at Hastings, and 9-37 against Essex on another rough pitch, at Westcliff in 1966, when he played in his first Test matches. His debut was against West Indies at Trent Bridge, where he did not take a wicket but bowled 43 overs for 86 runs in the second innings and batted with unexpected obstinacy to share in a last-wicket stand of 65 with Basil D'Oliveira. In the second Test he took the wicket of Rohan Kanhai but was unsuccessful otherwise, and he did not play in the last Test.

His first official tour, with the Under-25 side to Pakistan in 1966-67, was also not especially successful, and the tendency grew to regard him as a very good bowler in English conditions but ineffective on hard pitches overseas. He was not taken to the West Indies on the full tour a year later, but went with a Commonwealth side to Pakistan and to Ceylon, where, after rain, he had the astonishing figures of 8-10 and 7-33 against the Ceylon President's XI in Colombo.

Underwood's greatest triumph was to follow in 1968, in the last Test against Australia at the Oval. He had been quite successful in the three previous Tests he had played in that summer and, for good measure, had contributed a hard-hitting 45 not out at Leeds at No. 11. In the last Test his big chance came. In the first innings he bowled 54.3 overs with customary steadiness and took 2-89, but on the last day there was a thunderstorm, and when play became possible again only 75 minutes remained. If the pitch became difficult as it dried, Underwood was clearly the match-winner. Forty minutes passed before it did and then, after a wicket fell to D'Oliveira, Underwood took the last wickets in 27 balls to win the match with six minutes to spare, level the series, and finish with 7-50 himself.

In the three-match series against New Zealand in 1969, he was in devastating form, taking 24 wickets at 9 apiece, but there were still those who doubted his effectiveness in Australia. Nonetheless he played an important part in the recovery of the Ashes in 1970-71, containing the Australian batsmen while the fast bowlers recovered, and taking 16 wickets. At times since then he has been uncertain of his Test place. In 1972 he was omitted until the Fourth Test at Headingly where, on a pitch ideally suited to his style, he returned match figures of 10 for 82 to win the match and keep The Ashes in England.

Yet at the start of the 1973 season, he had lost his place again, though he regained it later in the summer.

**1** The Oval, 1968, and the end of Australia's second innings as Derek Underwood captures his seventh wicket to win the match for England with just six minutes to spare. On such a pitch, the Kent left-armer was nigh impossible to play.
**2** Underwood's bowling action.

Central Press

### UNDERWOOD Derek Leslie

Teams: Kent and England

| Test series | | Tests | Wkts | Average |
|---|---|---|---|---|
| 1966 | v West Indies | 2 | 1 | 172.00 |
| 1967 | v Pakistan | 2 | 8 | 16.12 |
| 1968 | v Australia | 4 | 20 | 15.10 |
| 1968-69 | in Pakistan | 3 | 8 | 25.50 |
| 1969 | v West Indies | 2 | 6 | 16.83 |
| 1969 | v New Zealand | 3 | 24 | 9.16 |
| 1970-71 | in Australia | 5 | 16 | 32.50 |
| 1970-71 | in New Zealand | 2 | 17 | 12.05 |
| 1971 | v Pakistan | 1 | — | — |
| 1971 | v India | 1 | 4 | 30.25 |
| 1972 | v Australia | 2 | 16 | 16.62 |
| 1972-73 | in India | 4 | 15 | 30.47 |
| 1972-73 | in Pakistan | 2 | 3 | 71.66 |
| 1973 | v New Zealand | 1 | — | — |
| Total | | 34 | 138 | 22.13 |

Career wickets: 1,207 *Average:* 18.89
Best Test bowling: 7-32 v New Zealand, Lord's, 1969
Best career bowling: 9-28, Kent v Sussex, Hastings, 1964
Highest Test score: 45* v Australia, Leeds, 1968
Highest career score: 80, Kent v Lancashire, Old Trafford, 1969

*Not out. Career figures up to the start of the 1973 season

Patrick Eagar

# Walcott

## Clyde Leopold (1926- )

The largest and most powerful of the 'Three Ws', Clyde Walcott wrote his name in the record books even more often than Sir Frank Worrell and Everton Weekes. By 1971, only three men —Herbert Sutcliffe, George Headley, and Clyde Walcott—had twice scored a hundred in each innings of a Test match, but only Walcott did it twice in the same series. His scores for West Indies against Australia in the Caribbean in 1954-55 were 108 and 39, 126 and 110, 8 and 73, 15 and 83, and 155 and 110. His 827 runs in that series had been exceeded only by Don Bradman, Walter Hammond, and Neil Harvey, and his five separate hundreds were the most ever made in a series. Yet they were made for the losing side, for Australia, captained by Ian Johnson, won the series 3-0.

This season was the highlight of a career that began, in common with those of Weekes and Worrell, in the war years. Strictly in terms of class, Walcott was perhaps a shade below them, lacking the compact soundness and lightning feet of Weekes and the elegance of Worrell. But he was a tremendous striker of the ball, a driver and hooker of immense power.

He was only 16 when he first played for Barbados and barely 20 when cricket lovers the world over were noting with awe the names of two young men, Worrell and Walcott. Playing for Barbados against Trinidad at Port of Spain, they put on 574 in an unbroken stand for the fourth wicket, the highest partnership on record for any wicket. A year later the Indians Hazare and Gul Mahomed beat it by three runs, but nobody has approached it since.

The first of Walcott's 44 Test matches were played against England early in 1948. In his first Test he opened the innings, which may surprise those who remember him farther down the order at the height of his career, but he achieved little in that series and kept his place mainly because of his wicket-keeping. He kept wicket again in England in 1950, at 6 ft. 2 in. breaking all conventions for wicket-keepers, only this time he made a lot of runs, including 168 not out in the Lord's Test, the first ever won by West Indies in England.

He had a poor tour of Australia in 1951-52, when he was no longer keeping wicket, and played the fast bowling of Lindwall and Miller indifferently. But when Len Hutton's England team arrived in the West Indies early in 1954, he entered on his most prolific period. In the series he made 698 runs, averaging 87, and his 220 in the second Test at Barbados was made in 6½ hours out of a

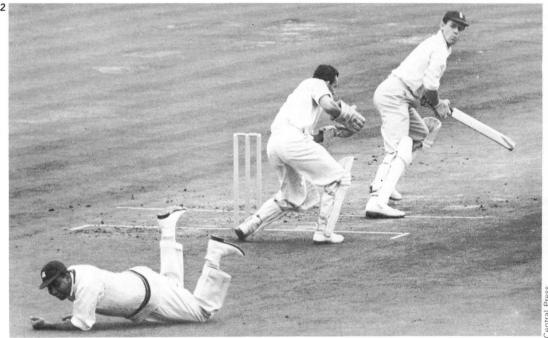

total of only 383. By now he was earning a reputation as a prop in a crisis, and it was his 116 in the second innings of the last Test that stood for some time between England and the victory that enabled them to draw the series.

His great series against Australia followed a year later, and his reputation was at its highest when he went to England in 1957. He started well with 117 and 49 against MCC, 115 against Notts, and 90 in the first innings of the first Test at Edgbaston, but a leg injury suffered there handicapped him thereafter and he made few runs. When England went to the West Indies in 1960 he was captaining British Guiana, as he was to do for some years more, but he played in only two Tests, and they were his last. He remained, however, an important figure in West Indies cricket, was awarded the OBE in 1965 for his services to it, and was manager of the 1969 team that toured England.

**1** Clyde Walcott may not have been quite the batting artist that the other two Ws—Weekes and Worrell—were, but few other batsmen could hit the ball with such immense power. His hooks, drives, and cuts flashed to the boundary at tremendous speed.
**2** A snick from Sheppard eludes Walcott in the slips. Earlier in his career Walcott had held his place in the West Indies side for his fielding ability—as a 6 ft. 2 in. wicket-keeper.

---

## WALCOTT Clyde Leopold

**Teams:** Barbados, British Guiana, and West Indies

| Test series | | Tests | Runs | 100s | Average |
|---|---|---|---|---|---|
| 1947-48 | v England | 4 | 133 | – | 22.16 |
| 1948-49 | in India | 5 | 452 | 2 | 64.57 |
| 1950 | in England | 4 | 229 | 1 | 45.80 |
| 1951-52 | in Australia | 3 | 87 | – | 14.50 |
| 1951-52 | in New Zealand | 2 | 199 | 1 | 66.33 |
| 1952-53 | v India | 5 | 457 | 2 | 76.16 |
| 1953-54 | v England | 5 | 698 | 3 | 87.25 |
| 1954-55 | v Australia | 5 | 827 | 5 | 82.70 |
| 1957 | in England | 5 | 247 | 1 | 27.44 |
| 1957-58 | v Pakistan | 4 | 385 | 1 | 96.25 |
| 1959-60 | v England | 2 | 84 | – | 28.00 |
| Total | | 44 | 3,798 | 15 | 56.68 |

**Career runs:** 11,820 *Average:* 56.55
**Highest Test score:** 220 v England, Bridgetown, 1953-54
**Highest career score:** 314*, Barbados v Trinidad, Port of Spain, 1945-46

*Not out.

Ray Green

# Walters

## Kevin Douglas (1945-    )

Few cricketers have had the experience, as Australia's Doug Walters has, of being hailed as a genius and written off as a mighty disappointment before they have passed their middle 20s. A brilliant start against England in 1965-66 was confirmed by an immensely successful series against West Indies three seasons later, when amongst other feats he became the first batsman in Test history to score a double hundred and a hundred in the same match. But before this, in England in 1968, and afterwards, in South Africa in 1969-70, at home in 1970-71 and in England in 1972 his technique looked suspect outside the off-stump.

Doug Walters's curiously mixed Test career began at Brisbane in December 1965, when, having already made 129 for New South Wales against MCC, he scored 155 in his first Test innings. Both in build and in background—he too came from a small town up-country—he brought back memories of Don Bradman. In temperament, also, he seemed supremely well equipped.

In his second Test, at Melbourne, Walters followed with 115, helping to save a match Australia looked like losing, and the fluency of his strokes, especially on the onside, was remarkable for a young man of 20. He lost no reputation in the rest of the series, for which he averaged 68, and he also looked a very useful seam bowler.

But soon afterwards he had to do his national service in the army, which prevented him from going on the 1966-67 tour of South Africa. Just how much the break hindered his development is hard to say, for though he went through the 1968 tour of England without making a hundred, he was back to his record-breaking best against West Indies. Injury kept him out of the first Test, but he followed with 76, 118, 110 and 50 run out, and finally 242 and 103. His total of 699 passed Neil Harvey's record for Australia against West Indies.

Which was the real Doug Walters? The tour of India in 1969-70 did not provide an answer, for although he made a valuable 102 in the last Test, he mustered only 286 altogether. And in South Africa, where his average of 32 was second best in an unsuccessful batting side, his only century on the tour came right at the end—against Western Province on a good batting wicket at Newlands.

In Australia in 1970-71, he began with a double hundred for New South Wales against MCC, but both this innings and his 112 in the first Test were made in a strangely unconvincing manner. Later, when the England bowlers gave him less on his legs and concentrated more on and around the off-stump, perhaps just short of a length, there appeared that same vulnerability to the short ball that the Springboks had exploited so successfully. The periods of fitful brilliance became fewer, and as many of his innings ended in an unworthy stroke it seemed as if his confidence had

Central Press

**Doug Walters's leg-side power was obvious, but bowlers found his off-side technique lacking.**

deserted him. In fact, he finished the series so unimpressively that not many would have expected him to be selected if there had been another match in the series.

Phlegmatically, he returned to form in the West Indies in 1973. Despite the technical defects that sparkling early promise may still be fulfilled.

| WALTERS Kevin Douglas | | | | |
|---|---|---|---|---|
| **Teams:** New South Wales and Australia | | | | |
| **Test series** | **Tests** | **Runs** | **100s** | **Average** |
| 1965-66 v England | 5 | 410 | 2 | 68.33 |
| 1967-68 v India | 2 | 254 | – | 127.00 |
| 1968 in England | 5 | 343 | – | 38.11 |
| 1968-69 v West Indies | 4 | 699 | 4 | 116.50 |
| 1969-70 in India | 5 | 286 | 1 | 40.85 |
| 1969-70 in South Africa | 4 | 258 | – | 32.25 |
| 1970-71 v England | 6 | 373 | 1 | 37.30 |
| 1972 in England | 4 | 54 | – | 7.71 |
| 1972-3 v Pakistan | 1 | 25 | – | 12.25 |
| 1972-3 in West Indies | 5 | 497 | 2 | 71.00 |
| Total | 41 | 3,199 | 10 | 49.98 |

**Career runs:** 10,140 *Average:* 46.09
**Highest Test score:** 242 v West Indies, Sydney, 1968-69
**Highest career score:** 253, New South Wales v South Australia, Adelaide, 1964-65

Career figures up to the end of the 1972-73 season

# Weekes

Everton de Courcy
(1925-      )

Everton Weekes, smaller in stature than the other two of the famous 'Three W's' who dominated West Indies cricket in the years after World War II, was the most brilliant on his day—and his day was a frequent occurrence. In New Zealand in 1955-56, he made five successive hundreds, by 1971 a feat only three batsmen had surpassed. And by then, no one had beaten or even equalled his feat of making five hundreds in successive Test innings, one against England in 1947-48 and four against India a year later in India. He was heading for a sixth when he was run out for 90 in his next innings.

Wonderfully quick into position, Weekes at times recalled Don Bradman in his range of ruthless, devastating strokes, which were played off front foot and back with flawless judgement and impeccable timing. He first played for Barbados in 1944, but his entry into Test cricket early in 1948 was disappointing for a batsman who already had a high reputation. However, in the last of the four Tests against England he made 141, an innings that is said to have been only just in time to save him from being left out of the team to go to India later that year. The sequel to it in India was remarkable. He averaged 111 in the Test series, in which he made 779 runs, and 90 in all first-class matches.

When he arrived in England in 1950, he had already acquired a big reputation, and it was soon being lifted even higher. An innings of 232 against Surrey was followed by 304 not out at Cambridge in five hours 25 minutes. Earlier in the match, Dewes and Sheppard had made 343 for the University's first wicket. He was kept within bounds for a month, and then made 279 against Notts, followed a fortnight later by 246 not out against Hampshire and 200 not out against Leicestershire. Not until he scored 129 in the classical partnership of 283 with Frank Worrell in the Trent Bridge Test did he make a hundred without turning it into a double hundred.

Like the other batsmen, he failed in Australia in 1951-52, but in the Caribbean and in league cricket in England he was a tremendous force. In 1952-53 he averaged 102 in the five-match series against India. A leg injury handicapped him against Len Hutton's England team a year later, but he still averaged nearly 70 and made 206 in the fourth Test in Trinidad. He was outshone by Clyde Walcott when the Australians visited the West Indies early in 1955, but made 139 and 87 not out in Port of Spain. His triumphant tour of New Zealand with a mainly young side followed, and in 10 innings he made 6 hundreds and averaged 104. Weekes was only 32 when West Indies went to England in 1957, and he seemed good for many more runs and records. But he was dogged by sinus trouble and injury, and it was not until the last match of the tour that he made his only hundred. Nevertheless, an innings of 90 with a broken finger in the Lord's Test was up to his very best form and is quoted as a gem of stroke play.

Back in the Caribbean he had a successful series against Pakistan, but during it he announced his retirement from Test cricket. When Peter May's England side arrived in 1959-60, they met Weekes as captain and coach of Barbados, whom he led to victory against them—without batting, but with some flighted leg-breaks with which he took 4 useful wickets for 38 in MCC's second innings!

---

### WEEKES Everton de Courcy

Teams: Barbados and West Indies

| Test series | | Tests | Runs | 100s | Average |
|---|---|---|---|---|---|
| 1947-48 | v England | 4 | 293 | 1 | 48.83 |
| 1948-49 | in India | 5 | 779 | 4 | 111.28 |
| 1950 | in England | 4 | 338 | 1 | 56.33 |
| 1951-52 | in Australia | 5 | 245 | – | 24.50 |
| 1951-52 | in New Zealand | 2 | 60 | – | 20.00 |
| 1952-53 | v India | 5 | 716 | 3 | 102.28 |
| 1953-54 | v England | 4 | 487 | 1 | 69.57 |
| 1954-55 | v Australia | 5 | 469 | 1 | 58.62 |
| 1955-56 | in New Zealand | 4 | 418 | 3 | 83.60 |
| 1957 | in England | 5 | 195 | – | 19.50 |
| 1957-58 | v Pakistan | 5 | 455 | 1 | 65.00 |
| Total | | 48 | 4,455 | 15 | 58.61 |

Career runs: 12,010  Average: 52.90
Highest Test score: 207 v India, Port of Spain, 1952-53
Highest career score: 304*, West Indians v Cambridge University, Cambridge, 1950

*Not out.

---

Wonderfully quick into position, Everton Weekes possessed a range of ruthless, devastating strokes that were played off both the front and back foot with flawless judgement and impeccable timing, bringing him hundreds of runs.

Press Association

Sport & General

# Worrell

## Sir Frank (1924-1967)

Famous as one of the 'Three Ws' of West Indian cricket, Frank Worrell was little less prolific than Everton Weeks and Clyde Walcott and was more elegant than either of them. But he became more than just a highly successful batsman. He captained West Indies on that tour of Australia in 1960-61 which, though West Indies lost, captured the imagination of the cricketing world, and he knitted together the different factions of West Indian cricket as never before.

He was captain again on that other triumphant venture to England in 1963, after which he retired. In 1964 he was knighted for his services to cricket, and, an immensely respected figure, he continued to work for cricket and for West Indies in a wider field until his sadly premature death of leukaemia in 1967 at the age of 42. The distinction he won in the last few years of his life was gained by courage, breadth of vision, dignity, and a capacity for leadership, and he was accorded the then unique tribute for a cricketer of a memorial service in Westminster Abbey.

As a cricketer, Worrell was a batsman of sound and orthodox method, wonderfully quick into position. Slim and a little above medium height, he was a fine driver and an especially skilful exponent of the late cut. If Walcott reflected power and Weeks quickfooted pugnacity, Worrell batted with the balanced grace of the artist.

He was also a left-arm bowler who, in the West Indies hey-day of the early 1960s, played a valuable part in the attack at a lively fast-medium pace. But in his early days in Barbados he was a slow left-arm bowler, and it was mainly in this role that he first played for Barbados in 1942.

It did not take him long to display his batting talents, though, and as early as 1943-44, when only 19, he was making 308 not out against Trinidad at Bridgetown, sharing with John Goddard in an unbroken stand of 502—then the world's best for the fourth wicket. Though twice exceeded in the next few years, once by Worrell himself with Walcott, it was still, in 1971, the fifth highest stand ever recorded for all wickets. His unbroken 574 with Walcott, to which he contributed 255 not out, was made two years later against Trinidad at Port of Spain and was the world's best ever fourth wicket stand and was still, in 1971, only three runs away from the record for all wickets.

By the time Gubby Allen's MCC team arrived in 1947-48, Worrell had moved to Jamaica, for whom he played thereafter. His first Test was the one in Trinidad, and he made 97 in his first Test innings. In his second Test, he scored 131 not out, the first of his nine Test hundreds.

Already recognized as a batsman of the highest class when he went to England in 1950, Worrell made six hundreds there, two of them in the Tests, in which he averaged 89. His innings of 261—made in 5 hours 35 minutes—in the third Test at Trent Bridge is still cited as one of the classics.

The next few years were relatively lean ones, though of the West Indies side to Australia in 1951-52 Worrell was one of the few to reproduce something like his best form. He took 6-38 at Adelaide in the Test West Indies won, and made 108 at Melbourne in the next Test, which they only just lost. He was unfit for much of Len Hutton's tour of West Indies in 1953-54, though he made 167 in the Trinidad Test. With a highest score of 61 he had a modest series against Australia a year later, but in England in 1957 he lost none of the lofty reputation earned seven years before. He headed the overall averages, carried his bat through the innings at Trent Bridge, where his 191 not out did much to save the match, and headed the bowling averages.

After his rescuing act with the bat in that Third Test, he almost repeated the feat with the ball in the next match of the series. A wonderfully sustained spell of 38.2 overs at Headingly brought him 7 for 70 and restricted England's first innings to 279. It was all in vain, as West Indies slumped to the second of their three innings defeats of that series. In all matches, Worrell had a marvellous tour, making nearly 1,500 runs in the summer at an average of over fifty, and taking his share of wickets at a reasonable cost.

Since 1948 Worrell had played successfully in the Lancashire League and had studied at Manchester University. Now he took the course in sociology that was to lead to his appointment as Warden of the University College of the West Indies. In time, he also became a senator in Parliament, but before that he embarked on the final triumphant stage of his playing career.

He had a good series against England in 1960, though his 197 not out in the first Test at Bridgetown in a stand of 399 with Gary Sobers was a marathon and rather untypical affair of 11 hours 20 minutes. Later that year he was made captain of the West Indies team for the tour of Australia, which ended with a ticker-tape drive through Melbourne. He was still a valuable batsman and bowler, though others such as his successor Gary Sobers were now commanding the scene as batsmen. But he had become almost a father figure who welded together with tremendous effectiveness the great talents of such players as Hall, Kanhai, Sobers, Hunte, Gibbs, Nurse, and the turbulent Griffith. Though they lost narrowly in Australia, West Indies won conclusively in England in 1963. Frank Worrell ended his long Test career at the Oval, acclaimed by a cricketing world that within four years was to be saddened by his untimely death.

1 Worrell acknowledges the applause that greeted his 200 at Trent Bridge in 1950.
2 His batting tended to dominate his career, but he was an invaluable left-arm medium pace bowler. With the ball, too, Trent Bridge was a happy ground. In 1957, he took seven England wickets for 70 runs there.

*Central Press*

*Keystone*

## WORRELL Sir Frank Mortimer Maglinne

Teams: Barbados, Jamaica, and West Indies

| Test series | | Tests | Runs | 100s | Avge | Wkts | Avge |
|---|---|---|---|---|---|---|---|
| 1947-48 | v England | 3 | 294 | 1 | 147.00 | 1 | 156.00 |
| 1950 | in England | 4 | 539 | 2 | 89.83 | 6 | 30.33 |
| 1951-52 | in Australia | 5 | 337 | 1 | 33.70 | 17 | 19.35 |
| 1951-52 | in New Zealand | 2 | 233 | 1 | 116.50 | 2 | 40.50 |
| 1952-53 | v India | 5 | 398 | 1 | 49.75 | 7 | 37.57 |
| 1953-54 | v England | 4 | 334 | 1 | 47.71 | 2 | 96.50 |
| 1954-55 | v Australia | 4 | 206 | – | 25.75 | 3 | 103.66 |
| 1957 | in England | 5 | 350 | 1 | 38.88 | 10 | 34.30 |
| 1959-60 | v England | 4 | 320 | 1 | 64.00 | 6 | 38.83 |
| 1960-61 | in Australia | 5† | 375 | – | 37.50 | 10 | 35.70 |
| 1961-62 | v India | 5† | 332 | – | 88.00 | 2 | 60.50 |
| 1963 | in England | 5† | 142 | – | 20.28 | 3 | 34.66 |
| Total | | 51 | 3,860 | 9 | 49.48 | 69 | 38.73 |

Career runs: 15,025 *Average:* 54.24
Highest Test score: 261 v England, Trent Bridge, 1950
Highest career score: 308*, Barbados v Trinidad, Bridgetown, 1943-44
Career wickets: 349 *Average:* 28.86
Best Test and career bowling: 7-70 v England, Trent Bridge, 1957

*Not out. †Captain

# Test cricket—
# the great grounds

The pavilion at London's Kennington Oval was threatened by redevelopment plans in 1973.

# Lord's Cricket Ground

## 1

The most famous cricket ground in the world, Lord's derives its name, not from any association with the aristocracy (as is sometimes thought), but from its founder, Thomas Lord (1755-1832). A Yorkshireman of farming stock, Lord was employed as a bowler and general assistant at the White Conduit Club when, in 1786, he was asked by the Earl of Winchilsea and Charles Lennox, later Duke of Richmond, to open a private ground in London. This marked the foundation of MCC, which developed out of the White Conduit Club.

Lord opened his first ground in 1787 in what is now Dorset Square, close to Marylebone Station, but the lease expired in 1810, and with London expanding rapidly northwards Lord moved to another ground three-quarters of a mile away. Within three years, an Act of Parliament decreed that the new Regent's Canal should pass through the ground, so Lord moved again—a few hundred yards to the north-west. This is Lord's Cricket Ground of today.

Though Lord opened this third ground in 1814 and ran it until he retired in 1825, it was an MCC member, William Ward, who was mainly responsible for its survival. The original rent had been £100 per annum, but the price of land was rising fast and when Lord retired he obtained permission to build houses on the site, cutting down the playing area but increasing the value of the lease under which he held the ground.

Happily, the significance of this move was not lost on William Ward, a fine player whose 278 for MCC against Norfolk in 1820 remained the highest score on the ground for over 100 years. A director of the Bank of England and later MP for the City of London, he was a far-seeing businessman and he bought out Lord for £5,000.

In time Ward and his family handed on their interest to J. H. Dark, who as time passed wanted MCC to buy the freehold. There was, however, a strange reluctance to do this, even when it was auctioned—for £7,000—in 1860, and it was not until 1866 that the club became the owners at £18,000. The sum was advanced by a member, William Nicholson, a later President of MCC.

Another £18,000 was paid in 1887 for what is known as the Nursery, so called because the area of nearly four acres was until then a flower and fruit nursery. Various other pieces of land were bought until the property grew to the area it covers today and included land along Grove End Road and up Elm Tree Road. One more attack had to be resisted in 1888 from the Great Central Railway, which wanted to take over the ground through which its railway was

going to run. But this was settled and the line runs through a tunnel under the nursery ground.

In 1890 the present pavilion was built with its fine Long Room, and in 1898 the Mound Stand. The Mound and Tavern occupied one side of the ground while a low stand ran round the rest of the perimeter to the Pavilion until the 1920s, when the Grand Stand, with Father Time on top, was built and a second tier was put on the stands at the Nursery End. In 1934, a members' stand south of the Pavilion was built, and in 1957 the Warner Stand to the north was added, this including press and television facilities.

In the mid-1960s, the famous old Tavern was demolished, partly because its catering facilities were too antiquated and partly because of property development in the south-west corner. The big new stand may lack some of the character of the old Tavern, but it fits agreeably into the dignified surroundings that have helped to make Lord's a unique ground on which cricketers all over the world hope to play once in a lifetime.

Middlesex play on the ground as tenants of MCC and through the years it has been the scene of traditional services and schools matches that have enabled many ordinary cricketers to play on the ground. However, in the 1960s MCC regretfully had to cut the number of these matches down in order to spare the 'square'. When some 90 days cricket was being played on it, the square had a bare and weary look, and a season of bad pitches in 1968 caused great concern, forcing MCC to reduce the amount of cricket played there.

The capacity of Lord's is hard to estimate. It has held 34,000, but in an age when the spectator's comfort is more frequently considered, it is a long time since this figure was approached. Much depends on how many people are allowed to sit on the grass. For the purpose of the Gillette Cup final, which is sold out annually, admission is only to seats in the stands, and the gate is around 21,000.

The Lord's Test match is now the highlight of the season. Before Test matches began, the most important fixture was Gentlemen and Players, which was still popular when it was discontinued in 1963 after the abolition of amateur status. Apart from odd interruptions, Eton and Harrow have met at Lord's since 1822. The first century was made there in 1816 by E. H. Budd, and it was Percy Holmes who in 1925 beat William Ward's highest score when he made 315 not out for Yorkshire against Middlesex. The next year, Jack Hobbs topped this by one run, scoring 316 not out.

More famous matches and famous innings have been played at Lord's than on any other ground

Sport & General

2

**LORD'S IN DANGER. THE M.C.C. GO OUT TO MEET THE ENEMY.**

**1** Since the 1920s, when the Grand Stand was erected, the Father Time weather vane has presided over matches at Lord's. **2** A panorama of the world's most famous cricket ground on an occasion when it is assured of a capacity crowd—the final of the Gillette Cup. **3** Thomas Lord, who in 1787 opened his first ground in Dorset Square and later moved to the present ground which still bears his name. **4** A cartoonist's impression of MCC reaction to an Act of Parliament in 1891 authorizing the building of tunnels that would run from Marylebone Station under the eastern fringe of Lord's. **5** The Lord's Tavern, from the street. In the 1960s the famous Tavern was replaced.

in the world, and many of its historic moments are recorded in the museum that stands just behind the Pavilion, beside the squash and real tennis courts. Lord's was the scene of 'Cobden's match' in 1870, when F. C. Cobden took three wickets with the last three balls of the match to win the University match for Cambridge by two runs; or 'Fowler's match' in 1910, when R. st G. Fowler made 64 for Eton when they were on the verge of defeat and then took 8 Harrow wickets for 23 to win the match; of countless famous innings by W. G. Grace; of Don Bradman's peerless 254 in the Test match of 1930; and of Hedley Verity's 15 wickets in the 1934 Test.

One of the most bizarre incidents on the ground occurred during the England-Australia Test match in 1926. Early on Monday morning, it was found that water had saturated a part of the square during the night, someone having connected a hose with the water supply. It had penetrated to the pitch, but only in the middle and no harm was done. The incident was never satisfactorily explained, but nowadays the ground is guarded throughout the night.

# The Oval

The traditional scene of the final and often decisive Test of an English series, the Kennington Oval has a special place in cricket history. For one thing it staged the first Test ever played in England, in 1880.

The beginnings were modest, for the area was originally meadow land and it had a brick house, barns and stables when it was purchased in auction in 1826 by the Rev William Otter, later Bishop of Chichester. He intended it for the minister's house, but came to the conclusion that it was not a practical proposition, and he decided to use the land for a market garden. In 1836 Otter asked for a building lease, but died before anything developed.

The Trustees refused to accept the terms offered by the owners, the Duchy of Cornwall, and it was taken over by the Montpelier Cricket Club in 1845. They arranged for 10,000 turves to be transferred from Tooting Common, and cricket began later that year. The Surrey Club shared the ground for a time and thrived, whereas Montpelier's fortunes declined and they eventually disappeared. Even so, the future of Kennington Oval was in doubt and Surrey were thinking of leaving. The Duchy of Cornwall were considering using the ground for a building scheme, but the Prince Consort intervened and a new lease was arranged.

In 1877 a new tavern was built and the last and largest of the gas-holders, which have always been a landmark at the Oval, was erected. The present pavilion was completed 20 years later, and in 1934 the fence round the ground was replaced by a brick wall and the Hobbs Gates erected 'In Honour of a Great Surrey and England Cricketer'.

Requisitioned during World War II, the Oval became a searchlight site and later a prisoner-of-war transit camp, although no prisoners were accommodated there. Considerable damage was done to the playing area by high-explosive bombs and incendiaries, but the ground was repaired with the help of 40,000 turves from Gravesend, and cricket resumed in 1946. Plans for the 1970s are for a complete reconstruction, with a large development scheme to include a hotel, flats, shops and a reduced playing area.

Apart from cricket the ground has staged tennis, hockey, rugby, and soccer. The first FA Cup final was played at Kennington Oval in 1872 and for 19 continuous years from 1874 to 1892, and England's first six home matches with Scotland were staged there. Soccer returned for a time in the 1950s when the Corinthian-Casuals, the amateur team, used the ground.

A crowd of 40,000 saw the first Oval Test, in 1880, when England,

*Above,* **The Oval, scene of the first Test played in England and many times host to the last and sometimes deciding match in a series.**
*Right,* **The Oval crowd, many of them West Indian, after the fifth Test in 1963.**

with W. G. Grace scoring 152, beat Australia by 5 wickets. Two years later Australia gained revenge by 7 runs, England being put out for 77 when needing only 85 to win. Another thrilling game, perhaps the most exciting in English history, came in 1902 when Australia were beaten by one wicket and Hirst and Rhodes, the last pair, hit off the 15 needed at the fall of the ninth wicket with 13 singles and a two.

The ground subsequently became known as a batsman's paradise, especially in the 1930s with Donald Bradman so dominant. He made 232 there in 1930 and shared a stand of 451 with Ponsford in 1934 when Australia scored 701 and won by 562 runs. In 1938 England ran up the record Test total of 903 for 7. An emotional moment came in 1948 when Bradman, in his last Test, and needing only 4 runs to average 100 in all Test innings, received a tremendous ovation from the warm-hearted Oval crowd but was bowled by Hollies for a duck.

Bowlers have had more success in recent years and a big moment came in 1952 when India lost five wickets for six runs at the start of their innings and were all out 98. In modern times the Oval has been good to England: from 1951 to 1969 they were beaten only twice in 19 matches, 10 of which were won.

# Melbourne Cricket Ground

The scene of the first-ever Test match, in 1877, the Melbourne Cricket Ground, or MCG as it is known to most Australians, is the biggest cricket ground in the world. Its capacity was already much larger than that of any other cricket ground when it was further enlarged to accommodate the Olympic Games of 1956. Then, as well as the athletics programme and the opening and closing ceremonies, the football and hockey finals were also held there. On most days 100,000 people filled the ground, most of them seated, and this number or more attend the most important Australian Rules football games played there.

The record crowd for a cricket match is the 90,800, who paid £A65,054 (£52,041 sterling) on the second day of the fifth Test between Australia and West Indies in 1960-61. The largest attendance for a whole Test was the 350,534 who watched the third Test of 1936-37 in which Australia, having lost the first two Tests to G. O. Allen's England team, started the revival that led to final victory.

The Melbourne Cricket Club was founded on November 15, 1838, when Melbourne itself was not much more than three years old, and the club's ground was moved to its present site beside the Yarra River in 1853. The surroundings are still very pleasant, though the ground is only 15 minutes walk from the centre of the city, and many spectators walk there through attractive gardens. The MCG itself once had its pastoral attractions, but now, after its many additions, it has become a huge amphitheatre in which people look down on the cricket, many of them from under cover.

The Pavilion is not imposing, being situated over third slip to a batsman taking strike at the City End, but to play in, or even to

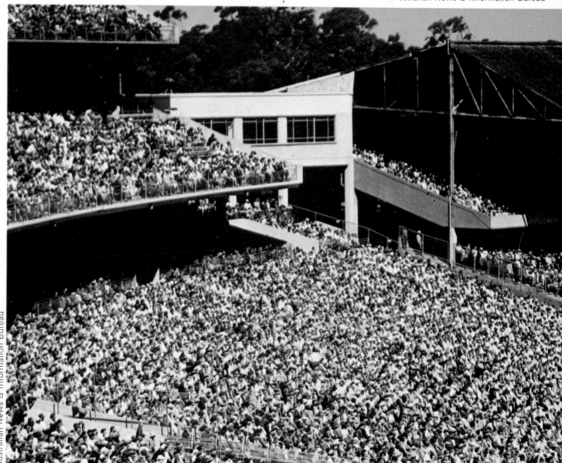

*Top left,* **The MCG, the largest cricket arena in the world.**
*Top right,* **Bill Lawry, an almost permanent fixture at the MCG, batting against England.** *Above,* **Shirt sleeves and hats are the order of a sunny day for spectators at a Melbourne Test.**

watch, a Melbourne Test match is a memorable experience. Either one or two Tests are held on the ground in every Test series.

Victoria play their Sheffield Shield matches on the ground, and nowadays the MCG provides one of the best pitches in Australia. Indeed, it was there in 1926-27 that Victoria made the highest ever score of 1,107, against New South Wales. In the days of uncovered pitches, however, those at Melbourne could be as vicious as any in Australia, and in 1931-32 South Africa were bowled out for

36 and 45.

The first English team to play in Australia played on the ground on New Year's Day, 1862, and 15 years later, on March 15, 1877, the first of all Test matches began. Australia won it by 45 runs, but England won the second on the same ground a fortnight later. In 1911-12, two of the most famous feats in Test cricket took place on the MCG.

There has seldom been a more sensational start to a Test match than to the second of that series when Australia found them-

selves 38-6 on a good pitch after Sydney Barnes had taken four wickets in five overs for just one run. And in the fourth Test six weeks later, Hobbs and Rhodes set up their record-breaking opening stand of 323.

Don Bradman made his first Test hundred at the MCG in 1928-29, and many others afterwards. It was also the scene in 1954-55 of Colin Cowdrey's first Test hundred and in 1965-66 of Bob Cowper's 307 in the last Test against England. This was the seventh score of over 300 on the ground, four of which were made by Bill Ponsford, whose 437 for Victoria against Queensland in 1927-28 was, over 40 years later, still the highest.

# Sydney Cricket Ground

It is not just because the Sydney Cricket Ground is in a great city that it earns its place among the two or three finest grounds in the world. It is because it has the genuine atmosphere for cricket. Rugby league and rugby union internationals are played on it; the Empire Games of 1939 were held on it. But first and foremost it is a cricket ground, a fine place to play and watch the game.

Few of the stands are modern, but they are comfortable and, with their turrets and pinnacles, contribute to the ground's character. The Hill, the big grassy bank at the Southern, Botany Bay, end of the ground, is perhaps the best-known vantage point of any cricket ground in the world. For a major match, thousands of critical spectators, well equipped with beer, sit packed densely together, sustaining a wealth of pungent comment. At the other end, beside the magnificent, relatively modern stand named after M. A. Noble, is a smaller grass bank, the Paddington Hill.

The ground is administered, not by the New South Wales Cricket Association as is often thought, but by the Sydney Cricket Ground Trust, a body with direct responsibility to the City Council. New South Wales play their Sheffield Shield matches on the ground, and in each Test series there is one Test match, sometimes two, there. Its capacity for cricket is approximately 50,000.

Considering the hammering the ground takes during the football season, its powers of recovery are astonishing. In the days when Bulli soil was used, the Sydney Cricket Ground provided some of the best pitches in the world, as the records of Bradman and Hammond testify. Since the supply of that soil was exhausted, however, the pitches have been less reliable and have taken more spin than most in Australia. Nevertheless they have produced some memorable cricket, and it was there that Ray Illingworth's team won the two Test victories that took the Ashes back to England in 1971.

Incidents in the last Test of that series, when beer cans were thrown onto the field and Illingworth led the England team off, recalled turbulent events soon after the ground was opened in 1878. Then, riots interrupted a match between Lord Harris's English team and New South Wales. Between these unsavoury happenings, though, the ground has witnessed much splendid cricket. Donald Bradman, when only 21, made his 452 not out there, the highest first-class innings until Hanif Mohammed exceeded it in Pakistan nearly 30 years later.

The first Test was played there in February 1882, and it was there in 1886-87 that England recorded their lowest-ever total against Australia. Turner and Ferris bowled them out for just 45. That match apart, however, it has tended to be a particularly happy ground for England. At the end of Illingworth's tour, 18 of England's 42 victories in Australia had been won at Sydney. One famous victory was in 1903-04. Though Victor Trumper made 185 not out in Australia's second innings, R. E. Foster replied with 287, which until Andy Sandham's 325 for England against West Indies in 1929-30 was the highest in Test cricket. The stand of 130 between Foster and Wilfred Rhodes was, in 1971, still England's best for the last wicket.

Walter Hammond, who was nearly always at his best in Sydney, began with 251 in his first Test there, in 1928-29, and four years later made 112 in one Test and 101 and 75 not out in the other. On his third tour, it was 231 not out.

After World War II, Don Bradman returned to the scene of his youthful triumphs to make 234 in the first post-war Test on the ground, sharing in a stand of 405 with Sid Barnes, who also made 234. And it was in Sydney in 1954-55 that Peter May made a second innings century which started the revival that led to Len Hutton's side retaining the Ashes. Later in the tour, the other Sydney Test met unprecedented opposition from the weather—and the match did not start until after lunch on the fourth day.

Just as every Australian side that comes to England loves to win at Lords, an England success at Sydney is sweet and satisfying.

*Above,* **Summer scenes on The Hill, renowned throughout cricket circles for the wit and other comments of its inhabitants.**
*Below,* **Alan Davidson bowls to Peter May in a Sydney Test.**

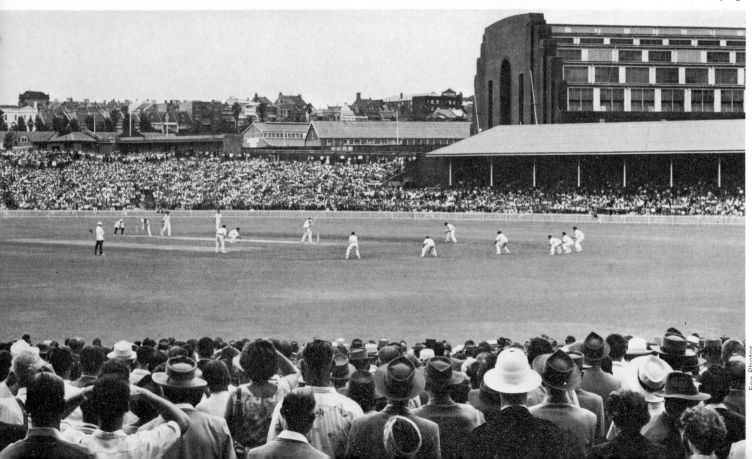